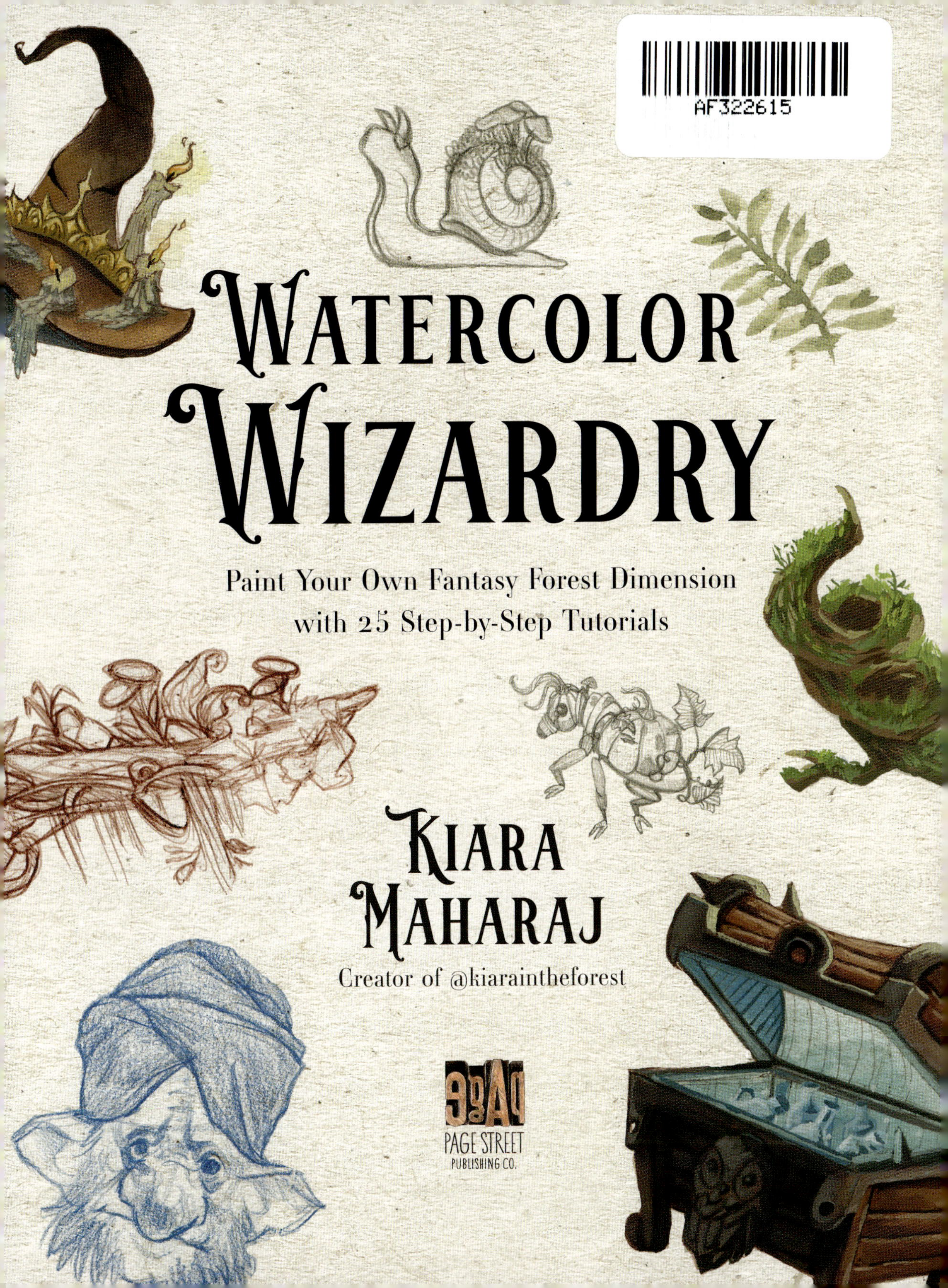

Watercolor Wizardry

Paint Your Own Fantasy Forest Dimension
with 25 Step-by-Step Tutorials

Kiara Maharaj

Creator of @kiaraintheforest

PAGE STREET
PUBLISHING CO.

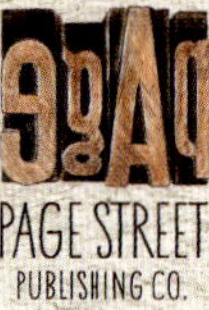

PAGE STREET
PUBLISHING CO.

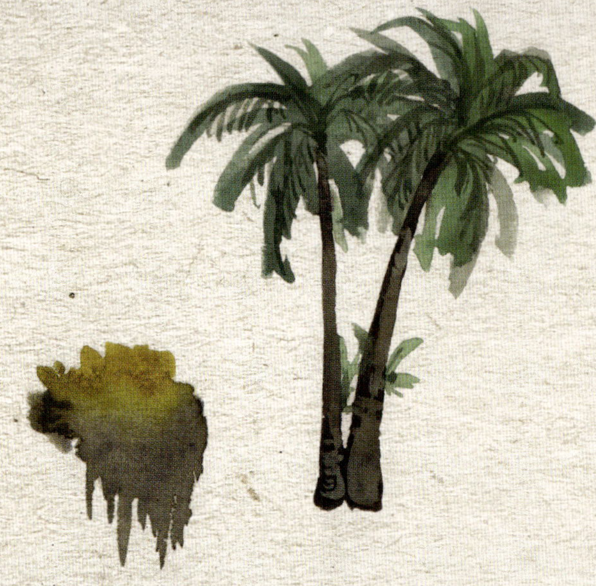

First published in 2026 by
Page Street Publishing Co.
27 Congress Street, Suite 1511
Salem, MA 01970
www.pagestreetpublishing.com

Distributed by Macmillan, sales in Canada by The Canadian Manda Group.

30 29 28 27 26   1 2 3 4 5

ISBN-13: 979-8-89003-417-5

Library of Congress Control Number: 2025940459

Edited by Sarah Monroe
Cover and book design by Emma Hardy for Page Street Publishing Co.
Artwork by Kiara Maharaj

Printed and bound in China

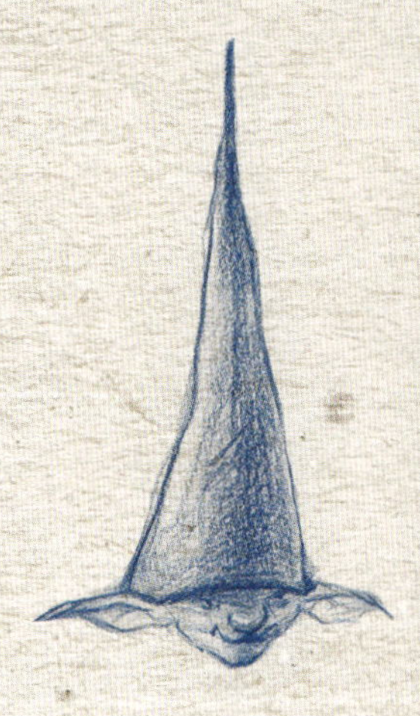

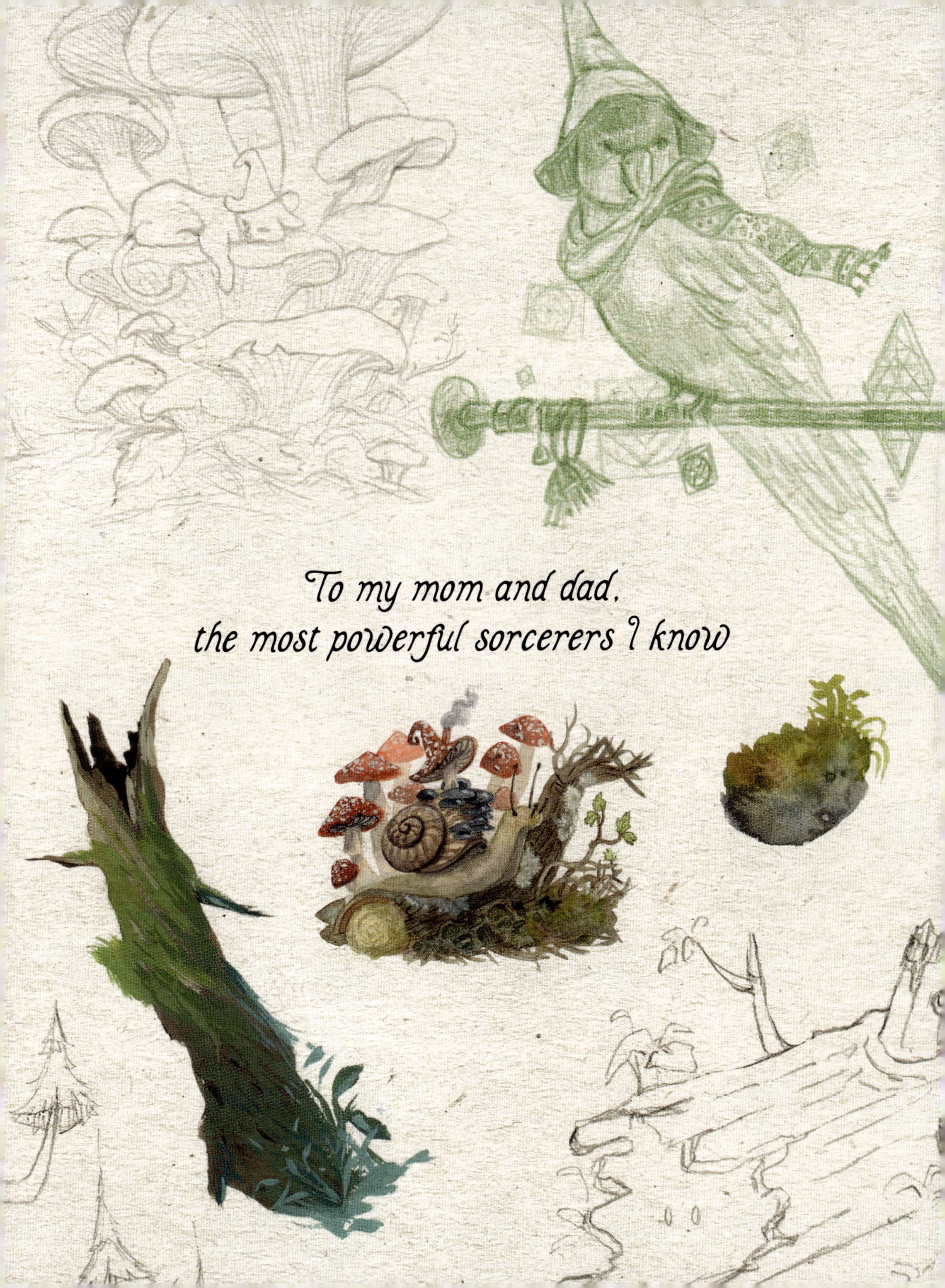
To my mom and dad,
the most powerful sorcerers I know

Contents

Introduction • 7

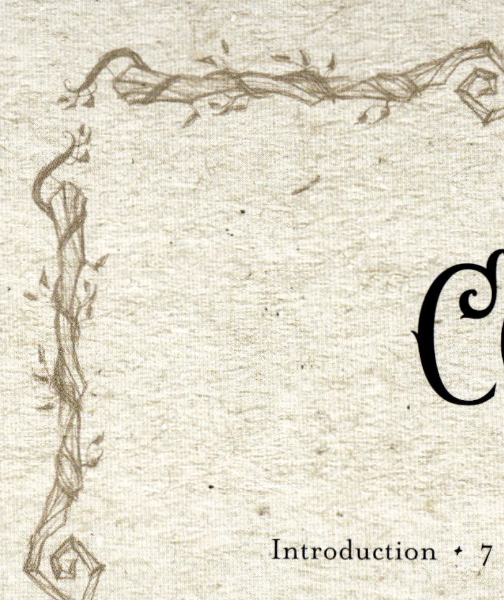

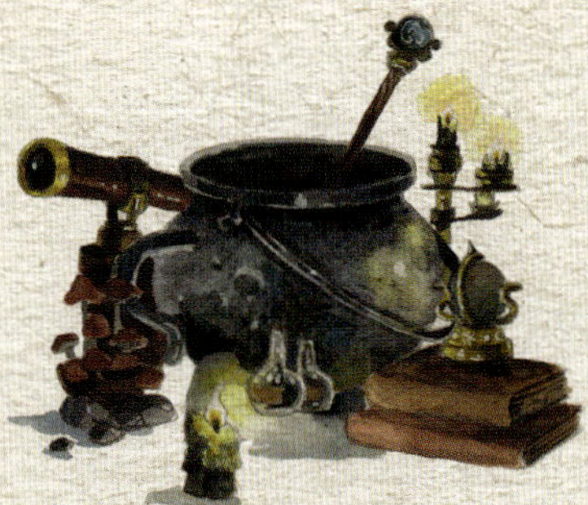

Chapter 1 • 8
Tools & Tricks of the Trade

Supplies List • 10

Characteristics of Watercolor
vs. Gouache • 13

Techniques Used in This Book • 15

Common Shapes and
Color Combos • 20

How to Trace the Sketch • 22

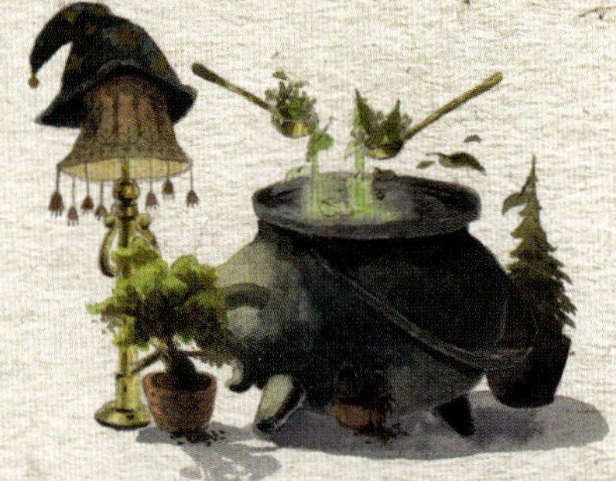

Chapter 2 • 24
Two Tablespoons of Trees

A Dimension Never Reveals
Its Directions • 26

The Tale of the Skeleton Tree • 32

Tentacles in the Tree Stump • 39

Eyes from the Shadows • 45

A Place for Adventurers to Rest • 52

Shadow Creatures of the
Shade Tree • 60

The Talking Leafhead Tree • 67

Fresh Flowers for the Homesick • 73

Portal to the Unknown • 79

The Grove of Wonders • 85

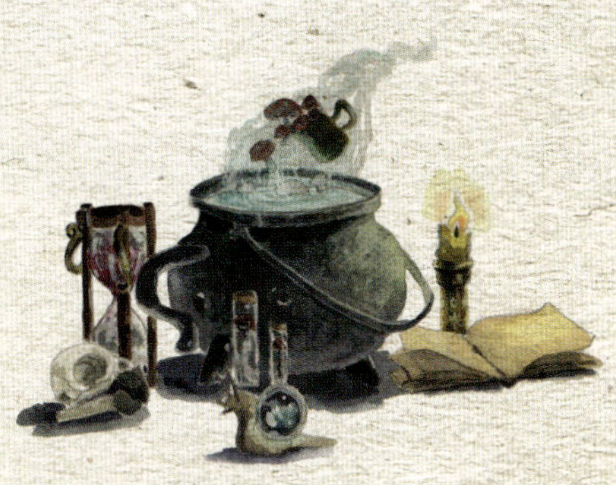

Chapter 3 · 92
A Dash of Mushrooms

The Pixie Party House · 94

The Mushroom Wizard · 100

The Path of the Toadstool · 107

A Fungivore in the Underbrush · 114

Secrets of the Spores · 121

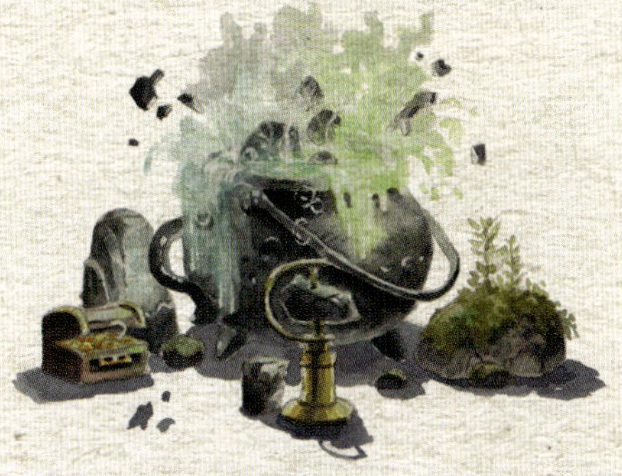

Chapter 4 · 128
A Handful of Rocks

The Caves of Cadmus
the Uncanny · 130

Rune Magic and Rock Rituals · 137

A Simple, Safe,
Slithering Stream · 143

A Goblin's Gemstone Stash · 149

Rocks of Past, Moss of Present · 155

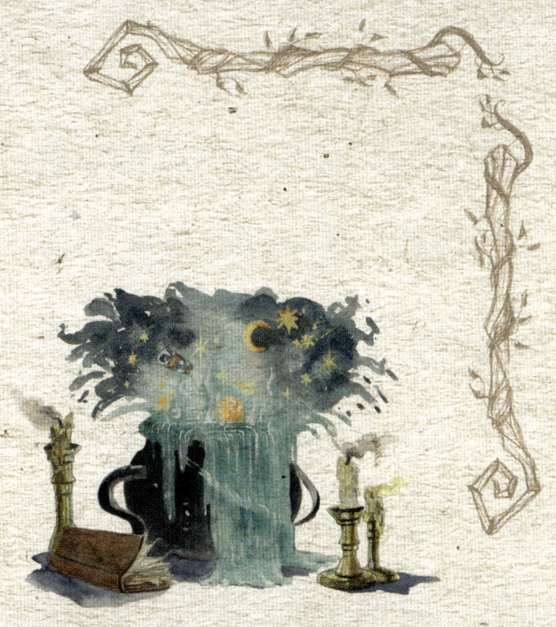

Chapter 5 · 162
And a Hint of Salt

The Book of Mosscraft · 164

The Wizard's Tower of Chambers · 170

The Waning Moonflies · 178

The Lantern Teahouse · 185

The Moss Dragon's Nest · 191

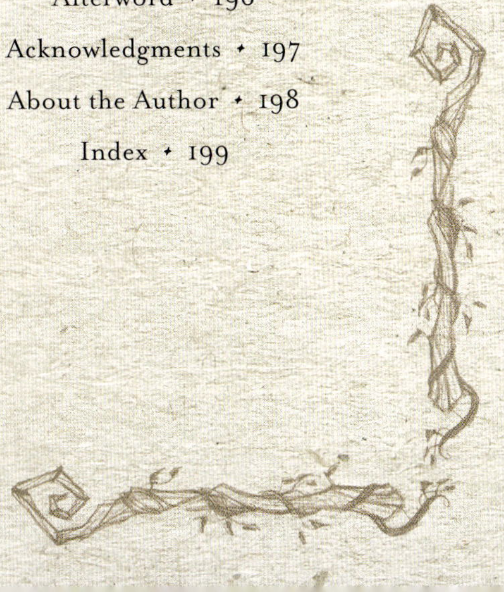

Afterword · 196

Acknowledgments · 197

About the Author · 198

Index · 199

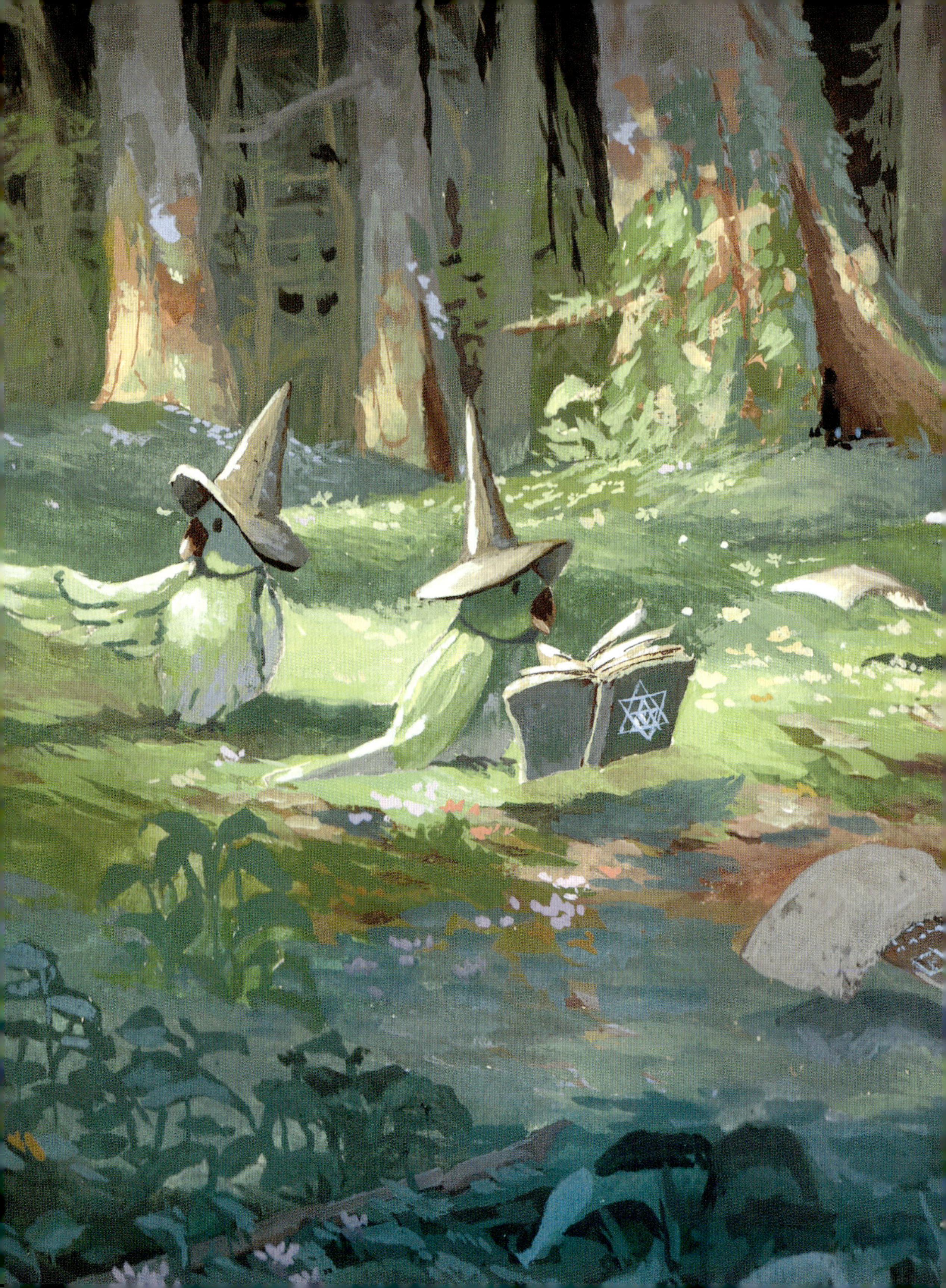

Introduction

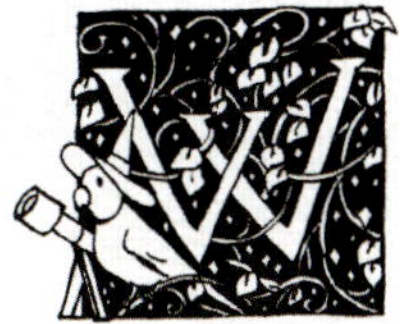

atercolor is wizardry. Think about it. You use a wooden staff (brush) and alchemy (paint derived from stone, rock, slate, blood, who knows what) to conjure (quite literally) *anything* from across the cosmos onto your scroll (watercolor paper). Logically, this can only lead to one conclusion:

Watercolor *is* wizardry.

And you? You are a wizard creating your own watercolor dimension.

What do wizards do? We create adventures, of course! We handpick our heroes and trouble them for the rest of their lives. We ignite the world with flair and drama and riddles. We also have the courtesy to send unwilling victims—I mean, *heroes* and *heroines*—to fulfill their destiny in otherworldly lands!

We have been doing this for centuries all over the world. Think of Merlin, who set the stage for King Arthur in Camelot, and all the legendary things *they* did. Or Gandalf the Grey approaching Frodo with a fresh set of problems he didn't ask for—I mean, *adventure.*

And in this book, that is precisely what we're going to do. We're going to create a forest dimension full of tree trickery, ancient moss magic, and trouble for our test subjects—I mean, *our adventurers.* And we're going to do it with the free-spirited medium that is watercolor.

In this book you can expect to be whisked away on the path to Watercolor Wizardry. Whether you're a beginner to watercolor or have dabbled before, the projects we'll create together are sure to get your creative muscles tingling: From dragons roaring in a lush green forest, to mysterious tentacle creatures sprouting from dead trees, to highly poisonous mushroom spores. Our dimension will be a beautiful forest full of moss and mystery, and tales of great heroes, heroines, and bards who journeyed through our forest. So if that's your thing, you've got just the perfect book in your hands.

This is not your regular watercolor instructional book. My goal for this book is to make you, the reader and wizarding apprentice, feel like the main character, immersed in the story and creation of the world. I, and my coven of parrot apprentices, will be your guide and mentor throughout this book.

I wrote each tutorial with the goal of inciting wonder and inspiration—and catering to your natural childlike mischievousness (perfect ingredients for a wizard).

Go on. Be a wizard.

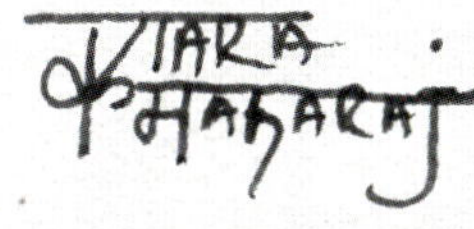
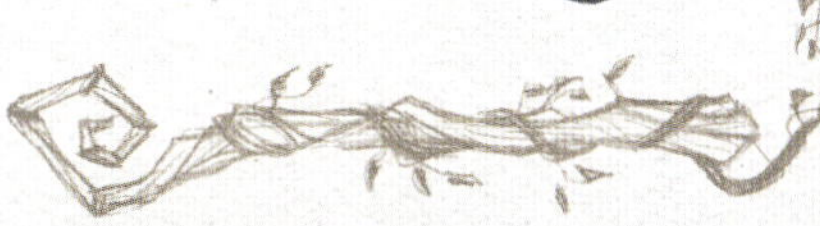

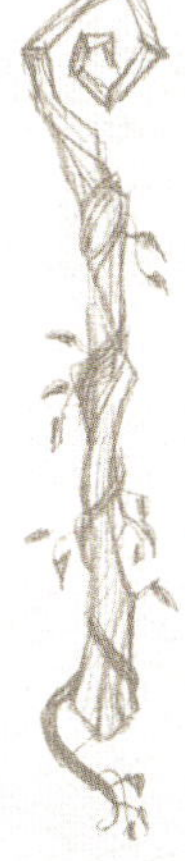

Chapter One
Tools & Tricks of the Trade

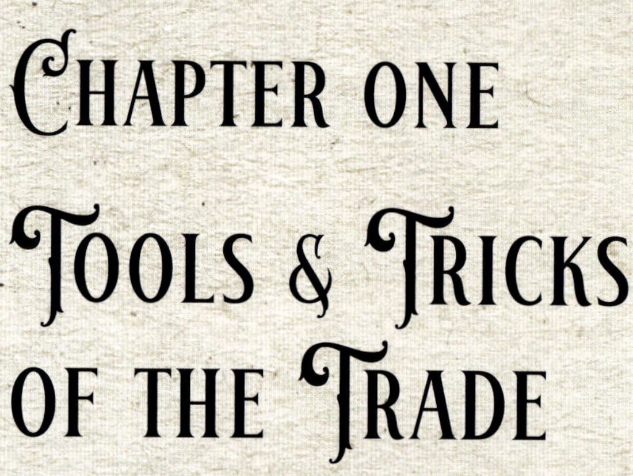

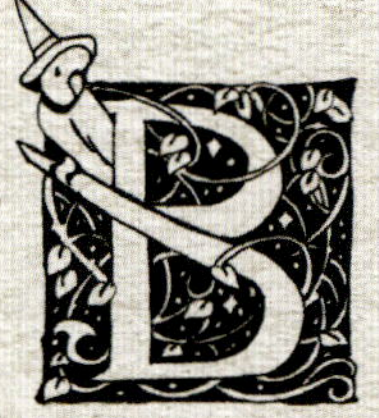

Before we begin the practical lessons of creating your very own watercolor forest dimension, we must first lay down some foundations. Theory, dear apprentice, is vital to any book-loving wizard.

In this introductory chapter, we're going to cover the essential supplies, learn key techniques for creating texture, and look at the shapes and common color combinations we'll be using throughout this book.

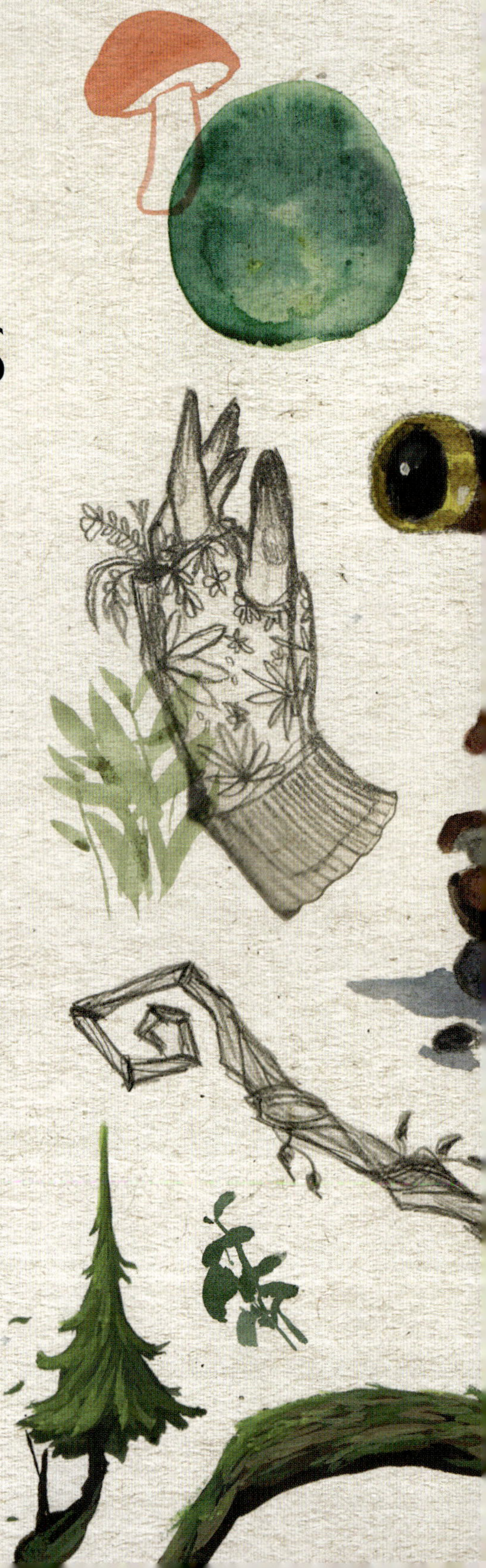

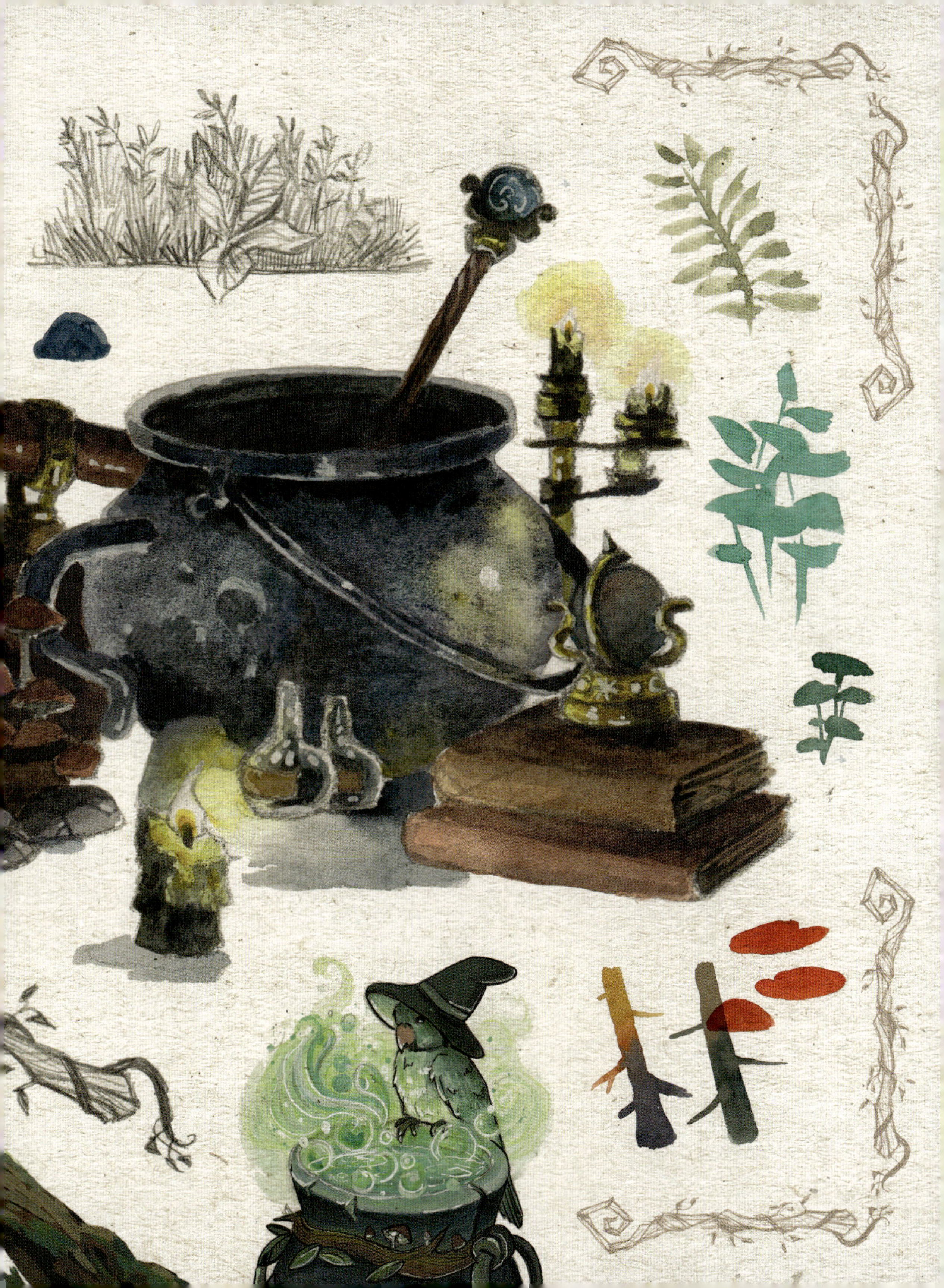

Supplies List

These are the basic tools you will need to acquire so you can follow the tutorials in this book. I have included the brands I use, but you can feel free to use a brand that you are more comfortable and familiar with.

Paint

The star of the show we'll be using to create all these paintings is *watercolor* paint. I will be using a set of eighteen colors from my local supplier, Prime Art. These are my favorite pigments at the moment, and the set includes all the colors I enjoy using to paint nature.

Additionally, I will also be using a few colors from the Daniel Smith watercolor range. A list of colors for each painting will appear at the beginning of the tutorial. For some of the paintings, we will also use gouache paint for finishing touches.

Full List of Colors

Watercolor

- Burnt Sienna
- Burnt Umber
- Carbon Black
- Cerulean Blue
- Crimson Lake Red
- Deep Blue
- Deep Green
- Gamboge
- Lemon Yellow
- Lunar Blue
- Payne's Grey
- Phthalo Blue
- Sap Green
- Titanium White
- Ultramarine Blue
- Vermillion
- Violet
- Yellow Ochre

Gouache

- Burnt Sienna
- Hansa Yellow Medium
- Titanium White
- Ultramarine Blue

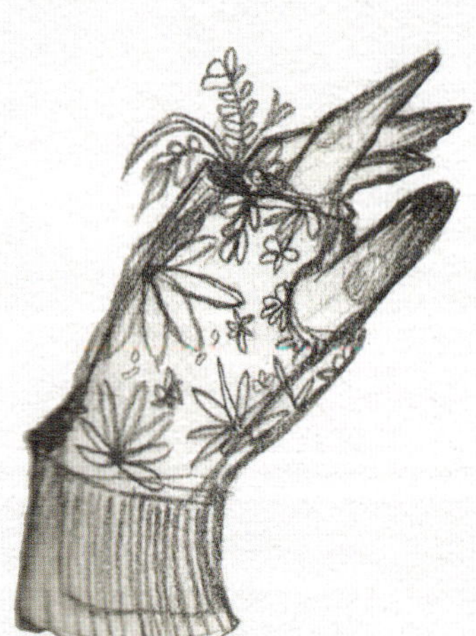

Paper

Ideally, you will need watercolor paper with a grammage of 140lb/300gsm. This refers to the thickness of the paper, and it means you can apply a lot of paint, water, and layers of color without the paper buckling or warping.

You can also use a watercolor sketchbook, which is what I used for some of the tutorials. My sketchbook is a 100% cotton paper watercolor book from Hahnemühle®. Additionally, I used a 140lb/300gsm agave paper pad from Hahnemühle, and Artistico soft press paper from Fabriano. I recommend testing a few types of paper to see which one you enjoy the most. There is no "perfect" paper—just different types, which give different effects and textures.

Watercolor paper can be described as having a *hot press* finish or a *cold press* finish. Hot press paper usually has a super-smooth surface, while cold press paper has a slight texture and roughness. My personal preference is cold press paper, merely because I enjoy having lots of texture in my paintings.

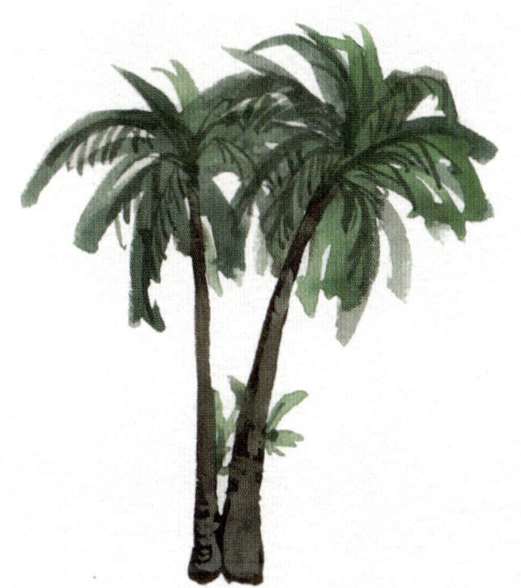

Brushes

There are dozens of different types of brushes to choose from, including different options in brush sizes, hair material, brands, medium to use them with, price, and so forth. However, throughout this book you will need only three sizes of *round* brushes, which is a commonly used type that is readily available at most art stores.

Specifically, you will need these sizes:

- 10
- 2
- 0

Additionally, the Lantern Teahouse tutorial (see page 185) uses a *rigger brush* size 0 to paint some rain. This is optional to create a dedicated brushstroke; you can alternatively use your round brush 0 to paint rain.

Palette

Like brushes, there are numerous options for palettes. You can use a plastic palette, a paint travel pan, or a stay-wet palette. When I'm working in my home studio, I tend to use an old plate from an ornamental tea set. I love the art printed on it and its small circular shape. Mixing watercolor mediums on a ceramic surface is also a lot more satisfying to me.

Additional Materials

You will also need these supplies:

- An HB graphite pencil to draw your sketches

- Thin printer paper (90gsm or less [20lb bond paper])

- A cloth or paper towel to wipe your brushes

- A jar of clean water to clean your brushes

- Three color pencils: Dark Brown, Glacier Blue (or any light-blue color), and White

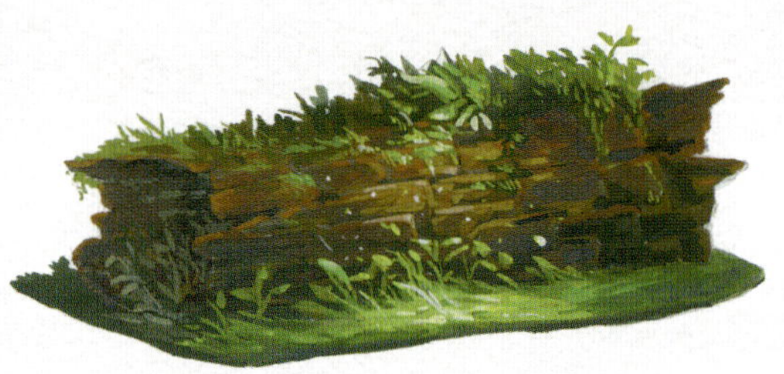

Apprentice Notes:

There are other supplies you may enjoy using together with water-color, such as Gelly Roll® pens, ink pens, masking fluid, or washi tape, but these are not necessary for the projects in this book.

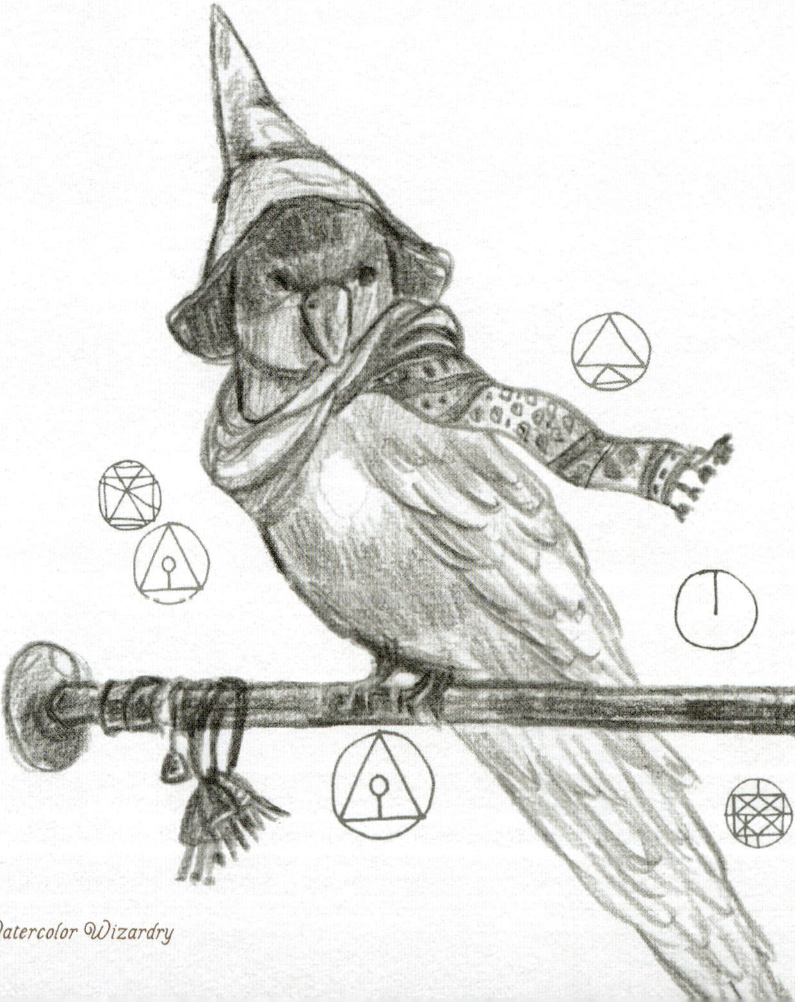

Characteristics of Watercolor vs Gouache

Gouache is a sister to watercolor. They share a lot of similar qualities, yet they are distinctly different.

I first learned how to paint with watercolor, and then I switched to gouache a few years ago. It quickly became my favorite medium because of the vibrant colors, the matte finish, and the impressionistic effect it allows me to create. However, as I was doing the artworks for this book, I fell in love with watercolor again.

After working with both mediums, I decided it is important to have a section in this book to highlight their similarities and differences. Both watercolor and gouache are heavily used in illustration, and both have wonderful storytelling capabilities. While this book is primarily a *watercolor* instructional book, you can also attempt to paint these illustrations using gouache. It would be a fun exercise for you to try them both out and compare how they differ for yourself.

Opacity

The first characteristic that differentiates watercolor from gouache is its *opacity*. Opacity refers to how transparent or opaque a pigment is. Oil and acrylic are both *opaque* paints, which means they can be layered over each other without the color beneath showing through. However, it is also possible to make certain oil and acrylic mediums more transparent.

Watercolor is notoriously a transparent medium. If we painted a swatch of yellow and then painted blue over it, the resulting color would be green. Without mixing the primaries, we can achieve a secondary color just by layering. This is because the color from the bottom layer shows through the top layer.

In comparison to watercolor, gouache is more opaque. Paint from above layers can completely cover the color below them. This makes the medium great for painting on black paper, for example, or doing studies of landscapes and portraits before attempting a larger oil painting.

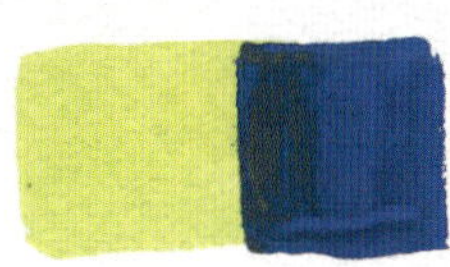

Both watercolor and gouache, however, interact with *water*. The more water you add to them, the more transparent they get. To get the most thick and opaque color, use the paint directly from the tube, with little or no water at all.

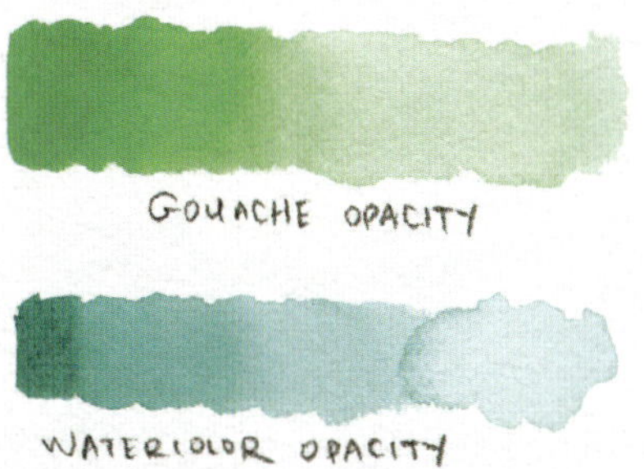

Another important thing to note is that you can make watercolor more opaque by mixing it with white watercolor or white gouache paint. Use only a small amount, so the overall value of the color doesn't change drastically.

The major difference in opacity between the two mediums serves as a great advantage to artists. While it is difficult to rectify a mistake in pure watercolor, we can use gouache paint over watercolor paint to change colors, fix errors, and paint final bold details and pops of color. For some of the projects in this book, we will use this advantage. If you don't have white gouache available for these finishing details, you can also get a similar effect from a white pencil or a white pen.

Drying Effect

Both watercolor and gouache colors look different after they have dried on the page. It's important to understand how the colors shift, so we can accurately predict what colors we'll get once we apply paint to the page.

Gouache notoriously dries with a *matte* finish. This means that while the paint is wet, the color can appear lighter because of reflections. Once it dries, the color shifts to a darker value, eliminating any glossy reflections.

Watercolor, however, dries *lighter*. An accurate way to predict how light the color would be is by noting how much water you used. The more water mixed with the color, the lighter it will be, and vice versa.

Layering

This characteristic is a follow-up from the first point about *opacity*. As noted, opacity affects the entire painting process and how we layer the colors, which is one of the largest differences between watercolor and gouache.

Because watercolor is a transparent medium, a light color (such as yellow or white) often does not show up when it's applied over a dark color (such as grey or dark green). For this reason, the watercolor-painting process involves working from *light to dark*. Watercolorists paint their first layers using a lot of water and laying out the lightest colors first, before using thicker and darker layers over it.

Gouache paint can behave differently. Light yellow or even white *can* be painted over dark colors like black and grey. Therefore, you can paint from *dark to light*, laying a base silhouette of black, and then bringing the light forward.

Techniques Used in this Book

The Bead Method

This method is a way to create smooth gradients using one of the most natural forces on earth: gravity. Water always flows *downward*. So, using this law, watercolorists blend colors together naturally by painting on an inclined surface. It's a good idea to try this method out before beginning the tutorials in this book.

Step 1

First, raise your sketchbook at a slight angle. You can use another object, like a small block or another book, to rest the top of your sketchbook on. The angle of inclination will determine how fast and far your paint will flow.

If you're using a sheet of paper, then stick the paper onto a hard surface, such as a desk easel or a wooden board, and then raise the board at an angle.

Step 2

Next, dip your brush into some water, and mix the first color of your gradient. Apply this color as a square swatch onto your paper. You will notice a "bead" of water forming at the very bottom of the paint. This method involves following that bead, working quickly so the water doesn't dry.

Step 3

Now clean your brush, and mix the next color in your gradient. Apply this color directly below the bead of water. Notice that the bead now flows further downward with the *new* color, creating a seamless gradient.

Step 4

Finally, repeat the above step, and add a third color in your gradient. Now you can let the paint dry. Observe how the colors have naturally blended—smoother than the effect would be if you painted on a flat surface.

The Wet-on-Wet Technique

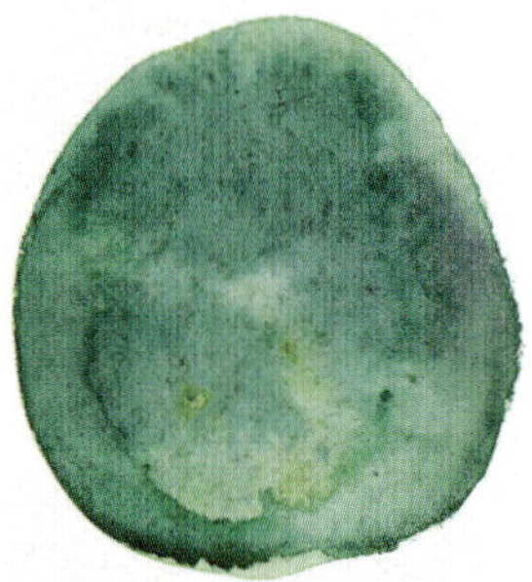

This technique is one of the most popular watercolor methods. With this method, you can create numerous textures, glowing effects, and transitions between colors.

In this book, we use *The Wet-on-Wet Technique* to paint fungi on wood, in Chapter 3.

Test this technique yourself:

Step 1

Use a wet brush and a watery mixture of any watercolor. Apply this color onto your watercolor paper.

Step 2

Working quickly while the paint is still wet, pick another color from your palette mixed with a fair amount of water (slightly more water than paint). Dab spots of this color into the wet paint.

Step 3

Notice how the second color pushes the first color away, creating tiny spirals and strands.

Step 4

Wait for the paint to dry to see the finished texture.

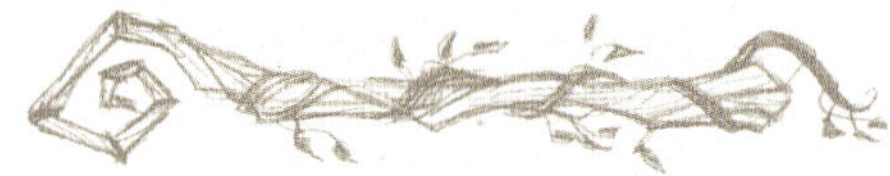

The Glazing Method

This technique involves layering multiple colors over each other to achieve depth and texture, or multiple layers of the same color to enhance the color. A secondary layer of paint is called a *glaze*.

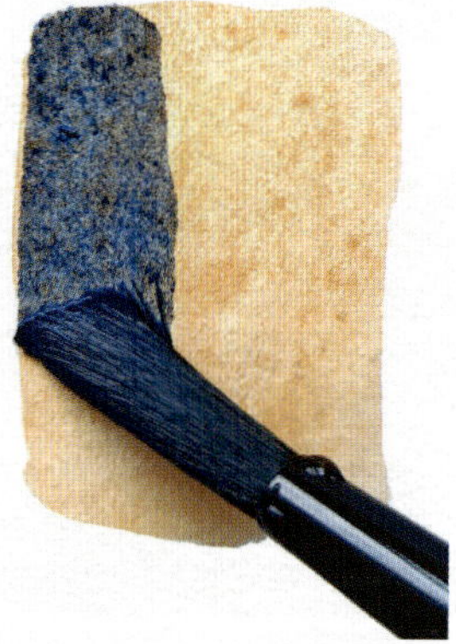

In this book, we use glazing to paint a chaotic jumble of sticks, leaves, grass, and stones.

Try this technique yourself:

Step 1

Paint two swatches of Yellow Ochre onto your watercolor page. Let it dry.

Step 2

On the first swatch, paint another layer of Yellow Ochre over the dry paint. Notice how the yellow has deepened by glazing the same color over itself multiple times.

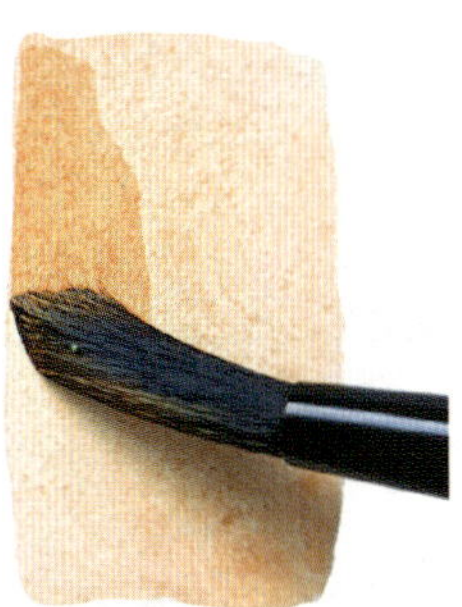

Step 3

On the second swatch, use Cerulean Blue with an equal part of water, and paint over the Yellow Ochre. Let it dry.

Step 4

Notice how the second swatch created green by glazing blue over yellow.

You can go further by applying more glazes of other colors over the Yellow Ochre and discover new shades.

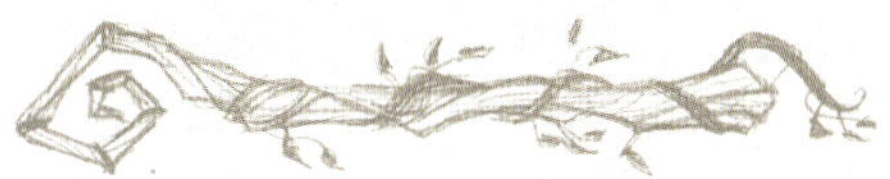

The Inverse Painting Technique

Inverse painting refers to painting the negative space around an object, to bring forward the object itself. For watercolor, we often use this technique to paint shadows *around* an object, instead of the object itself.

In this book, we use inverse painting to bring out sticks, twigs, branches, and other foreground elements in Chapter 3 and Chapter 5.

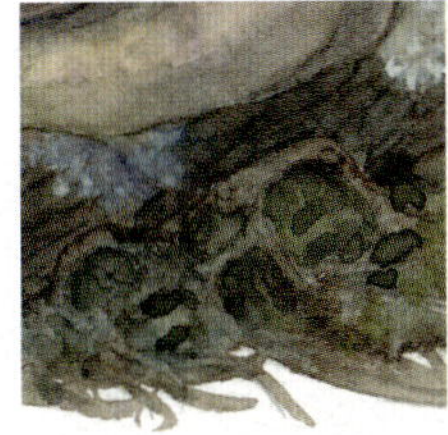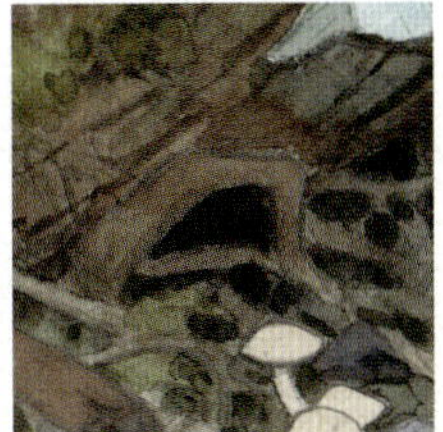

Try this technique yourself:

Step 1

Paint a swatch of Burnt Sienna with an equal part of water onto your page. Let the layer dry thoroughly.

Step 2

Now mix a darker color using Burnt Sienna + Ultramarine Blue, and imagine a stick on the page. Paint the negative space *around* the stick, to bring out the stick itself.

The Lifting Technique

A fun technique to utilize with watercolor mediums is *lifting*. This involves using a clean, dry brush and dragging it over wet paint. You will notice the brush *picking up* some of the color of the paint, making it lighter on the page.

This technique can be used to create *fades* into the page, or correct mistakes, or even create glowing effects.

Here's how you can try it for yourself:

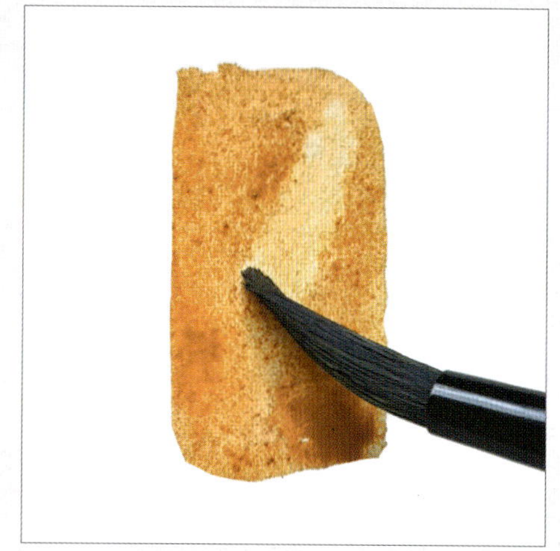

Step 1

First, apply a watery mixture of any watercolor paint onto your watercolor paper.

Step 2

Next, clean your brush with a cloth, and make sure the bristles are properly dry.

Step 3

Drag this dry brush over the paint you applied in Step 1. You want to be able to see the difference between the original swatch, and the lifted color, so only drag your brush across one side of the swatch.

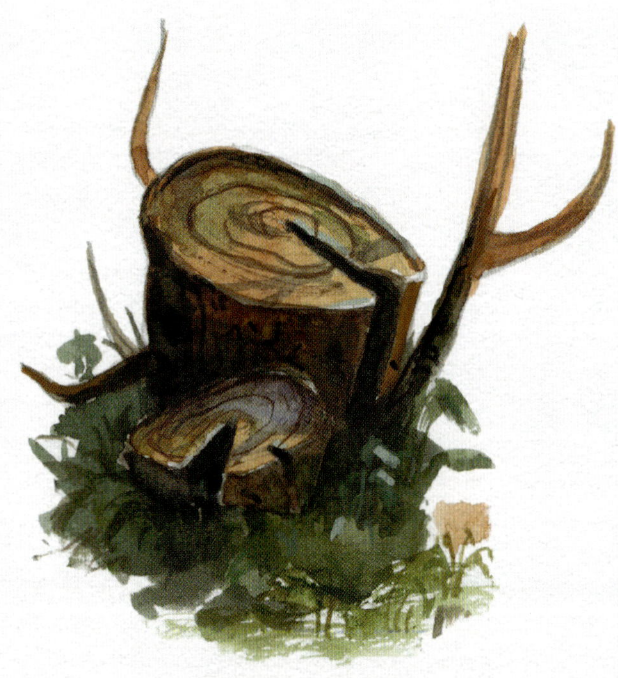

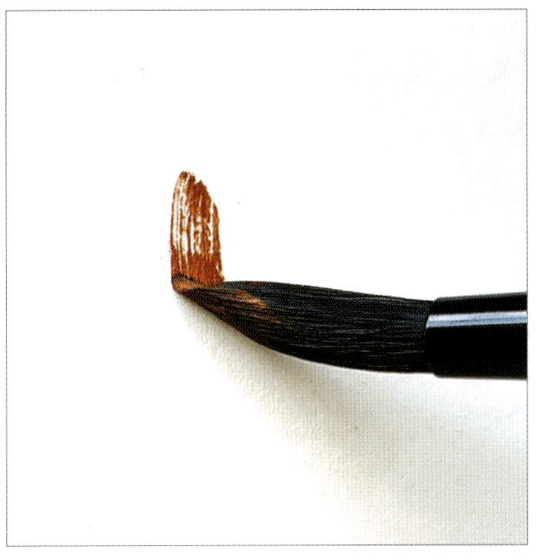

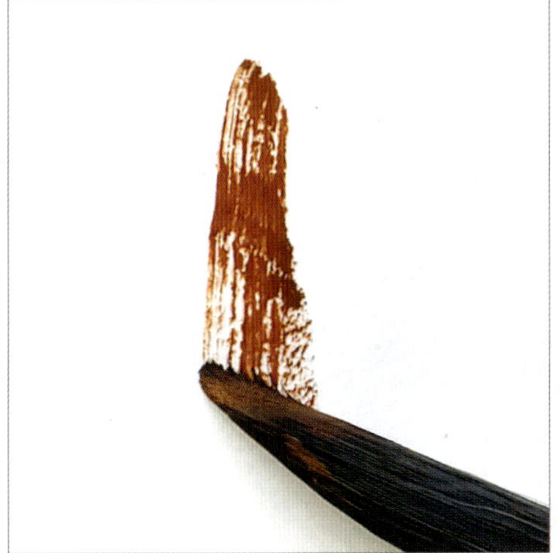

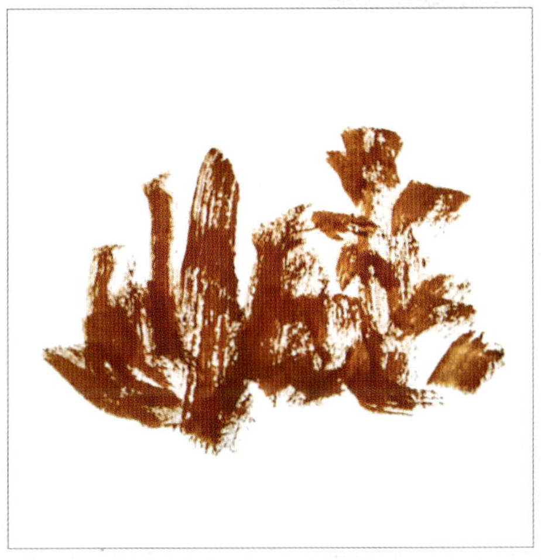

The Dry Brush Technique

This technique involves using a dry brush and paint from the tube to create rough textures on the page, allowing watercolorists to quickly paint distant trees, foliage, and various other textures, like sand, rock surfaces, walls, rust, and more.

Here's how you can try this technique for yourself:

Step 1

Use your round brush 10, and make sure the bristles are completely dry.

Step 2

Dab the brush in some Yellow Ochre watercolor paint.

Step 3

In quick and sudden movements, drag the brush across your watercolor paper. Observe how rough the resulting stroke is.

Step 4

Use this technique to paint the shape of a line of trees.

Common Shapes and Color Combos

The Language of Shapes

Beautiful paintings have one thing in common: beautiful shapes. Shapes are a powerful language artists use to create beauty, dynamics, interest, and pleasing eye candy in a painting. Shapes can be as simple as a circle, or as complex as a ten-pointed leaf, curving from being dried in the sun.

When you walk through a garden or forest, what are the shapes that instantly catch your eye?

In this book we use the language of shapes to communicate *suggestions* of the object we want to paint. Because painting every single detail of every single leaf on a tree is not only tedious, but also doesn't result in a pleasing painting, we can use shapes to simplify our task and create more beauty.

Here are all the common shapes we use in this book for mushrooms, leaves, foliage, plants, flowers, rocks, and sticks. Each tutorial will specify when to refer to this section when painting the silhouette of plants and foliage.

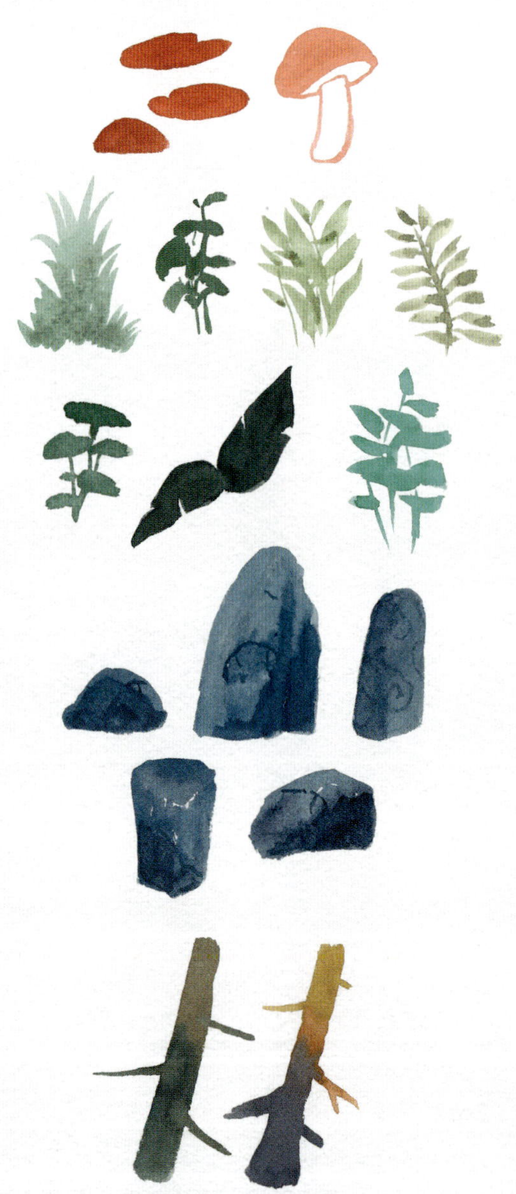

Common Color Combos in This Book

These are the commonly used color mixtures and gradients we use in the book. For any mixtures throughout this book, we will use an equal part of each color, unless otherwise stated. For example, to mix a dark-brown color, we will use an equal part of Burnt Sienna + Ultramarine Blue. In another case, to mix a light-green color, we will use Sap Green + a touch of Gamboge.

Feel free to refer to this section and practice mixing these colors as often as you'd like.

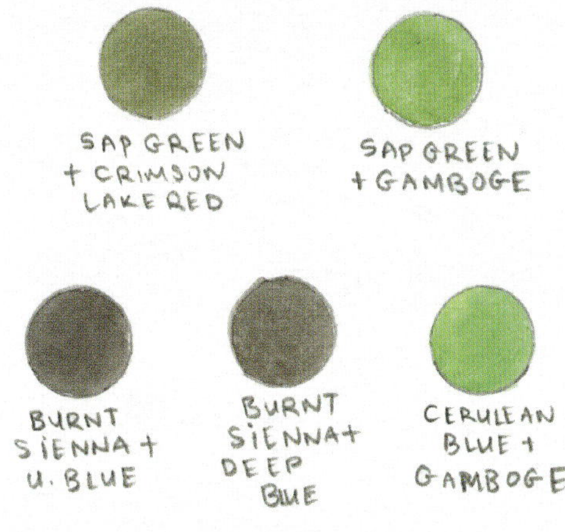

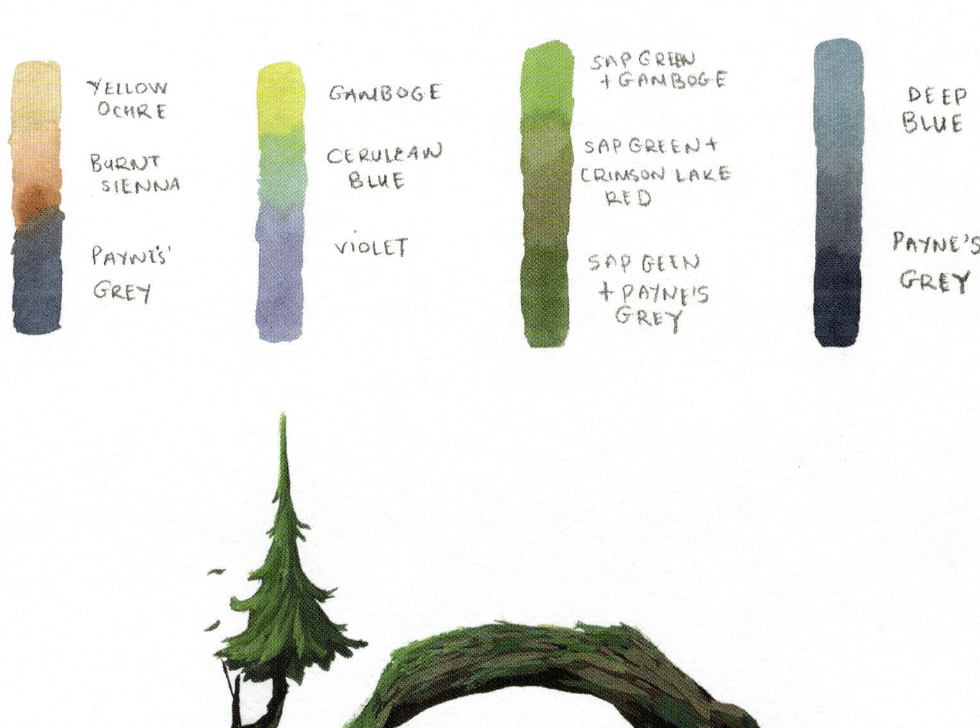

How to Trace the Sketch

All the tutorials include a base sketch and design of the overall artwork. Before we begin painting, you will want to draw the sketch yourself or trace the image onto your watercolor paper using a light box or bright window. However, watercolor paper can be very thick, making it difficult to trace a drawing even when using a light box. Here is an alternative method to create a traced image.

You will need the following:

- Thin printer paper
- A graphite pencil or graphite stick (HB or darker)
- Watercolor paper

Step 1

Place the thin printer paper over the drawing you wish to trace from this book. Because the paper is so thin, you should be able to see the lines of the illustration peeking through. Carefully use your HB pencil to trace the lines. Make sure to hold the page firmly in place, and avoid moving it until you are done with the trace.

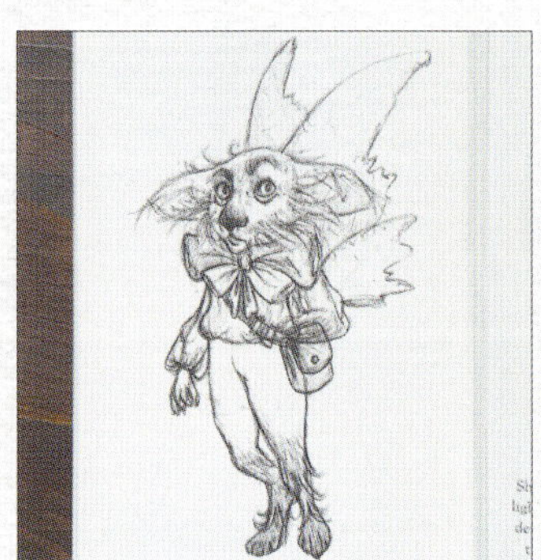 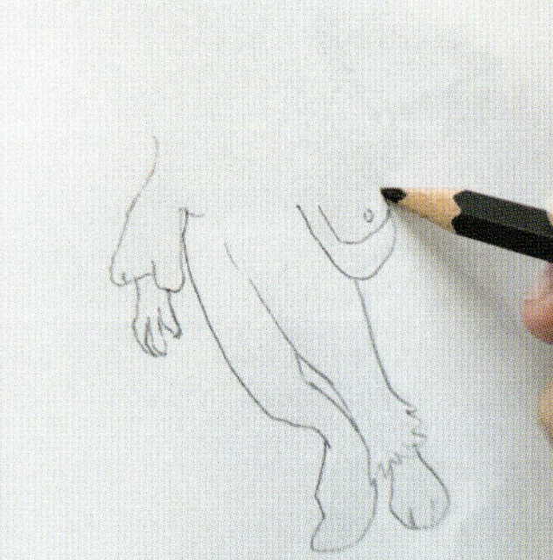 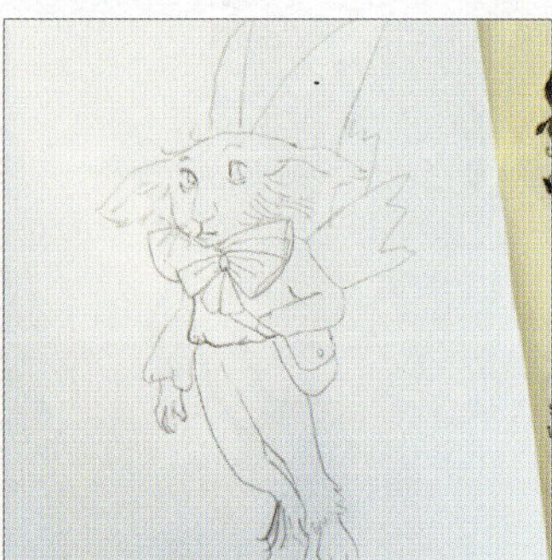

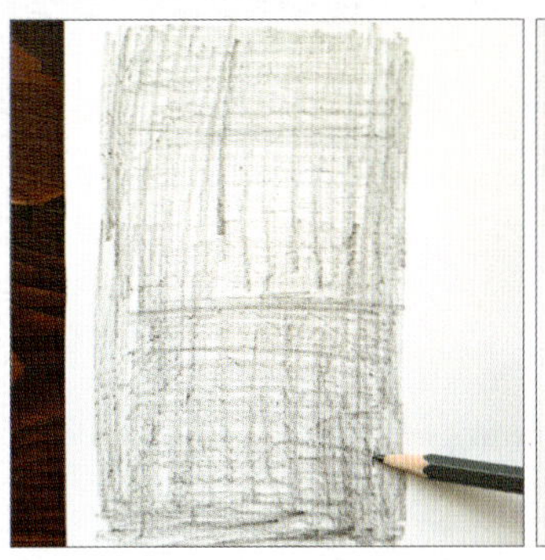
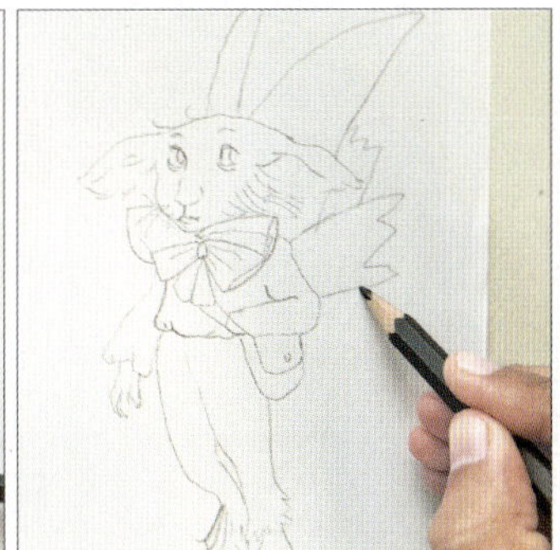
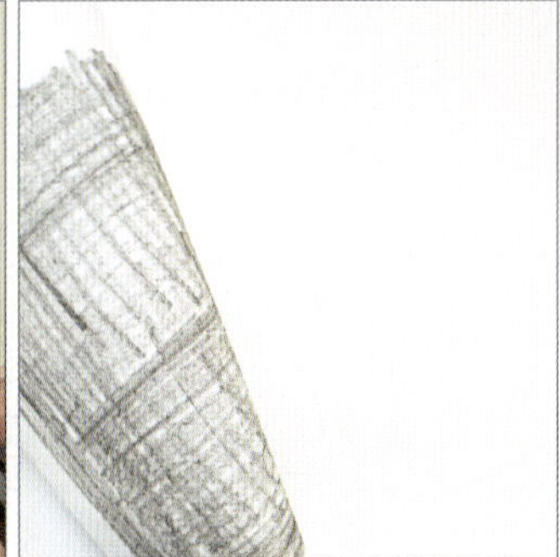

Step 2

Lift the printer paper with the traced drawing. Use the graphite pencil or stick to color the reverse side of the printer paper.

Step 3

Place the graphite page you just colored over your watercolor paper. Make sure the graphite side is facing down and the image you traced is facing you.

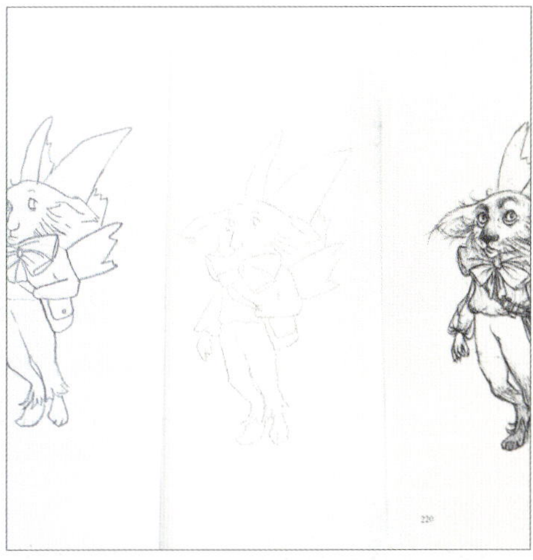

Step 4

Now use your HB pencil to draw over the lines of the trace again. Make sure you don't move the paper; hold it firmly in place over your watercolor paper for a smooth transfer. Cover all the lines while pressing the page in place.

Step 5

When you've traced over all the lines, remove the printer paper. You should be left with a lightly drawn copy of the sketch transferred on your watercolor paper. You can now darken the lines with your free hand based on what you see in the reference. Feel free to also include your imagination and alter the drawing as you prefer; add more mushrooms, leaves, trees, characters, and so forth as desired.

Now that we've covered the essentials, you are ready to begin your watercolor journey. Fire up your wand—and let's dive in.

Chapter Two

Two Tablespoons of Trees

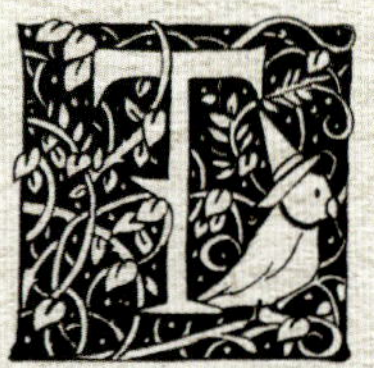 rees are the heartbeat of forests. Without them, there would be no home for birds to nest, no shade for humans to rest, and no base for magic to manifest.

In this chapter, we're going to explore all the twisting trees that can exist in an ancient, powerful forest. Such a forest is teeming at the brim with secrets and sorcery—from creatures lurking in the dark hollows of tree trunks, to networks of tree roots grappling the very ground beneath our feet, to freshly brewed tea leaves and a dark tale to accompany our travels.

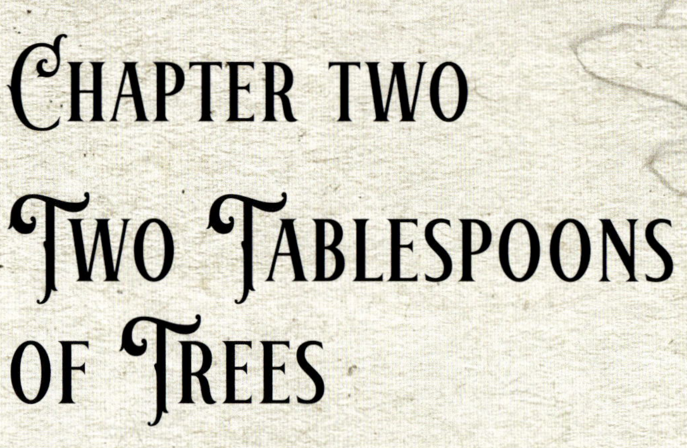

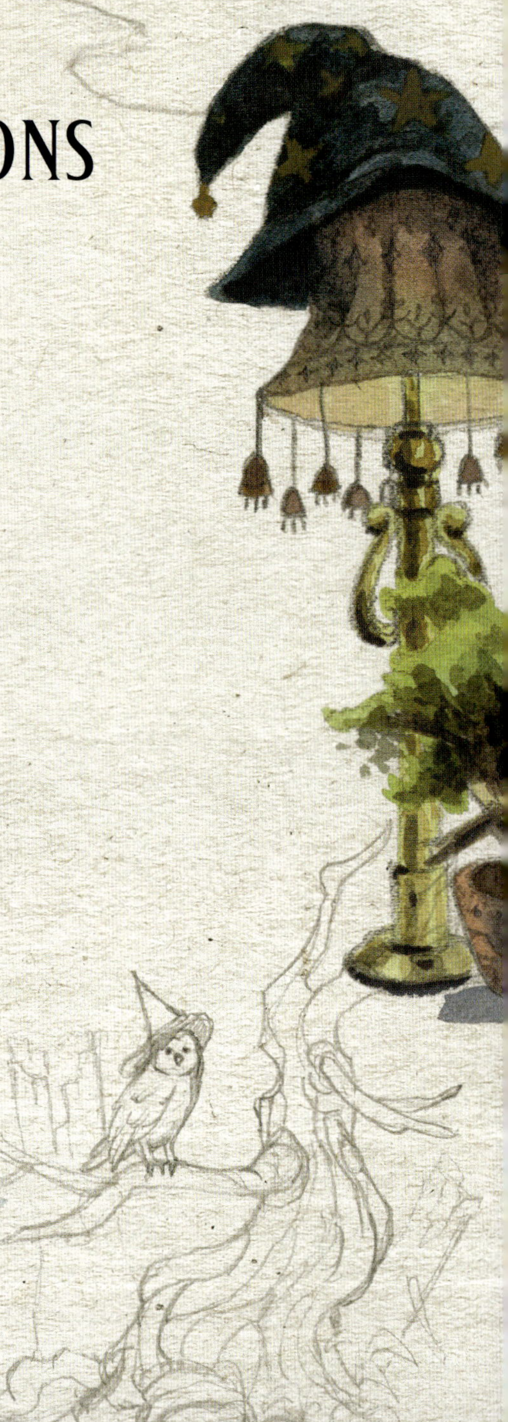

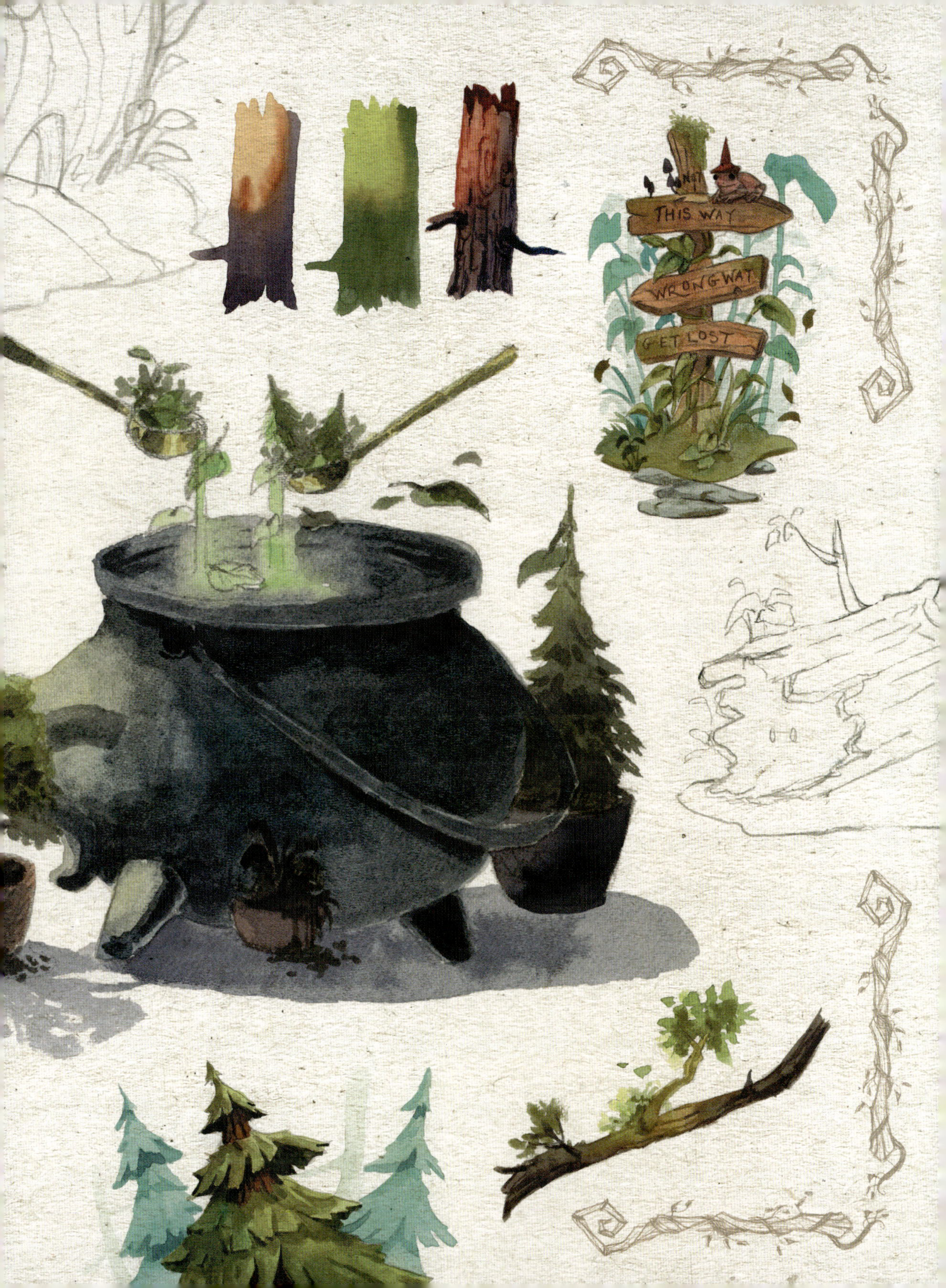

THIS WAY
WRONG WAY
GET LOST

A Dimension Never Reveals its Directions

uch like how modern-day magicians never reveal the secret to their parlor tricks, ancient, mysterious dimensions created by powerful wizards do the same thing. We never leave a map. And if there is a treasure buried deep in the dimension, the directions leading to it are always vague, full of riddles, and packed with multiple meanings.

In this project, we're going to paint a sign labeling certain directions. But, of course, they will be leading our adventurers to all the wrong ways.

Brushes

Round brush 2, 10, 0

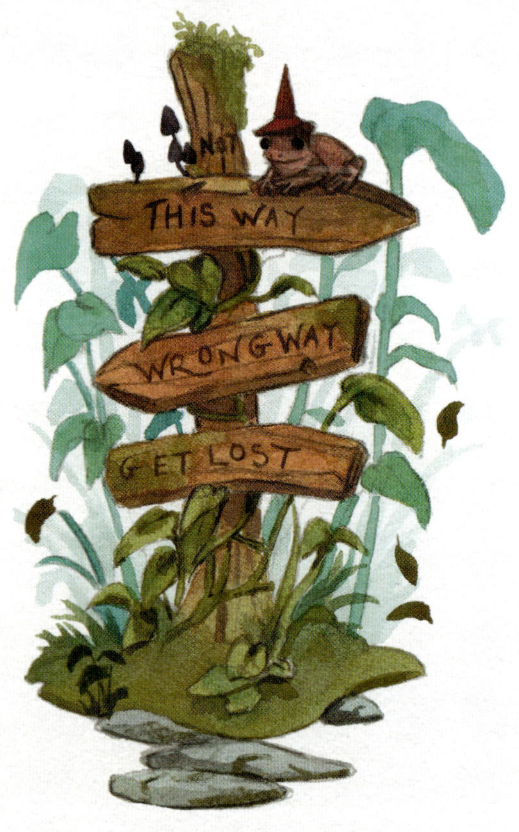

Colors

Cerulean Blue

Gamboge

Yellow Ochre

Burnt Sienna

Sap Green

Crimson Lake Red

Ultramarine Blue

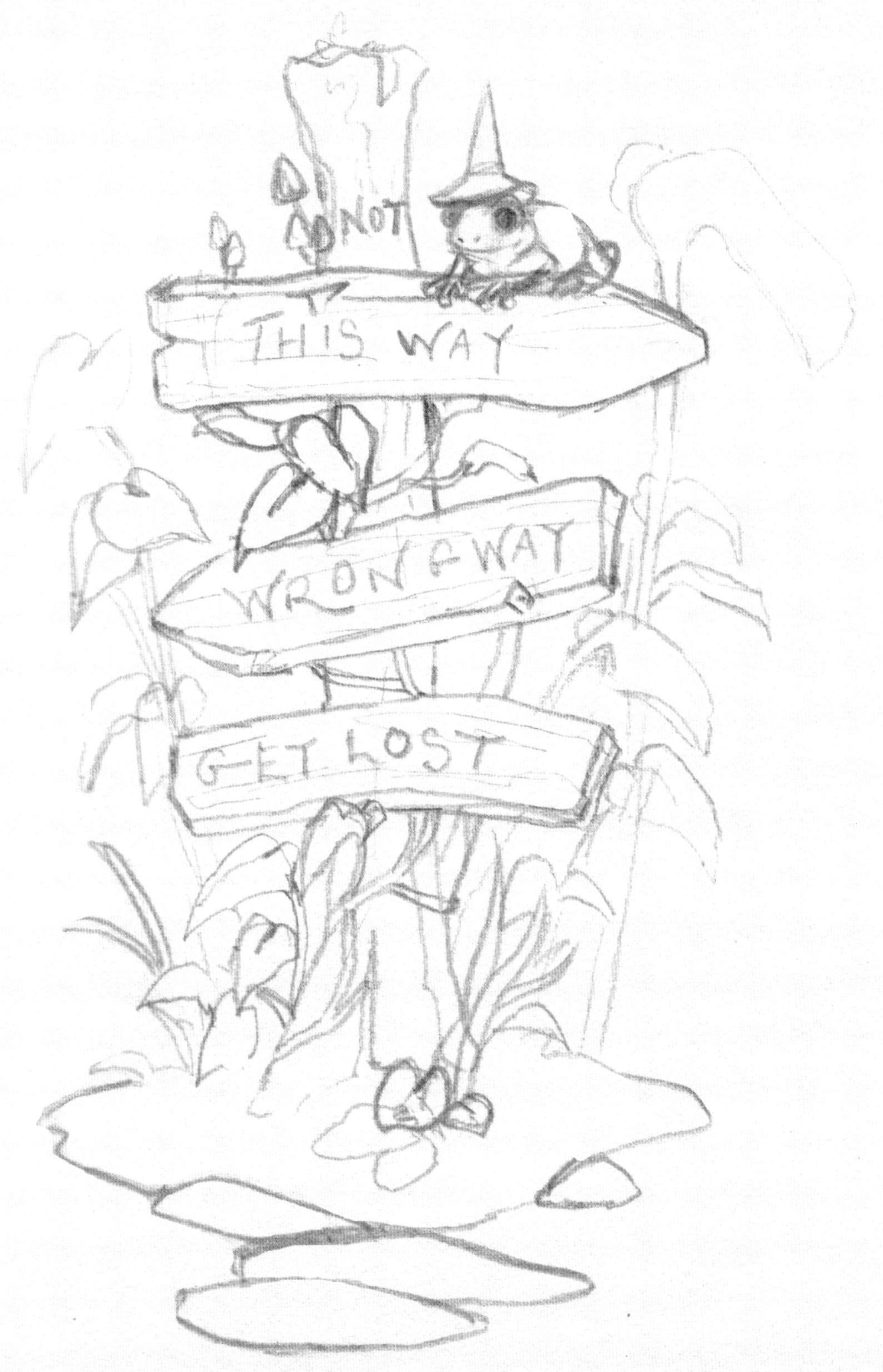
DO NOT
THIS WAY
WRONG WAY
GET LOST

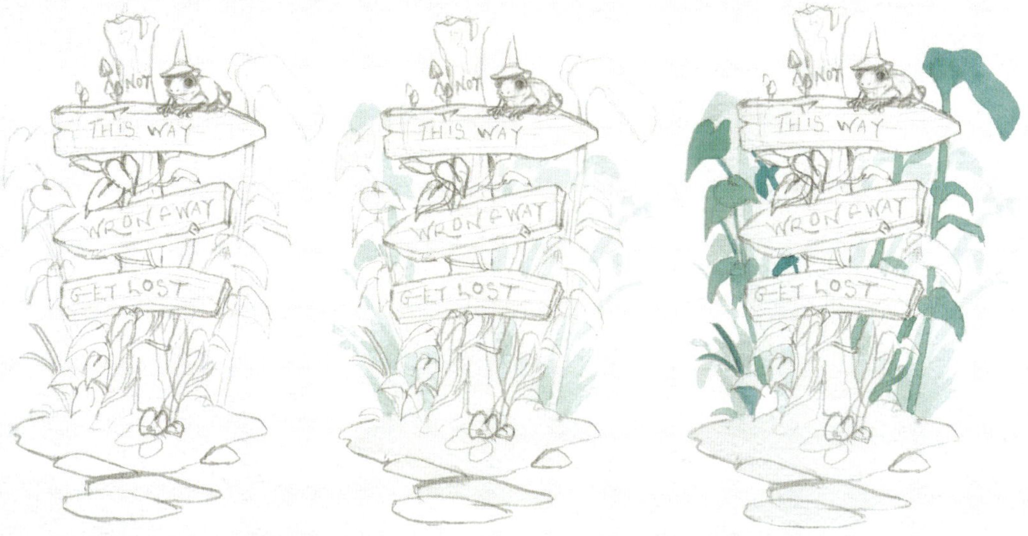

Step 1

Trace the sketch onto your watercolor paper or redraw it using my image as a reference. The key shapes of the drawing to keep in mind are the blocky wooden signposts surrounded by tall leaves overlapping each other.

Step 2

Start painting the furthermost background with your round brush 2 dipped in a lot of water. Use Cerulean Blue + Gamboge, completely diluted so you can work transparently.

Now paint the shapes of tall grass blades and leaves. These don't have to be very precise because they will be pushed to the background. Add more Cerulean Blue the further down to the ground you paint.

Let the paint dry thoroughly.

Step 3

Repeat the same technique as Step 2 for tall leaves and grass closer to the foreground, but use less water in the paint mixture so that we begin to work on a more opaque layer. Let the paint dry.

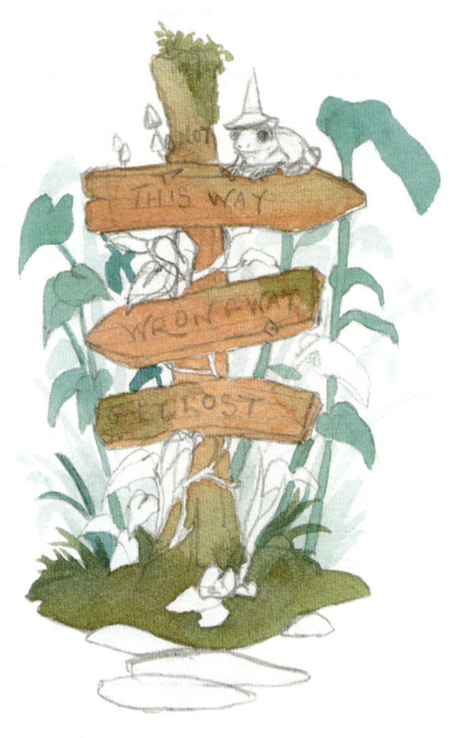

Step 4

Switch to your round brush 10. Start painting more opaquely, using an equal part of water and paint. For this step we're going to create a neat gradient for the wood and grass, so use *The Bead Method* from Chapter 1 (see page 15), and ensure that your sketchbook is raised at a slight angle.

Mix a wood color using Yellow Ochre + a touch of Burnt Sienna, and begin applying it to the top of the wooden sign. While the paint is wet, dab spots of Sap Green + Crimson Lake Red for random spots of moss growing on the wood. Cover all the areas of the wooden sign. As you reach the ground, add more Sap Green + Crimson Lake Red.

Work quickly to create a gradient transition to the grass. Mix a touch of Cerulean Blue into the Sap Green + Crimson Lake Red mixture, and apply that to the back of the grass. Paint silhouettes of grass blades and leaves.

Clean your brush, and use Sap Green + Crimson Lake Red + Gamboge for the lighter parts of the grass.

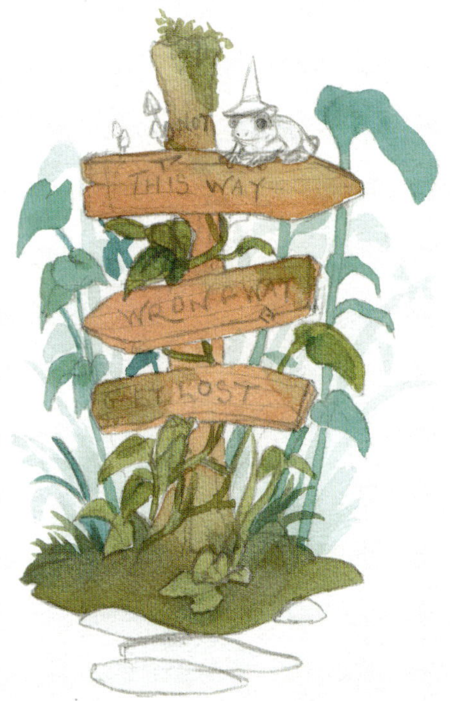

Step 5

Switch to your round brush 2 again. Use Sap Green + Yellow Ochre + a touch of Gamboge with an equal part of water to mix a light-green color. Apply this color to all the remaining leaves and vines curling around the wooden sign.

While the paint is still wet, add a touch of Cerulean Blue to the mixture, and dab spots of this color on the underside of leaves that are facing away or in shadow.

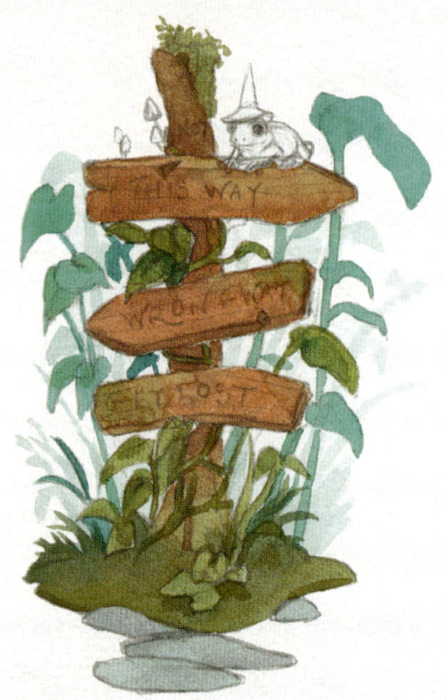

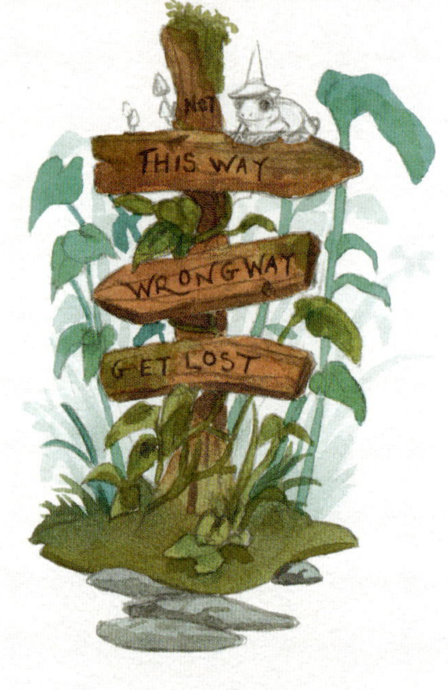

Step 6

Continue painting with your round brush 2. Mix a grey-purple color using Ultramarine Blue + Crimson Lake Red, diluted with a lot of water, and paint the stepping stones with this color.

Next, bring out the brown wood of the sign using diluted Burnt Sienna and *The Glazing Method* from Chapter 1 (see page 16). Make sure to leave the upper areas of the sign untouched, because they are facing the light. Then create a dark-brown color by mixing Burnt Sienna + Ultramarine Blue, and apply this color to the vertical wooden post behind the arrow signs.

Finally, for this step, create a dark-green color by mixing Sap Green + Crimson Lake Red, and apply it to vines that are in shadow, and the underside of leaves on the grass.

Step 7

Now let's slowly begin layering the details.

Use your round brush 0 and a thick mixture of Burnt Sienna + Ultramarine Blue to paint the words on the wooden sign. You can choose a specific font of your preference; in this case I just used a simple text with some exaggeration on the *W* and *R* to make it more whimsical. Use the same color and brush to paint the line texture across the wood.

Next, use your round brush 2 and the same color you used for the stepping stones. Define the bottom edges of the stones, and paint in a few cracks.

Then mix Ultramarine Blue + Crimson Lake Red for a dark-purple shadow color, and apply it to the vertical post, where the signs would be casting a shadow beneath.

Let these layers dry completely before moving on.

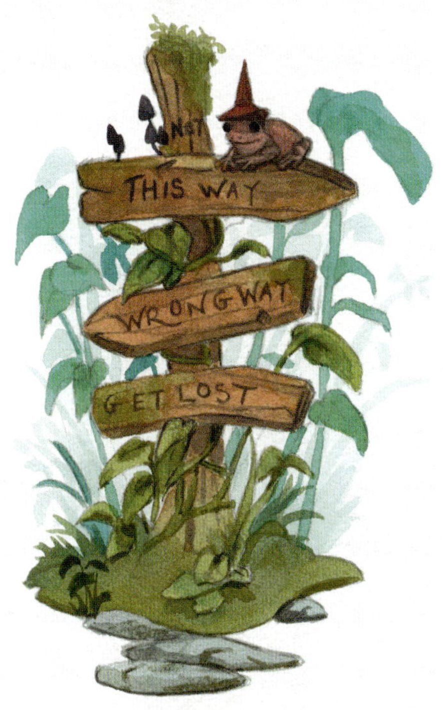

Step 8

In this step, let's bring the frog to life. Use your round brush 2 dipped in a fair amount of water, and paint the frog and its hat a light wash of Crimson Lake Red.

While that's drying, paint some silhouettes of leaves and grass blades in the foreground, using Sap Green + Crimson Lake Red.

Next, switch to your round brush 0 and mix Ultramarine Blue + Crimson Lake Red for a dark (almost black) color to paint the little mushrooms sprouting from the top of the wood. Use this same color for the eyes of the frog.

While those paint layers are drying, you can use this time to define some of the linework. Because there are so many overlapping elements in this illustration, use a dark-brown pencil to bring out the linework of the wooden sign, vines, the stepping stones, and the frog, and make the sign more readable.

Step 9

We're almost done with our mysterious sign. The last detail to add is some stray leaves falling in the wind. Use a round brush 2 and Sap Green + Crimson Lake Red to paint the shapes of these falling leaves.

With that, we can wrap up our wooden sign and leave it to confuse any visitors. Well done, dear wizard! Now our little project of chaos is one step closer to magic and wizardry.

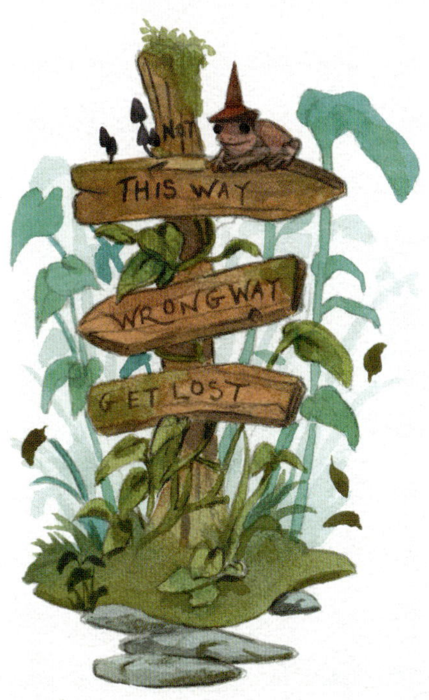

The Tale of the Skeleton Tree

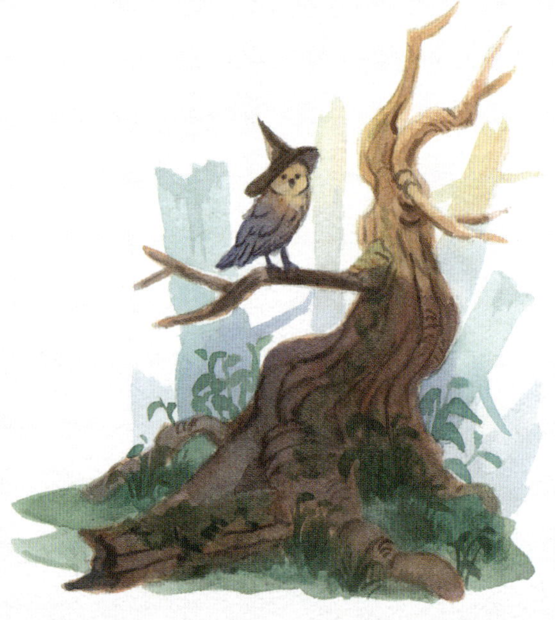

A skeleton tree is one that doesn't grow any leaves, no matter what season it is. The rest of the trees all around it will be in full bloom, but this one will be dry, cold, and moody, with a dark tale to tell. Its branches reach to the sky like fingers out of a grave, and its bark is grey and lifeless. Skeleton trees also make great homes for ghosts.

In this project, we're going to paint one of these skeleton trees for our dimension. We'll also paint a friend and colleague: an owl wizard named Boobok the Beady-Eyed, whom we've known for a while and who can share a tale with our adventurers. What exactly happened to this tree, and how did it end up the way it is?

Brushes

Round brush 10, 2, and 0

Colors

Cerulean Blue

Violet

Yellow Ochre

Burnt Sienna

Sap Green

Ultramarine Blue

Crimson Lake Red

Gamboge

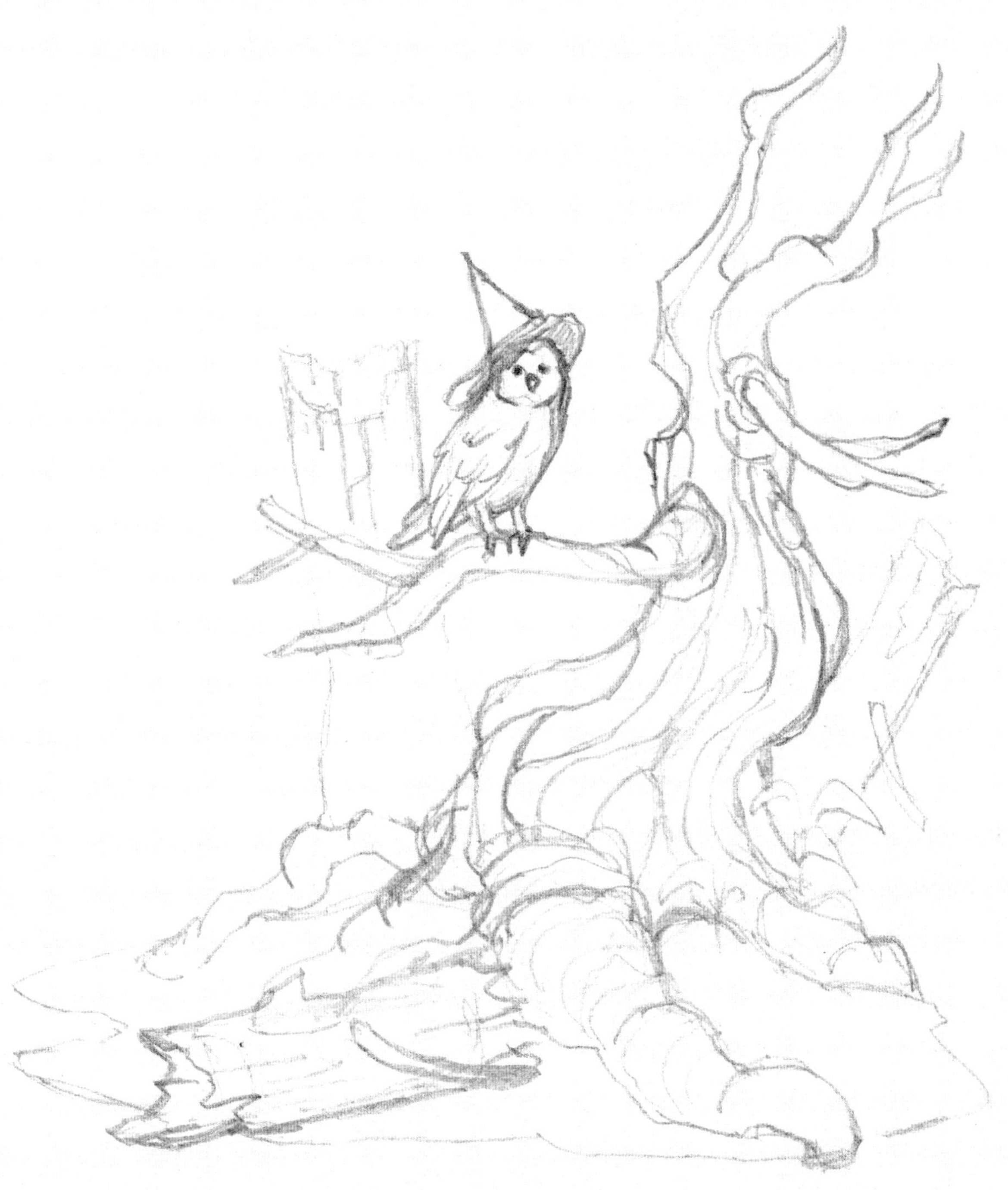

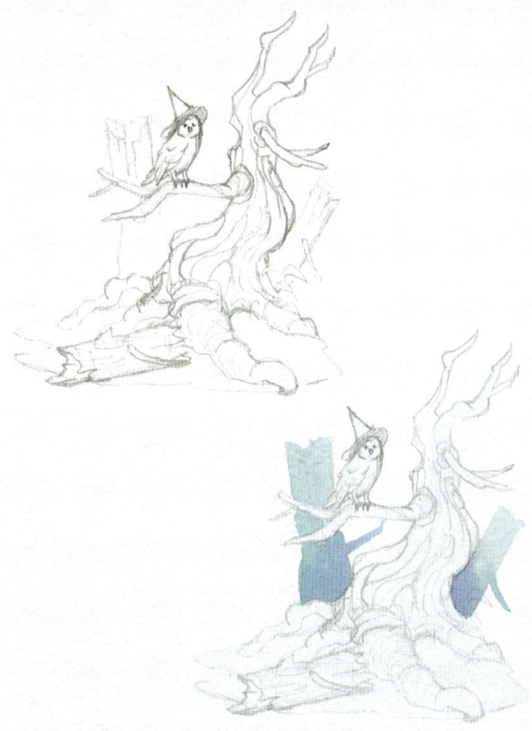

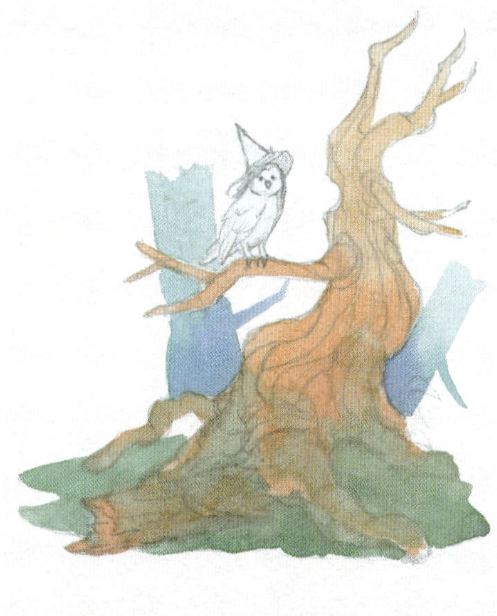

Step 1

Redraw or trace the sketch onto your water-color paper. The owl is the main feature of the drawing, so start with sketching his body and pointed wizard hat. Another key element of the drawing is the branch the owl is perched on. The rest of the drawing can be altered according to your imagination.

Step 2

Start painting with a round brush 10 dipped in a fair amount of water. Use diluted Cerulean Blue to cover the background tree trunks.

Because we want this scene to look a bit moody, use Violet at the bottom of the Cerulean Blue. These cool colors work together to give the scene a mysterious atmosphere.

Step 3

Using *The Bead Method* outlined in Chapter 1 (see page 15), for this step, raise your sketchbook at a slight angle, and work on a wet layer quickly with your round brush 10.

Start with Yellow Ochre, and paint the top branches of the tree. This is where the sunlight would be streaming in. As you paint the body of the tree, add Burnt Sienna.

For the grassy ground, use a mixture of Sap Green + Cerulean Blue, and let this green overlap with the Burnt Sienna. Later, when it dries, we can paint the effect of moss.

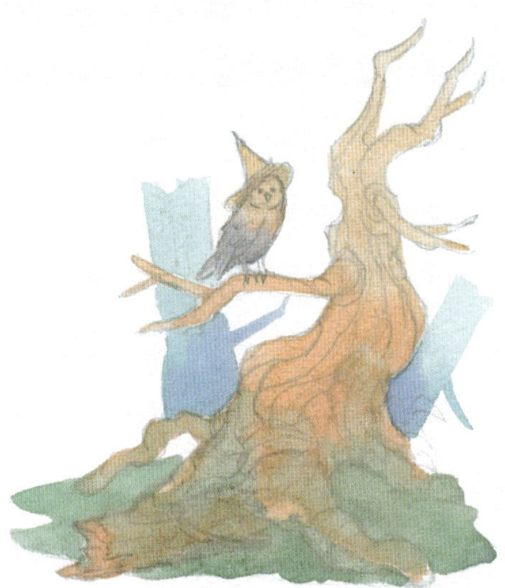

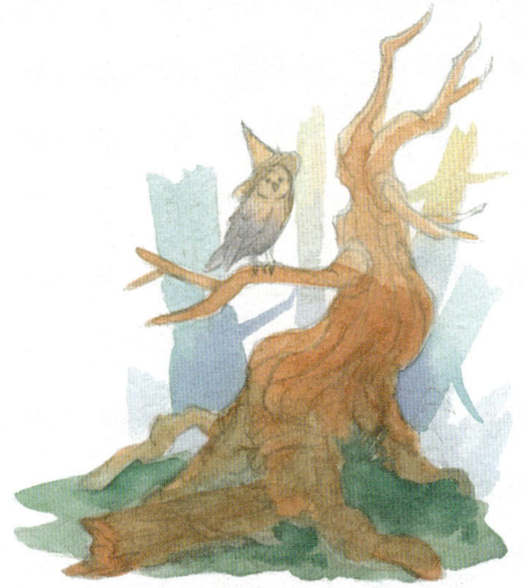

Step 4

Let's paint the base layer for the owl. First, use Yellow Ochre with a fair amount of water, and paint the top of the creature. As you reach his midsection, dab an angular line of Burnt Sienna. Clean your brush, and then paint the rest of the body with Violet + Ultramarine Blue.

This angular shadow gives us a sneak peek to what the moody lighting will look like when the illustration is done: half in shadow, half in light.

Step 5

Switch to your round brush 2 for this step. Add another layer of Burnt Sienna to the tree using *The Glazing Method* from Chapter 1 (see page 16), starting from the top of the branches where the curving branches would cast shadows.

Around the midsection of the tree, just below the owl, paint Burnt Sienna in a downward angle. Add another layer of Burnt Sienna over the tree roots and the fallen trunk.

Still using *The Glazing Method*, deepen the green grass with Sap Green + Ultramarine Blue.

While those are drying, use Violet to paint more tree trunks in the distance near the bottom of the illustration.

To push the contrast in the lighting even more, use a wet layer of Yellow Ochre for the top of distant trees, and add Violet + Ultramarine Blue with a lot of water near the bottom. Then use diluted Burnt Sienna for the right-most side of those trees, giving them some form.

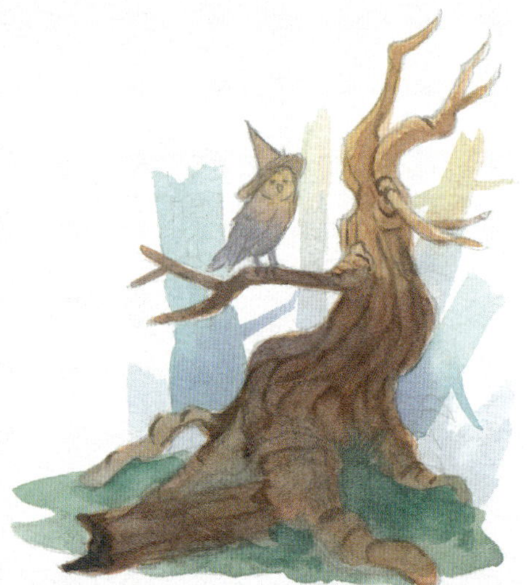

Step 6

In this step, we're going to establish the lighting and define it more by using *The Glazing Method.* Use your round brush 0, and mix Ultramarine Blue + Burnt Sienna to paint in the lines on the bark and across the tree. Loosely add circle textures and spots, which will dry later and create beautiful effects.

Next, use a round brush 2 and Burnt Sienna with an equal part of water. Apply it over the tree where you worked previously, on the curves of the bark, and the bottom half.

Then mix Violet + a touch of Ultramarine Blue, and exaggerate the bottom half of the shadow, covering the entire area.

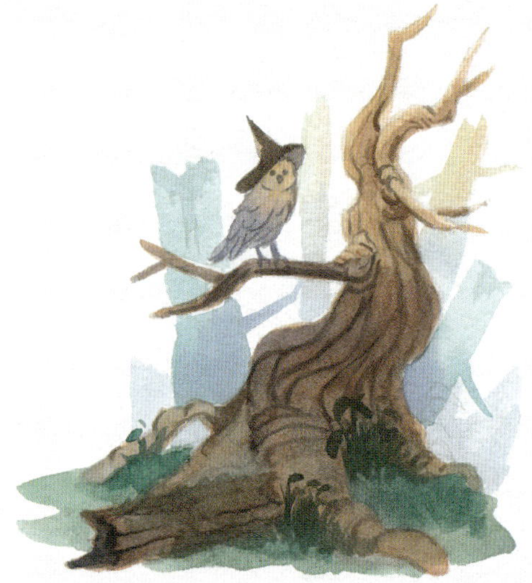

Step 7

Use your round brush 2 for this step. Add another layer of Cerulean Blue + Violet for detail on the inside of the tree trunks that are in the distance.

Then use Sap Green + Crimson Lake Red + Ultramarine Blue to paint silhouettes of leaves in the darkest areas near the tree roots.

Next mix Burnt Sienna + Ultramarine Blue to darken the lines on the tree trunk. Use this color for the owl's hat as well.

Finally, switch to your round brush 0, and use Violet to outline the feathers on the owl wizard. Erase any pencil lines that are still visible.

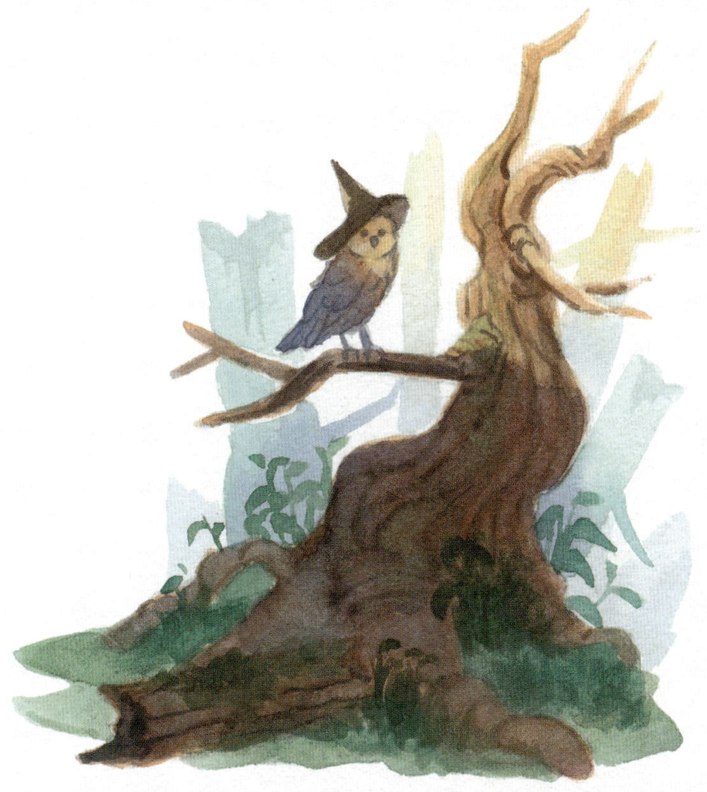

Step 8

We're almost complete with this illustration! All that's left is to add more purple to our tree and define the foliage.

Use your round brush 2 and pure Violet to glaze across the shadow part of the tree. Add another layer of Violet across the owl as well. Use Burnt Sienna for the transition between the Violet and Yellow Ochre on the owl's feathers.

Mix Sap Green + Cerulean Blue + Crimson Lake Red, and paint more leaves, stems, and grass blades around the tree roots. Dab some of this color into the Violet on the tree trunk, and let it granulate across the page for natural texture. In the light areas of the bark, use Sap Green + Gamboge with a fair amount of water. Don't paint too much moss on the bark, because we want the tree to feel a little bare and grey, like a skeleton.

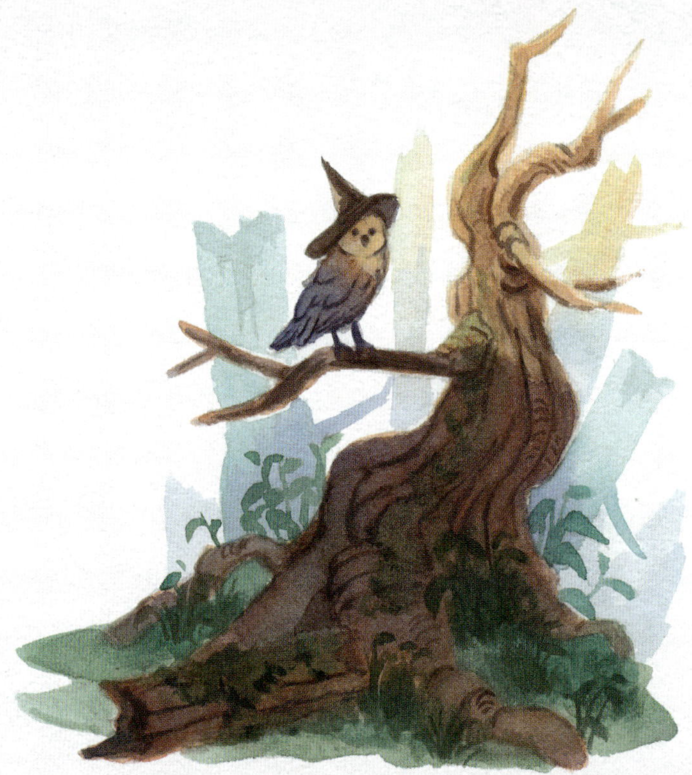

Step 9

To finish off this section of our dimension, use your round brush 0 and Burnt Sienna + Ultramarine Blue with very little water to paint over the lines on the tree bark.

Then mix Sap Green + Ultramarine Blue + Crimson Lake Red, and paint more details on the grass, adding more silhouettes of leaves and grass blades, and some spots of color variation across the grass.

Finally, use Violet to paint over the outlines on the owl's feathers, defining its form more since he is the star of this illustration. And that's another great job done! Our Owl Wizard, Old Boobok the Beady-Eyed, is ready to unleash a tale to visitors. Once upon an ancient time, a watercolor wizard had an idea . . .

Apprentice Notes:

Atmospheric scenes like these are a great way to play with moody lighting. Try these combinations for different times of day and mood:

Sunset: Yellow Ochre/Burnt Sienna/Payne's Grey

Night: Viridian/Lavender/ Ultramarine Blue

Red Lighting: Crimson Lake Red/ Crimson Lake Red + Violet

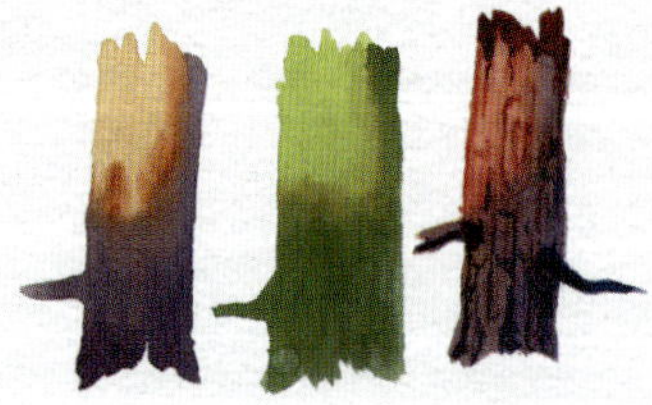

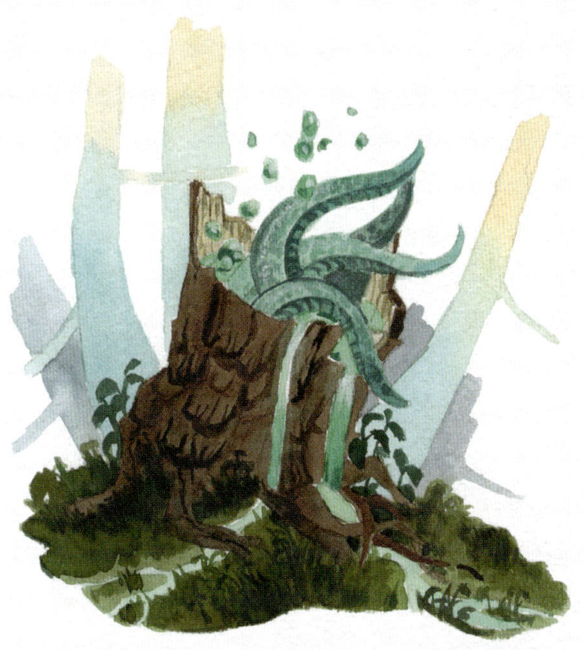

Tentacles in the Tree Stump

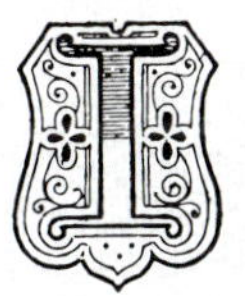

It's inevitable to stumble upon a tree stump while wandering a forest. However, in magical forest dimensions like ours, a tree stump is not a regular tree stump—it's teeming with danger. In this project, we're going to paint one for our adventurers to discover, not knowing what could be hidden inside this dead tree. Tree stumps are also one of my favorite things to paint because there are just so many beautiful colors and lighting you can play around with when painting them.

Brushes

Round brush 10, 2, 0

Colors

Yellow Ochre

Cerulean Blue

Gamboge

Burnt Sienna

Deep Blue

Sap Green

Crimson Lake Red

Payne's Grey

Deep Green

Titanium White

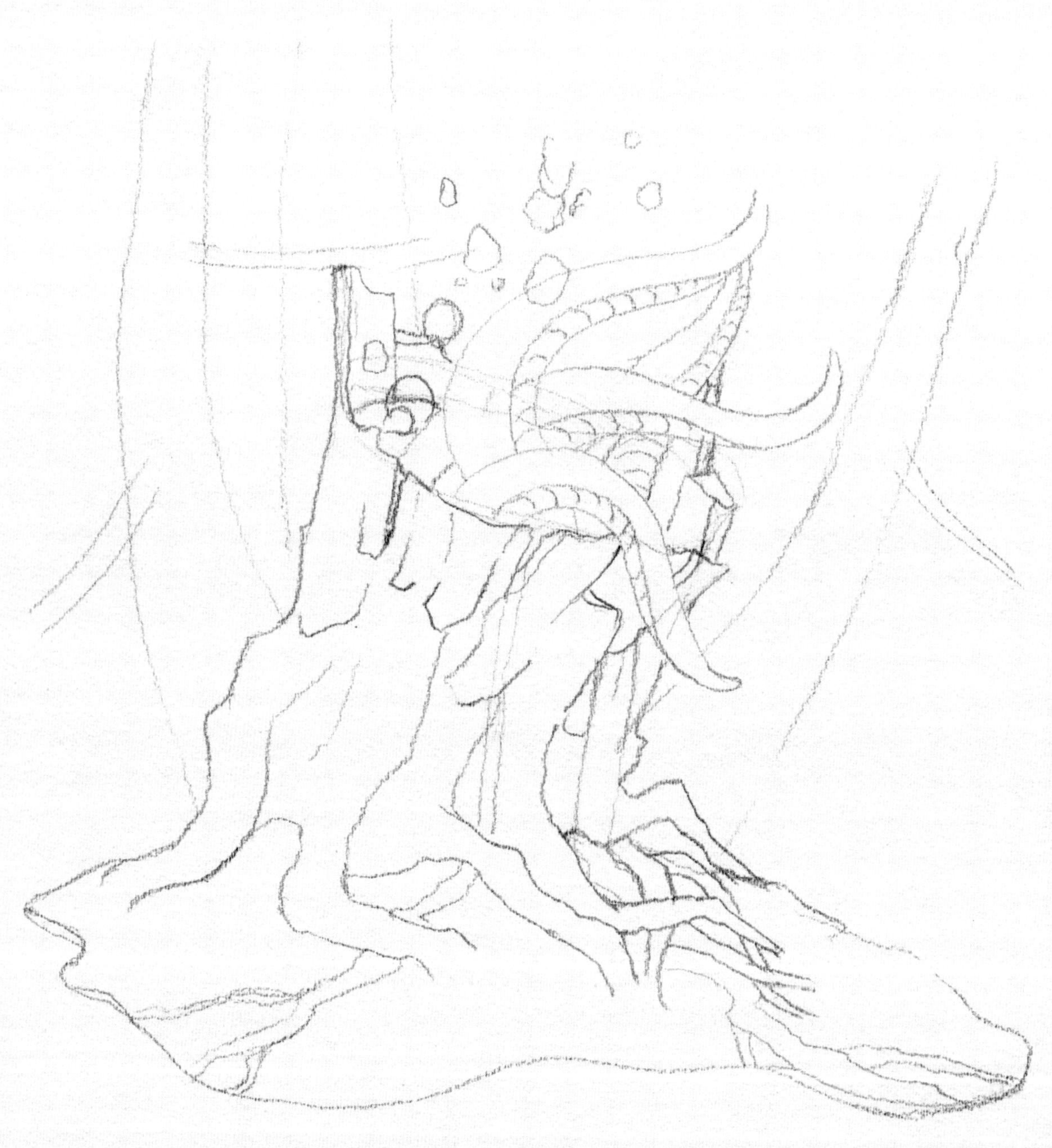

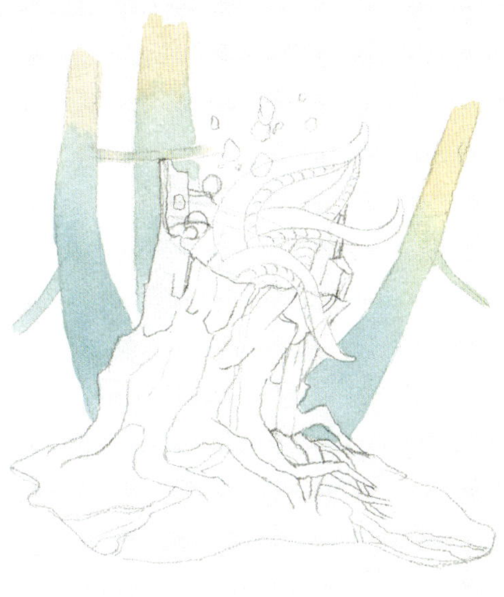

Step 1

Draw the sketch using the reference provided. Use an HB pencil, and don't worry about the darkness of the lines at first, because you can always erase the lines to make them less visible.

Step 2

Start with your round brush 10 dipped in a fair amount of water. Use *The Bead Method* described in Chapter 1 (see page 15), and paint with your sketchbook at a slight angle, so that the colors flow together and blend seamlessly.

Use Yellow Ochre mixed in an equal part of water, and paint the top of the tree branches in the background. Then, while the paint is still wet, dab spots of Cerulean Blue, which will mix with the yellow to create a green transition color. As you paint further downward, add more Cerulean Blue into the mixture.

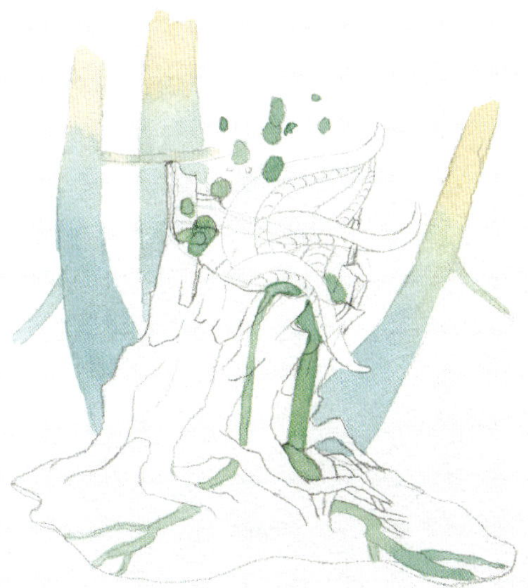

Step 3

Switch to your round brush 2. Mix Cerulean Blue + Gamboge to create an eerie green color, and paint the bubbles and potion pouring out of the tree stump.

Step 4

Continue painting with your round brush 2. Mix Burnt Sienna + Deep Blue to get a dark-brown color. Apply this color to the surface of the tree stump. To mix a darker shade of brown, add more Deep Blue into the color. Use this darker color to paint bark texture onto the stump, which we will define later.

Then mix Burnt Sienna + Gamboge for a light-brown color, and paint the inside of the stump.

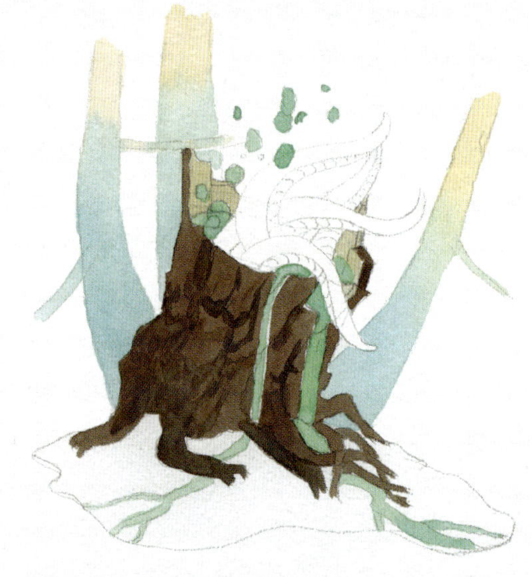

Step 5

For the grassy ground, mix Sap Green + a touch of Crimson Lake Red to get a desaturated green color. Apply this color on the entire ground. Paint the silhouettes of grass blades and leaves at the edges.

Next, mix Cerulean Blue + a touch of Gamboge for a similar yellow-green color, and paint all the tentacles. While the paint is still wet, dab spots of Cerulean Blue into the paint at the tips of the tentacles and on the inside of the curve.

Let this layer dry thoroughly before moving on.

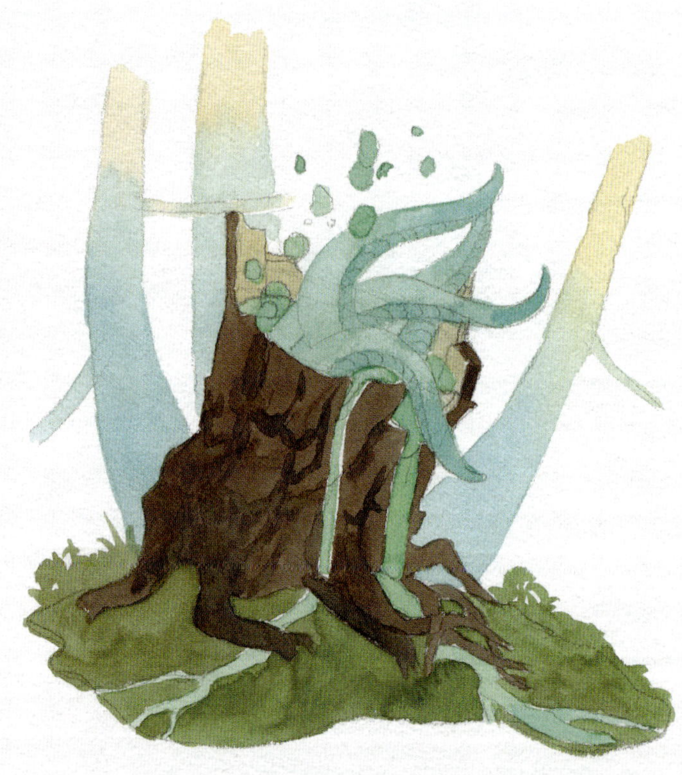

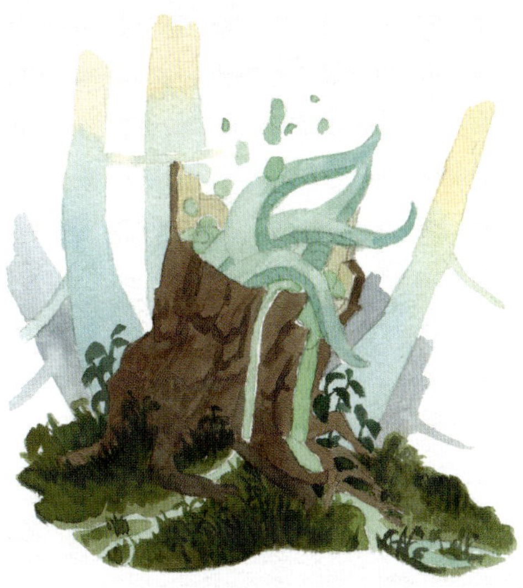

Step 6

Erase any unwanted pencil lines that are still visible. Mix Deep Blue + Payne's Grey, and paint the silhouettes of more branches and tree trunks in the furthermost background.

Paint another layer of Cerulean Blue on the inside curve of the tentacles.

Next, let's begin painting details. Mix Sap Green + Crimson Lake Red with an equal part of water, and paint strands of grass by the roots of the stump and hills facing away from the river. Then mix Deep Green + Crimson Lake Red, and glaze this darker color on the previous layer (see *The Glazing Method* from Chapter 1, page 16). To give the illusion of the eerie green liquid flowing through a lot of grass, use this dark-green color to paint silhouettes of grass and leaves over some of the small rivers at the bottom.

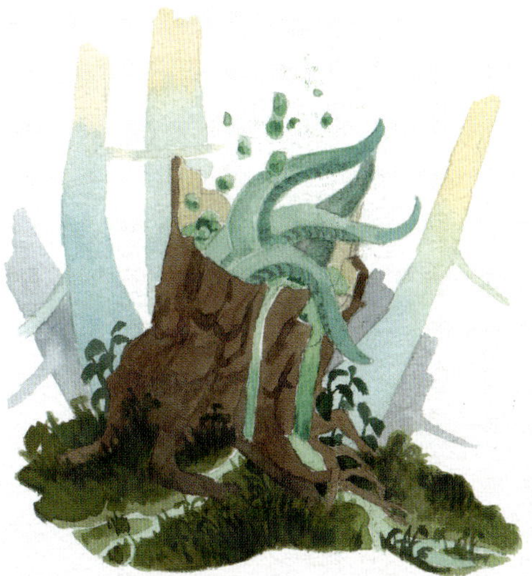

Step 7

Add a layer of Cerulean Blue at the bottom of the two falls, creating a fade into the existing color and enhancing the glow.

Next, mix Cerulean Blue + a touch of Payne's Grey to shade the tentacles. Apply this color on the lines on the inside and the outer curve. The furthermost tentacle will be the darkest; use more Payne's Grey in the mixture to cover this tentacle.

Then paint spots of Cerulean Blue into the bubbles as a shadow.

Step 8

Switch to your round brush 0. Create a thick mixture of Burnt Sienna + Deep Blue, and use this color to paint the outlines and texture on the bark of the wood. For the inside of the stump, use Burnt Sienna + Yellow Ochre.

Clean your brush. Then mix Cerulean Blue + Gamboge with a fair amount of water, and carefully glaze over the areas on the wood that are close to the pouring liquid. (See *The Glazing Method* from Chapter 1, page 16.)

Next, use the same color to paint spots on the tentacles, hinting at scales. Use pure Deep Blue to outline the shape of the tentacles so they don't disappear into each other.

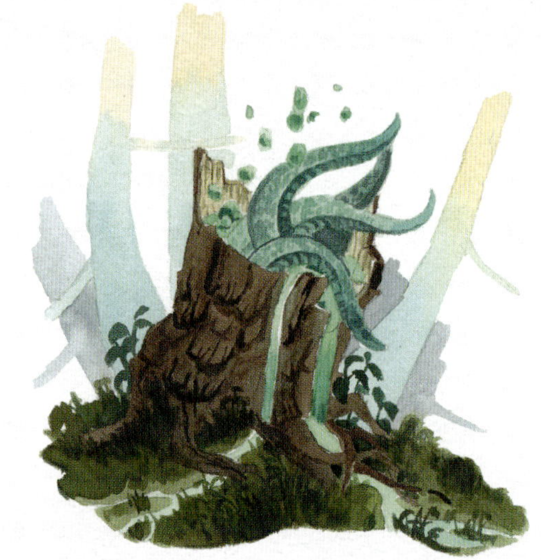

Step 9

In this final step, use Titanium White watercolor paint with your round brush 0 to paint the delicate highlight spots on the bubbles and the tentacles. Also apply this color, using a thick mixture, on the top of the falls, enhancing the movement.

With those highlights, our tentacle monster is complete! Beware, adventurers.

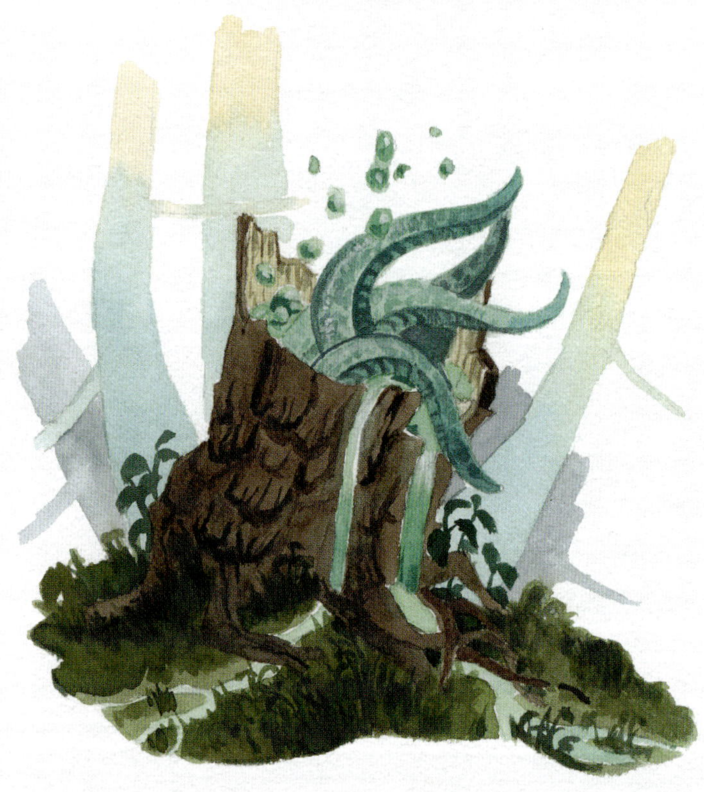

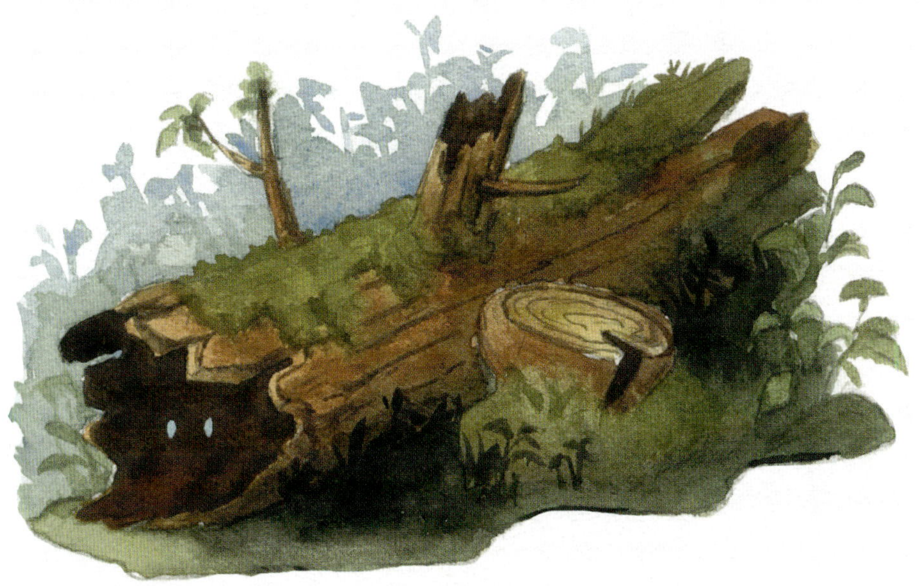

EYES FROM THE SHADOWS

As the head wizard of our forest dimension, we need to ensure that any adventurer who traverses our lands should always be monitored. In lieu of cameras, we can install magical friends who are adept at stealth to keep an eye on visitors. Such creatures enjoy shadowed crevices, hollowed out tree trunks, and the underside of leaves and bushes. If a stranger were to notice them in the shadows, they would appear as two little blue orbs . . .

In this project, we're going to paint some eyes peeking from the shadows, carefully hidden inside the darkness of a fallen tree log.

Brushes

Round brush 10, 0

Colors

Ultramarine Blue

Sap Green

Gamboge

Yellow Ochre

Burnt Sienna

Crimson Lake Red

Titanium White

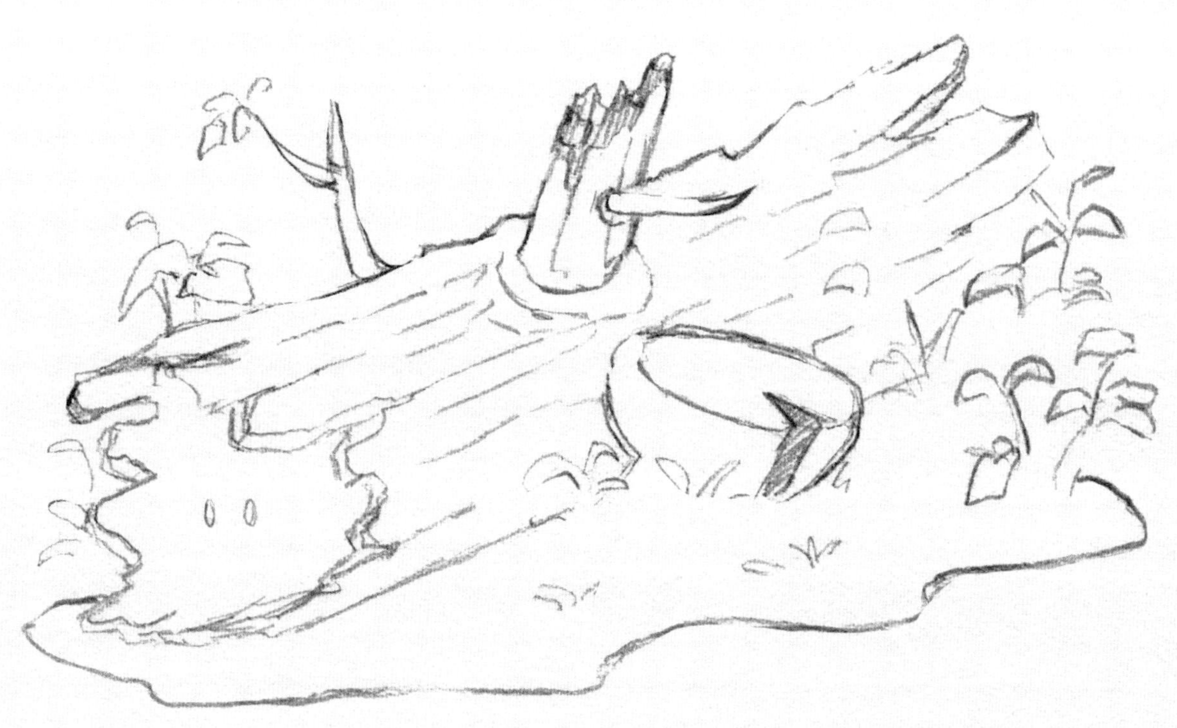

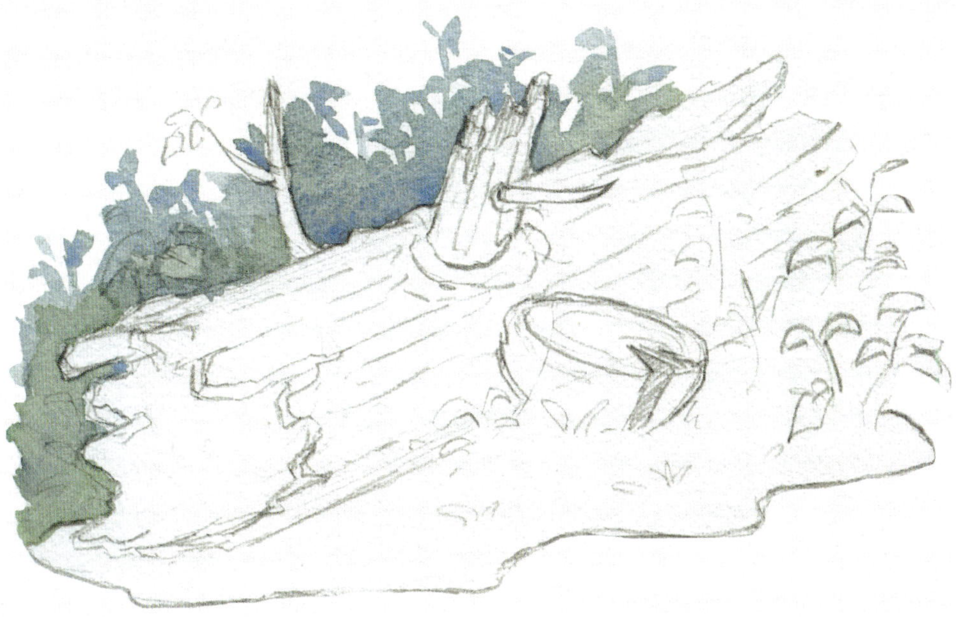

Step 1

Copy the drawing onto your watercolor paper using an HB pencil. The key shapes to transfer are the fallen log and the round stump nestled next to it. Make sure there is enough open space at the end of the fallen log to paint a pair of eyes.

Step 2

Let's start establishing depth in this illustration by painting the furthermost background elements; this will be an assortment of wild bushes, leaves, and stems. Using a round brush 10 dipped in a fair amount of water, we're going to work on a semitransparent layer. Mix Ultramarine Blue + Sap Green to get a beautiful teal color.

Now start painting loose silhouettes of wild leaves, attached by their stem. Feel free to refer to the Common Shapes and Color Combos section on page 20 in Chapter 1 to reexamine some of the leaf shapes we covered there.

While the Ultramarine Blue + Sap Green layer is still wet, add a touch of Gamboge using *The Wet-on-Wet Technique* outlined in Chapter 1 (page 16). Immediately you'll see the green become more intense. Quickly dab that green into areas of the Ultramarine Layer that are lower toward the ground of the log. These areas, because of the proximity to grass, will have more green.

Let the layer dry thoroughly.

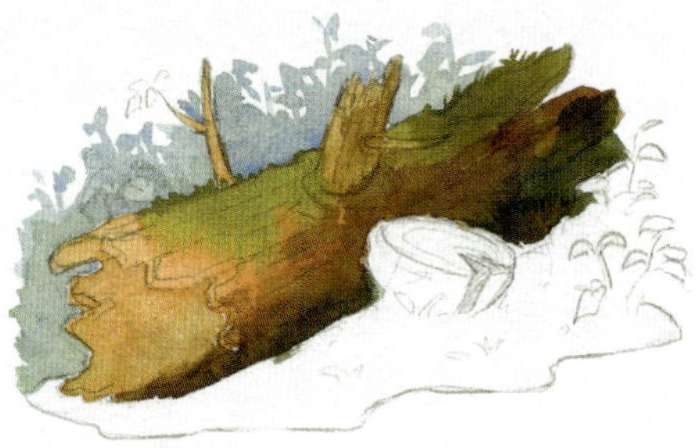 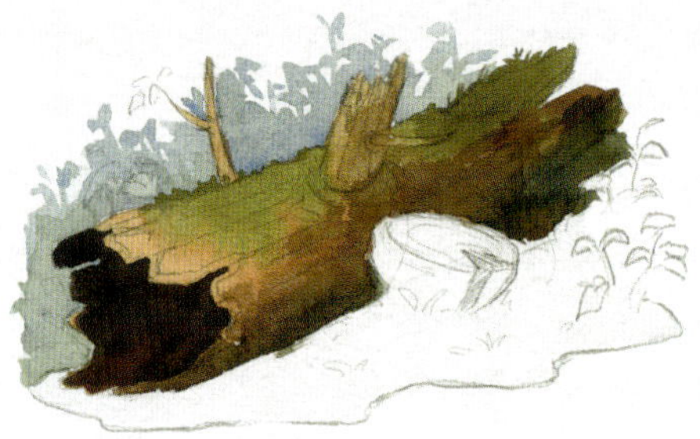

Step 3

We're about to paint the first layer of the star of the show: the log. Keep in mind the light source, which we can imagine to be striking the bottom left of the log from above. All other areas will have darker colors. We're also going to work quickly on a wet layer, so the water will naturally blend several colors together.

Use your round brush 10 dipped in water, and dab it in Yellow Ochre. Mix a hint of Burnt Sienna (very little, because we want more yellow here), and start by painting the left side of the log, right above where the eyes of the log creature would be.

Quickly, while the yellow is still wet, dip your brush in Sap Green mixed with a touch of Crimson Lake Red. These two colors are complementary; red reduces the intensity of the green. Now use *The Wet-on-Wet Technique* to dab the green into the wet Yellow Ochre on the top of the log, where moss would be growing.

Step 4

Again, while the layer is wet, and as you move to the right, mix a darker shade of green by adding a little bit of Ultramarine Blue. Then, toward the bottom of the log, mix a darker brown with Burnt Sienna + Ultramarine Blue.

Once the previous layer is completely dry, clean your round brush 10. Then, to create a dark-brown color, mix Ultramarine Blue + Burnt Sienna with just a little drop of water, making sure there is more blue in the mixture. Now start painting the darkest parts inside the log. This will be quite an opaque layer with less water.

While the layer is wet, add more Burnt Sienna as you paint the inside floor of the log. This makes the lighting inside the log a little warm, and it emphasizes the haze of the forest.

The key thing to keep in mind in this step is to preserve the shapes of the log, letting some of the background blue show through the cracks.

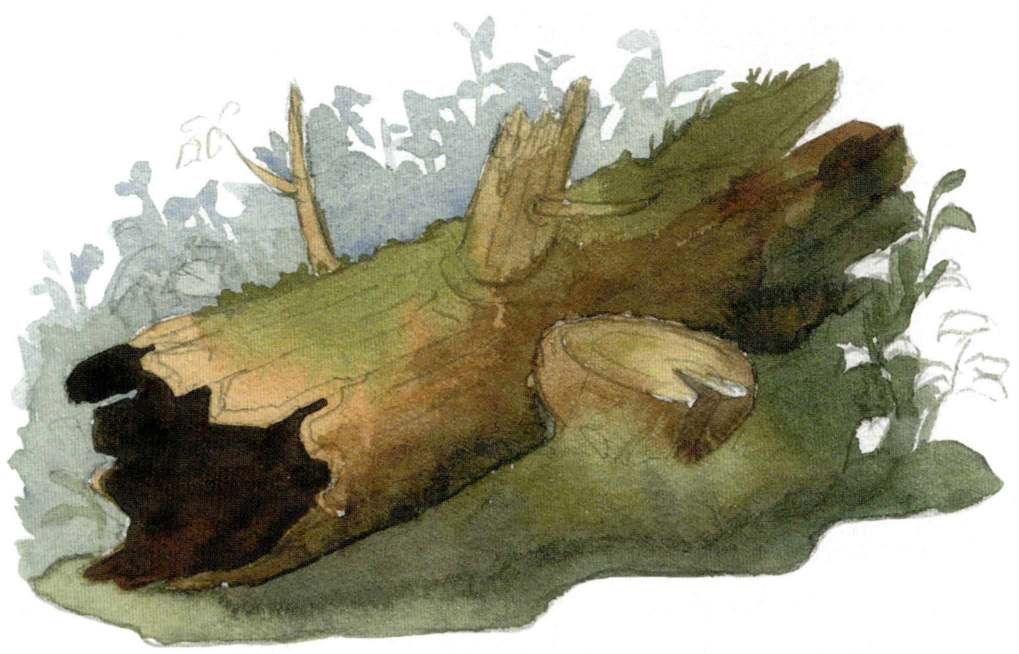

Step 5

Just as we painted the log in the previous step, we're going to work quickly on a wet layer to allow for colors to blend naturally. Also, we need to use *The Bead Method* from Chapter 1 (see page 15) for a smooth gradient, so be sure to raise your sketchbook at an angle for this step.

Let's start with Yellow Ochre and our round brush 10. Paint the top surface of the small tree stump. While it's wet, add Burnt Sienna to the Yellow Ochre, and apply the color to the round bark.

Create a dark-brown color by mixing Burnt Sienna + Ultramarine Blue to apply to the dark cut sliced into the stump. Now wipe your brush, and introduce Sap Green + Yellow Ochre to paint spots of grass directly below the round stump, where the light might be highlighting it.

For the dark areas of the grass, mix Sap Green + Ultramarine Blue + a little bit of Crimson Lake Red. We will slowly add more details in the next steps.

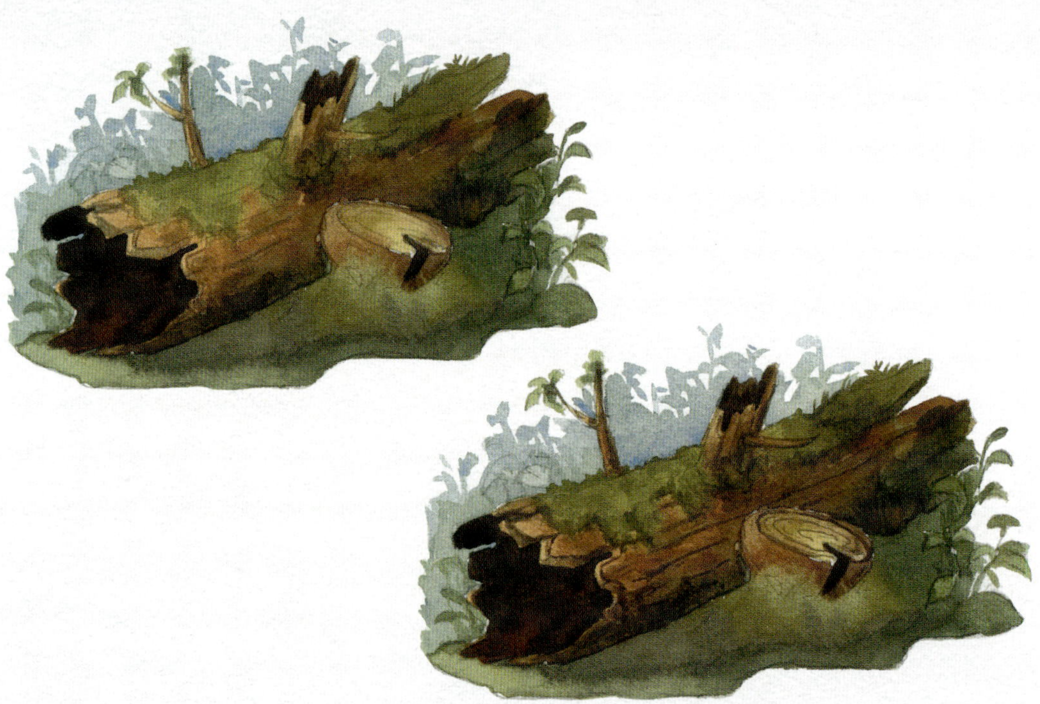

Step 6

Now we get into the delicious details! Mix Burnt Sienna + Ultramarine Blue for the inside of the smaller tree stump sticking out of the log. Use the same color to darken the slice on the round tree stump.

Then clean your brush, and use diluted Burnt Sienna and your round brush 0 for details on the bark of the log. Here, we can refine its shape and form more by adding variation in color.

Next, create a dark-green color by mixing Sap Green + Ultramarine Blue, and use the round brush 0 to paint shadow details on the moss. Even moss has form, which means certain areas will be in light, and other areas will be in shadow.

Finally, mix Sap Green + Yellow Ochre with a lot of water, and continue using the round brush 0 on the bark of the log. Use this color for the areas of the log that face toward the ground, and for the remainder of the leaf details sprouting from the ground and branches.

Step 7

Clean your round brush 0. Use the dark-brown color from the previous step (Burnt Sienna + Ultramarine Blue) to paint the outlines of the bark texture on the log and both stumps.

Then use the Sap Green + Yellow Ochre mixture, diluted with a lot of water, and the round brush 0 to add more color variation to the moss.

Next, use diluted Burnt Sienna to paint some final texture details on the log.

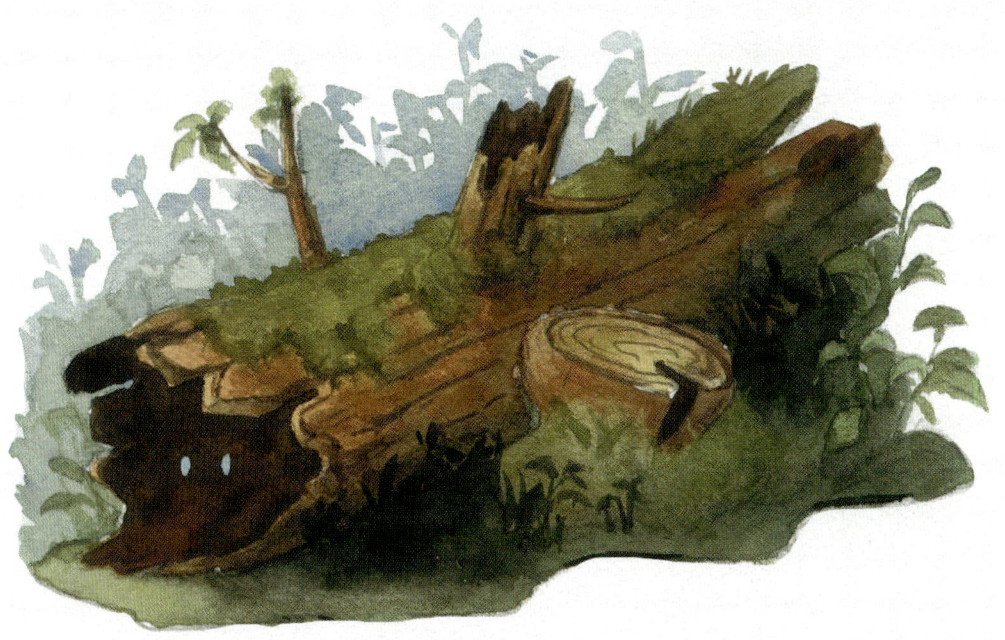

Step 8

We're almost done now. First, we're going to adjust the grass in the foreground. Mix the darkest green color using Sap Green + Ultramarine Blue + Crimson Lake Red, and use your round brush 0 to paint stems and leaves. Paint these leaves sprouting in the area below the log where the log would be casting a shadow, and behind the round tree stump. Use the same green to outline the ground shape where it curves.

The final step is to invite our creature. Use a thick mixture of Titanium White + Ultramarine Blue. Mix very little water so you have more control over the paint.

With the round brush 0, delicately paint two dots in the shadow inside the fallen log.

Step back and admire how this log has awoken to life! Painting moss on bark can be tricky, but as you have learned in this tutorial, by combining *The Bead Method* with some wizardry, it can be a much more enjoyable task. Now we have a handy friend watching our adventurers' every movement, every mistake, and every step out of line. Well done on creating a corner of magic in the world.

A Place for Adventurers to Rest

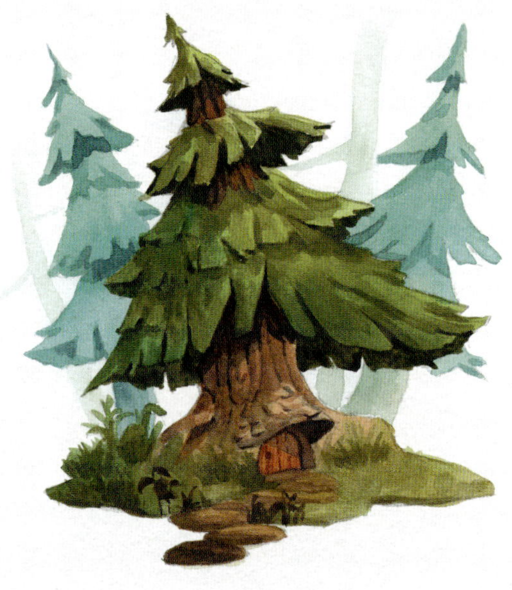

Let's be honest: Adventuring, while it's quite glamorous and honorable, can also be intensely exhausting. Can you imagine how tired our visitors could be? They're walking mile after mile and fighting monsters and creatures of the forest along the way. Any generous wizard would be kind enough to provide a resting place safe from threats: a cozy home nestled within a shady tree, complete with the scent of freshly made tea and baked goods wafting out of the door as strangers near it.

In this tutorial, we're going to paint a cozy, totally safe and nonthreatening nook: a bakery of one hospitable gnome who generously opens his door for our adventurers.

Brushes

Round brush 10, 2

Colors

Sap Green

Cerulean Blue

Gamboge

Burnt Sienna

Yellow Ochre

Crimson Lake Red

Ultramarine Blue

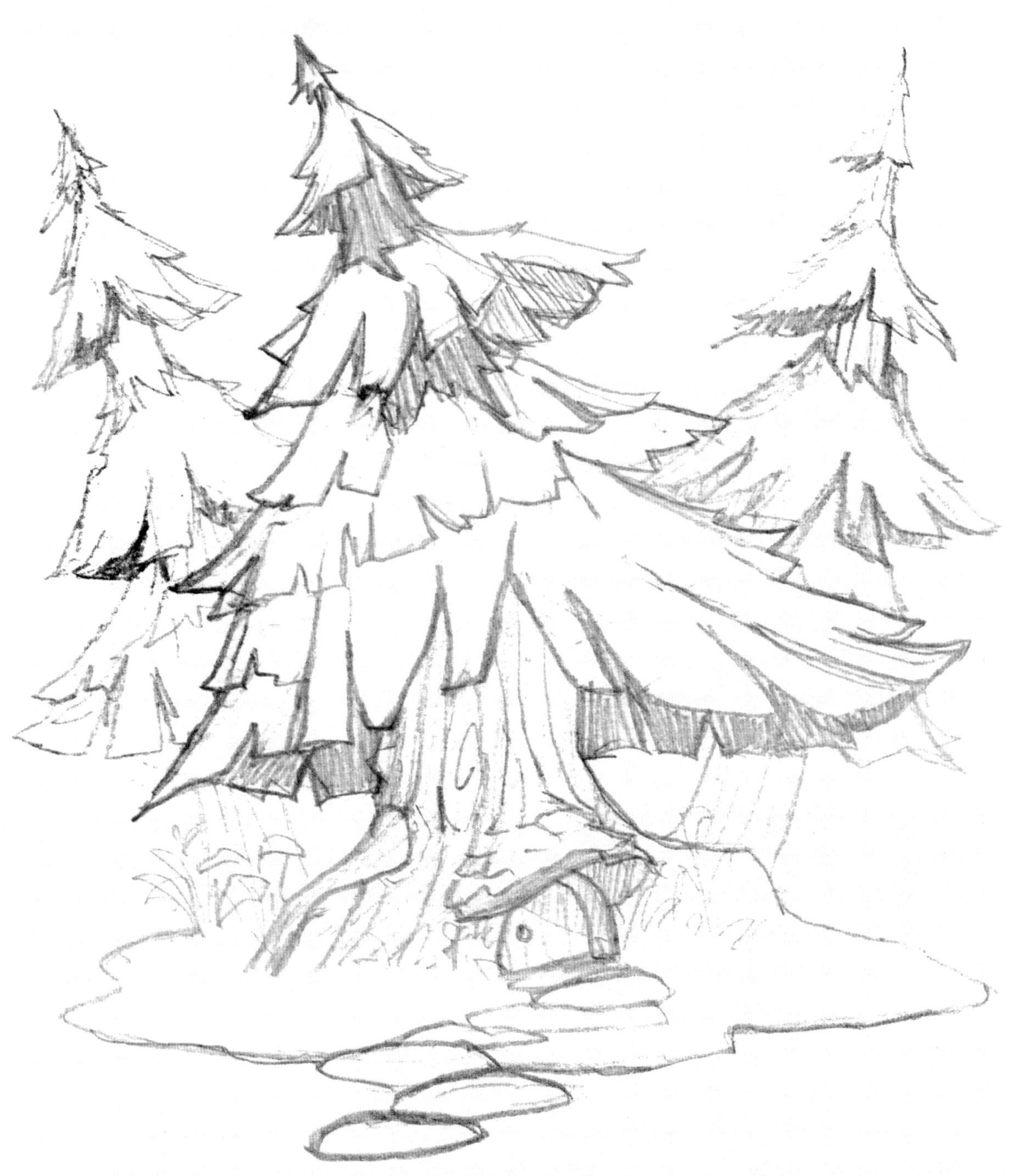

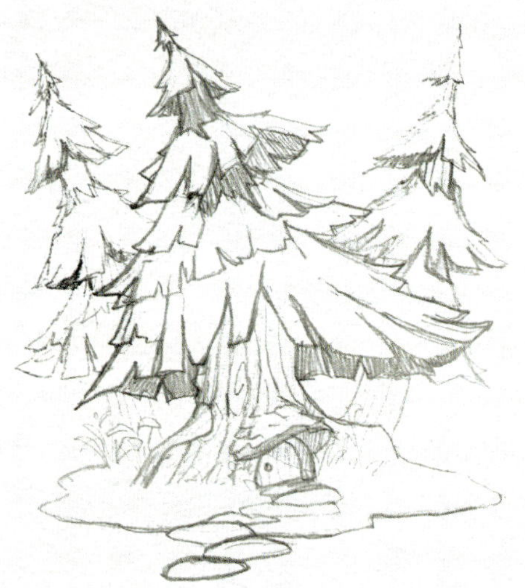

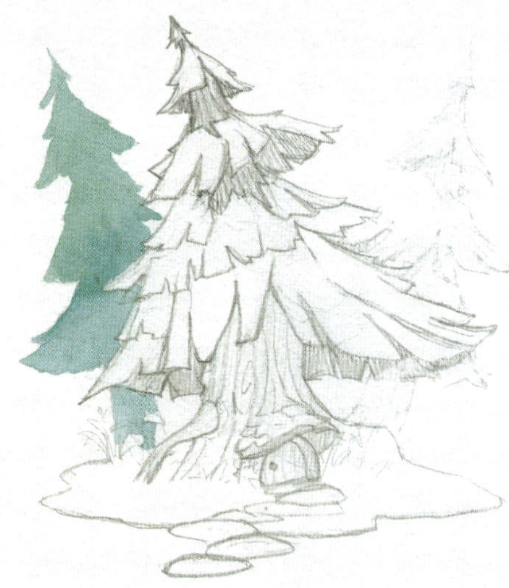

Step 1

Copy the drawing onto your watercolor paper. When drawing, feel free to change up the design according to your preference. The key shapes to transfer are the pointed trees that are slightly slanting, and the round curve of the door.

When you're done drawing, use an eraser to lighten the pencil lines of the two background trees. We want them to look as far away as possible from the main tree.

Step 2

Use your round brush 10, dipped in a fair bit of water. We're going to start by painting the two distant trees in the background. Mix Sap Green + Cerulean Blue, using a lot of water to reduce the opacity.

Raise your sketchbook at a slight angle so we can proceed to create a seamless gradient (see page 15 in Chapter 1 for *The Bead Method*). Start by painting the leftmost tree from the top, and let the water dribble down naturally. Dry your brush, and now add diluted Cerulean Blue as we paint further down the tree.

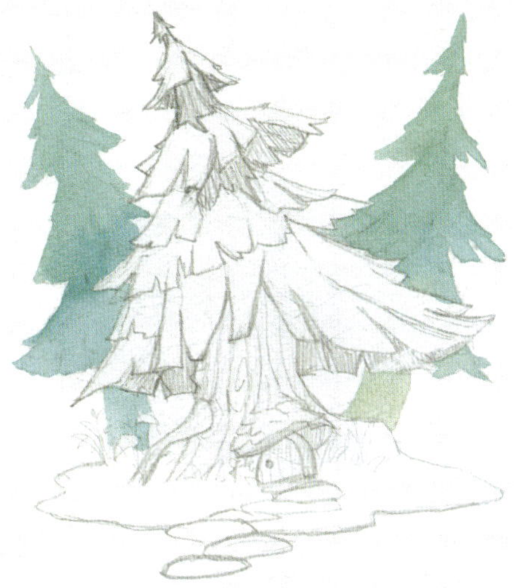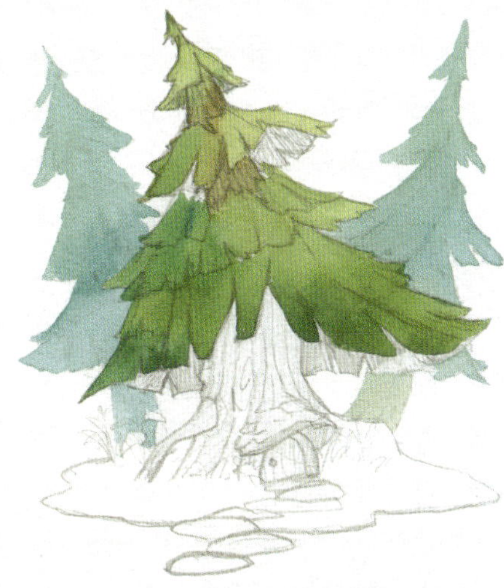

Step 3

For the tree on the farthest right, we'll use the same technique from Step 2.

Raise your sketchbook at an angle, and dip your brush into a fair amount of water. Use the Cerulean Blue + Sap Green mixture with water, and start by painting the top of the tree. Let the water flow downward with gravity.

Using a lot of water, mix Gamboge + a touch of Burnt Sienna. While your brush still has some of the Cerulean Blue on the hair, dab your brush into the new mixture. Add this color to the bottom of the tree, making a smooth gradient to the yellow-green.

Step 4

Now we're going to start painting the middle tree. We're going to create a gradient using *The Bead Method* here as well, so ensure that your sketchbook is at a slight angle.

Mix Sap Green + Yellow Ochre, diluted with a lot of water, and start applying the color from the top of the tree. Let the water flow downward. As you reach the bark on the tree, dry your brush and add a touch of Burnt Sienna with a lot of water. Then continue with the Sap Green + Yellow Ochre color for the right side of the tree's leaves.

While the paint is still wet, add some Cerulean Blue to the Sap Green + Yellow Ochre, for the left side of the leaves. This vertical and horizontal gradient creates a lot of form and interest in our illustration.

Leave the underside of the tree's leaves unpainted for now.

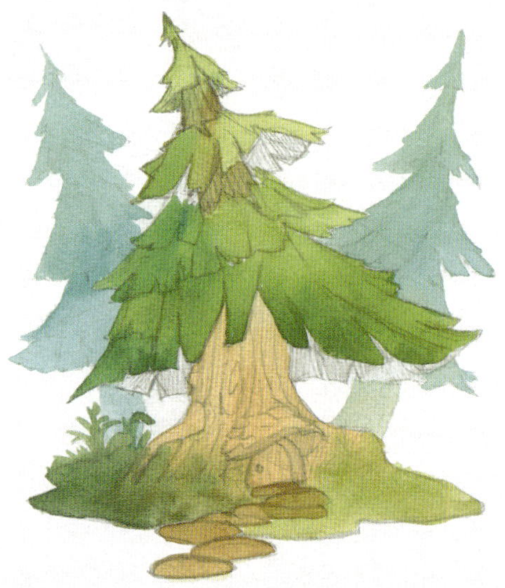 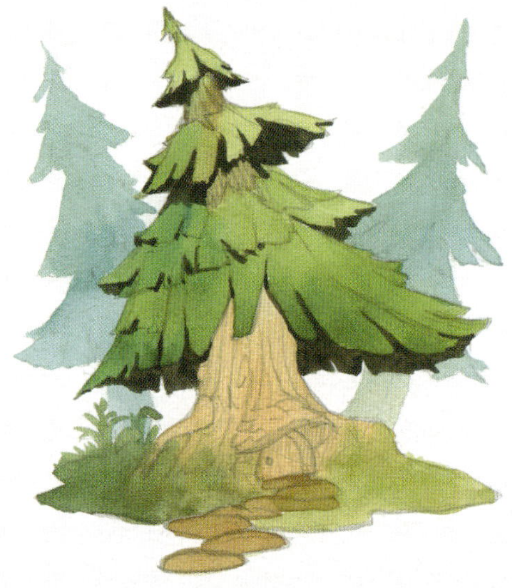

Step 5

Continue with your round brush 10. Paint the first wash for the bark of the main tree with Yellow Ochre + a touch of Burnt Sienna (more yellow than brown). Use a lot of water in this mixture, so we have a light-yellow base for the bark. Still using your sketchbook at a slight angle, start applying the color to the bark of the tree.

As you reach the grass ground, quickly add Sap Green + Yellow Ochre with a lot of water. Let the water mix these colors together naturally.

Work quickly while the paint is still wet. Add Cerulean Blue + Sap Green with a lot of water, and apply this color to the shadow side of the grass. Using this color, paint silhouettes of leaves and wild grass.

For the stones, use a light wash of Burnt Sienna + Yellow Ochre + Sap Green.

Let this layer dry thoroughly before we move on to painting depth and shadow.

Step 6

Mix a dark-green color with Sap Green + Crimson Lake Red + Ultramarine Blue, with very little water. We're going to need a thick, opaque layer for the shadowy under-side of the tree canopy. Use your round brush 10, and apply the dark-green paint on the areas we previously left unpainted.

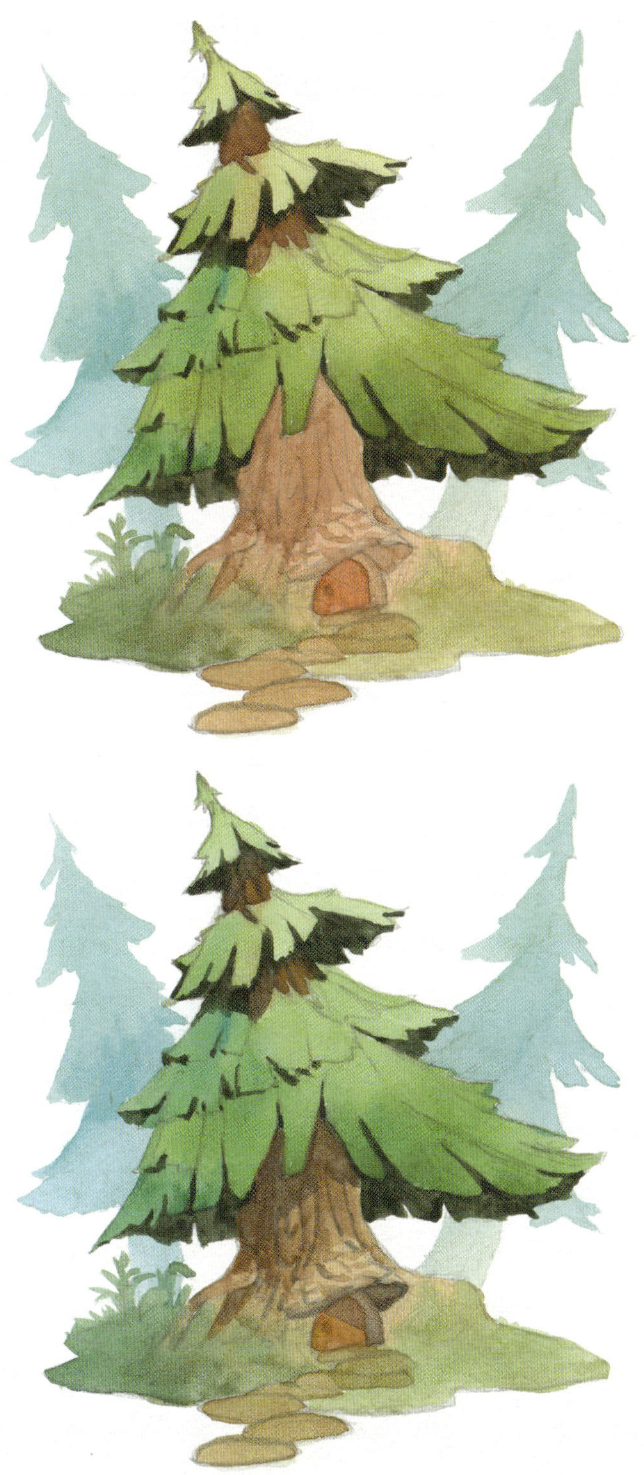

Step 7

Now that every area of our illustration is painted, we can move on to the exciting details.

First, mix a light-red color using Crimson Lake Red + Gamboge with an equal part of water. Paint the door this color to create a nice contrast with the greenery.

Next, use Burnt Sienna + Ultramarine Blue to darken the bark.

Step 8

In this step we're going to deepen our shadows. Use Ultramarine Blue, and a round brush size 2 dipped in an equal part of water. Apply this color to the bark at the top of the tree, the shadow cast across the trunk, and the inside of the door.

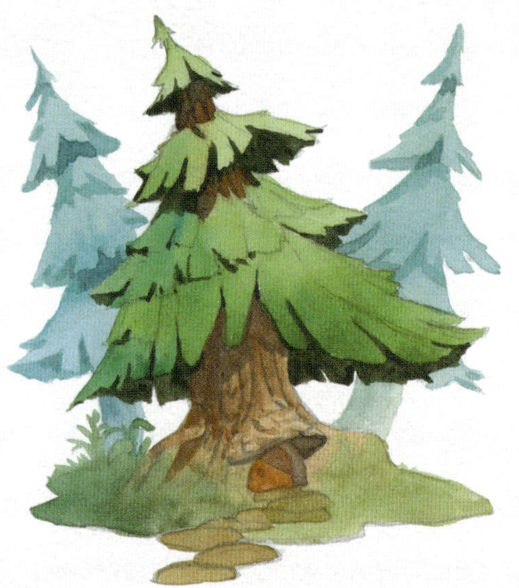

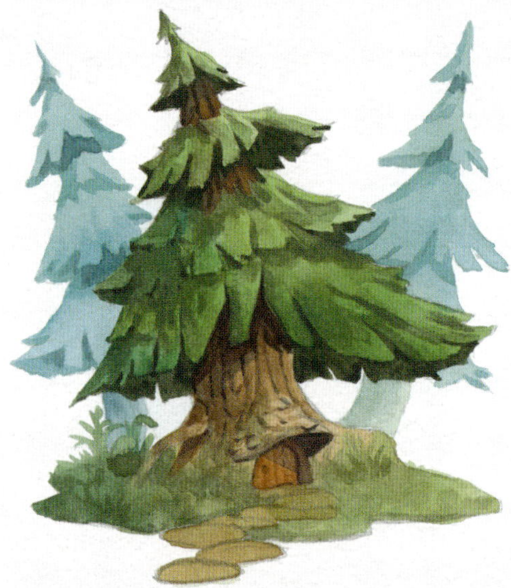

Step 9

Similar to how we created shadow and depth to the main tree in the previous step, we're going to add distant detail to the trees in the background. Mix Cerulean Blue + Sap Green + a touch of Ultramarine Blue. Using a round brush 2, apply this color to the shadow underside of the background trees. Create variation by letting some of the paint dry and then glazing over it, and by using more water in other random areas. We don't want the colors to look *too* blocky.

Step 10

Let's add further variation to make the illustration feel less blocky. Use your round brush 2 dipped in water, and now mix Sap Green + Crimson Lake Red. Apply this color in random areas on the leaves of the main tree. Keep your brushstrokes fun and loose. The more variation the better!

Create another shade of green by mixing Sap Green + Yellow Ochre, and apply this in loose strokes as well. In general, keep the light source in mind: the sun striking from the upper-right corner. Use the same loose technique to create variation in the grass.

Next, create a dark-purple color to deepen the shadows by mixing Ultramarine Blue + Crimson Lake Red. Apply this color beneath the leaves on the trunk, and to the inside of the doorway.

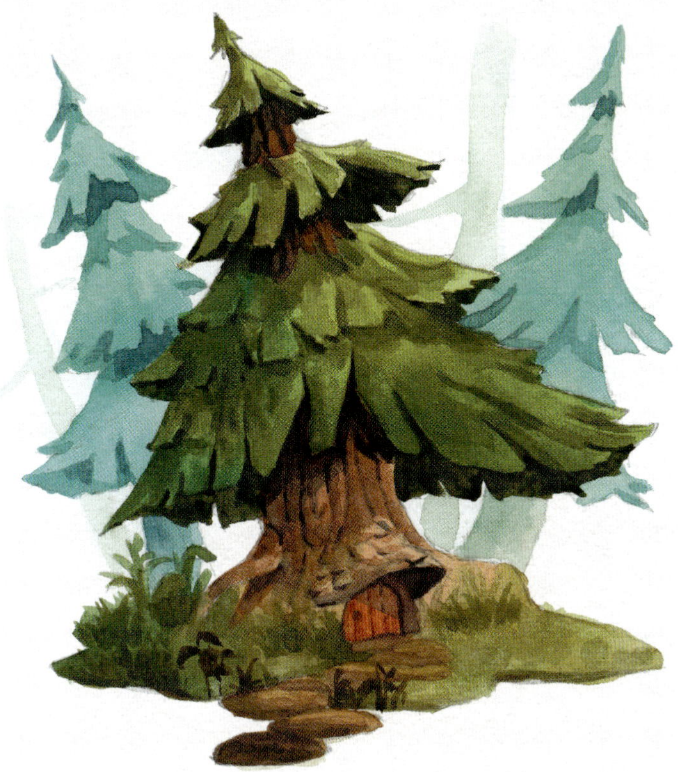

Step 11

We're almost done with this cozy nook! Use your round brush 2 for this step. We're going to finish this illustration with fine details.

First, mix Sap Green + Crimson Lake Red + Ultramarine Blue, and paint silhouettes of leaves and grass at the foreground. Use the same color to outline the stepping stones. Make sure to leave the upper area of the stones as it is, because the light is also striking them. On the foremost stepping stone, I imagine it will be receding into a shadowy area again, so paint with the dark color you just mixed.

Next, clean your brush, and let's add two more trees disappearing further into the distance. Mix Gamboge + Cerulean Blue with a lot of water, and paint the curve shape of a tree trunk on the left side. Do the same thing on the right side. Then use *The Lifting Technique* from Chapter 1 (see page 18). Clean your brush, and drag the paint upward to create a fade into the white of the page.

Let the paint dry completely.

Well done! We've successfully finished another area of our forest dimension. I know I said our adventurers will need a place to rest . . . but who knows what lies behind that door? Could be friend or could be foe. Either way, us wizards can step back and be proud of our handicraft.

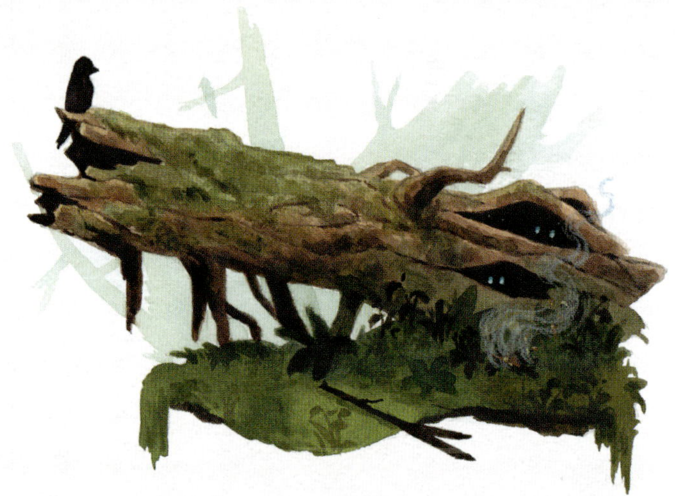

Shadow Creatures of the Shade Tree

Remember the surveillance creatures we created earlier to keep an eye on our adventurers? We should probably install more of them wherever the visitors may rest and start a fire. It's just good security practice. The surveillance creatures love dark, shadowed areas where they can easily hide. And I think I've found the perfect fallen log to install them in . . .

In this tutorial, we're going to paint an area where our visitors have started a fire and cooked food in the cool shade of a fallen tree. Unknowingly, a few of our shadow creatures will be watching them closely.

Brushes

Round brush 10, 2, 0

Colors

Yellow Ochre

Burnt Sienna

Sap Green

Crimson Lake Red

Ultramarine Blue

Gamboge

Cerulean Blue

Titanium White

Color Pencil

Glacier Blue

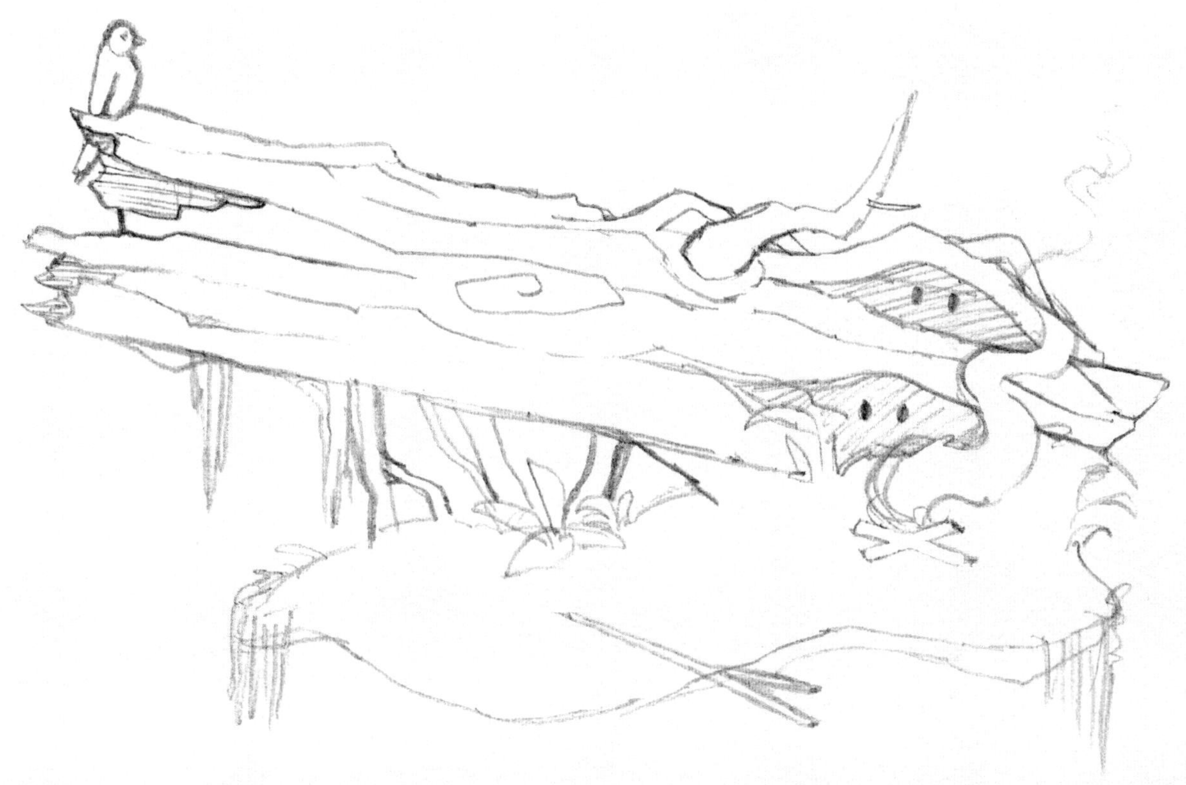

Step 1

Copy the drawing onto your watercolor paper using an HB pencil. For this tutorial, the key shape is the fallen log, and the interesting curve of the ground. Also draw curling smoke rising from a campfire.

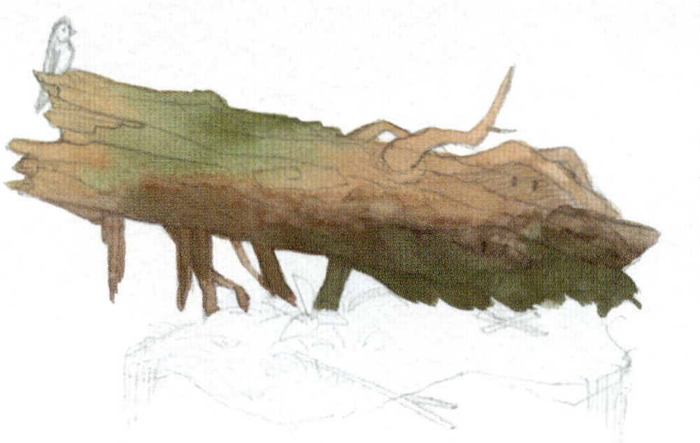 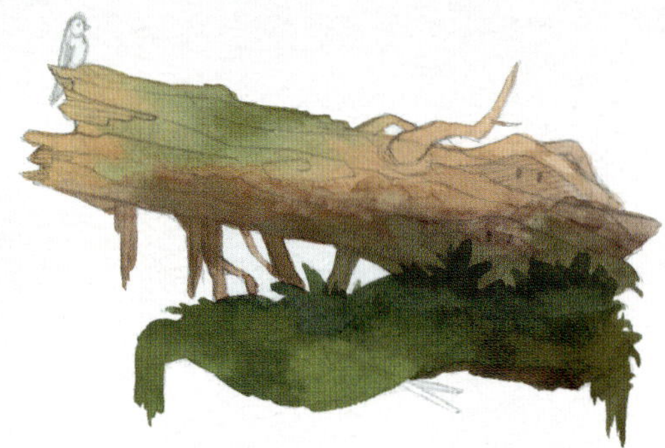

Step 2

Let's start with a wet layer to establish the base colors. Raise your sketchbook at a slight angle as described in *The Bead Method* from Chapter 1 (see page 15). Use your round brush 10 dipped in a fair amount of water. Mix Yellow Ochre + a touch of Burnt Sienna, and apply it to the fallen tree. Imagine the light striking the scene from the upper-left corner.

Work quickly while the paint is wet, and add a mixture of Sap Green + a touch of Crimson Lake Red to the upper part of the bark for suggestions of moss.

As you paint further down the trunk, add a darker shade of brown created with Burnt Sienna + Ultramarine Blue to the shadow parts. Mix a dark green with Sap Green + Ultramarine Blue for the shadow areas of the moss.

Where the light meets the shadow, dab some spots of water into the paint, and let it create natural textures as it dries.

Step 3

Now we'll paint the base layer for the grassy ground. Use the same amount of water as in the previous step, while the sketchbook is still raised slightly. Create a dark-green color by mixing Sap Green + Ultramarine Blue + Crimson Lake Red, and start painting from the top where the tree roots reach the ground. Paint silhouettes of foliage and leaf blades. (You can refer to the Common Shapes and Color Combos section from Chapter 1, page 20 to get ideas for different types of leaves.)

As you reach the left side of the grass, use lighter greens created with Sap Green + Gamboge. These spots of sunlight striking the grass add more interest and beauty to the scene. Use the same green to paint some falling vines.

For the bit of rock that is peeking beneath the grass, mix Burnt Sienna + Ultramarine Blue, and apply it while the green paint is still wet, making use of *The Wet-on-Wet Technique* described in Chapter 1 (see page 16).

Let this layer dry thoroughly.

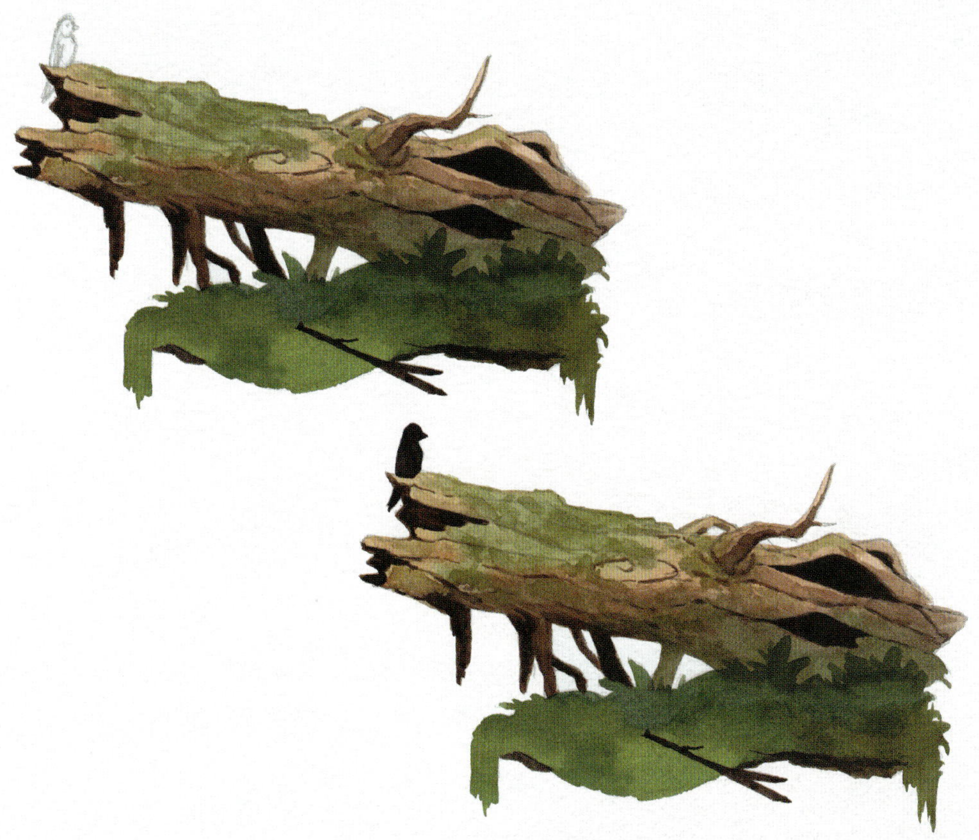

Step 4

Now we can begin to refine some of the outlines. Switch to your round brush 2 for this step, and use very little water.

Mix Burnt Sienna + Ultramarine Blue to get a dark-brown color, and paint the darkest areas of the tree trunk, where the hollow shadows are. Use the same color to outline the lines on the bark and to define the stick lying on the grass.

Next mix Sap Green + a touch of Crimson Lake Red, and randomly create variations of green on the moss. Let spots dry darker in areas where the moss casts a shadow on itself. In other areas where the light is striking, dab a drop of water and add a little Sap Green + Yellow Ochre.

Step 5

For the bird, use your round brush 0, with very little water. Mix a dark-black color with Yellow Ochre + Ultramarine Blue + Crimson Lake Red, and paint the entire form of the bird.

This little guy is a mysterious onlooker, neither visitor nor shadow creature. He's a denizen of the forest here to make our dimension extra magical.

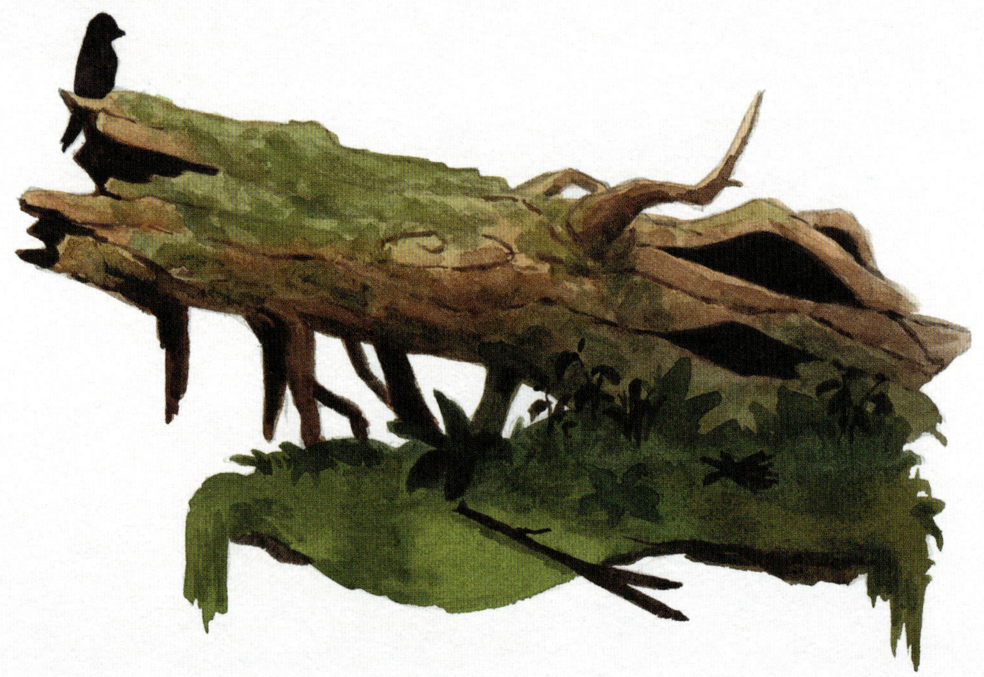

Step 6

In this step, we'll create more variation and interest.

First, using your round brush 0 and the dark-black color you mixed in Step 5, paint the firewood.

Next, create the darkest green color by mixing Sap Green + Ultramarine Blue + Crimson Lake Red. Use your round brush 2 to paint the shapes of grass blades, leaves, and stems beneath the hollow log where the firewood is. Then, with Sap Green + a little Crimson Lake Red mixed with an equal part of water, dab this color to areas of the grass where it's already a little dark. This creates the illusion of little hills and wild grass, which are natural elements on the forest floor. Use the same color and technique to define the shadows and variation on the moss, as well as a hint of a shadow beneath the stick.

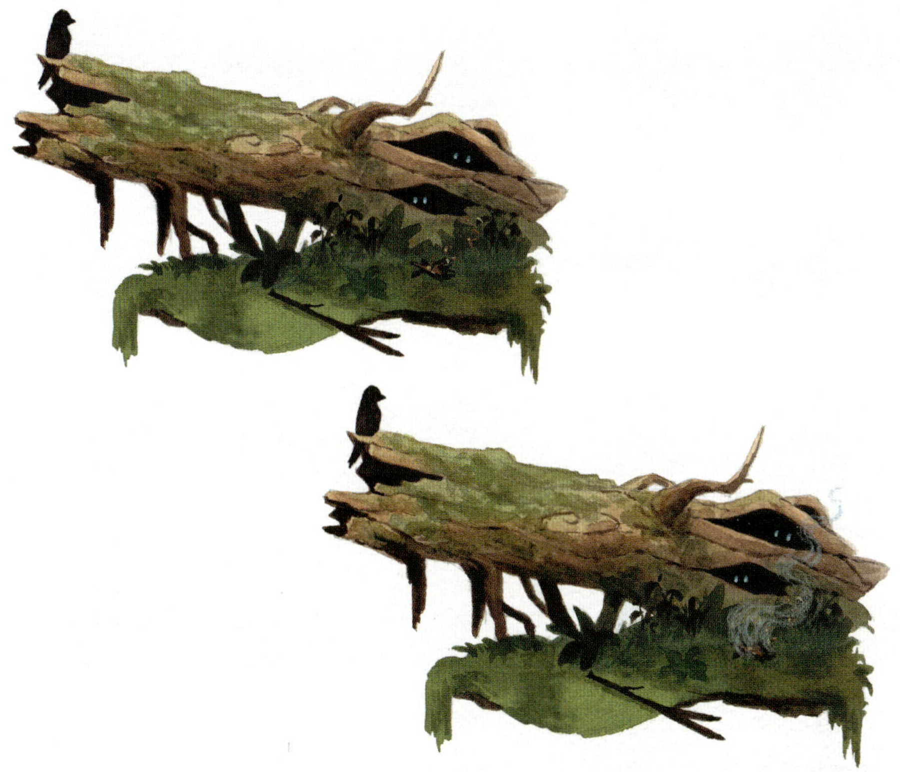

Step 7

Now let's paint the creepy blue orb eyes of our surveillance system. Use Cerulean Blue + a little bit of Titanium White to mix a bright-blue color. With your round brush 0, and very little water, carefully dab two pairs of eyes curiously set within the dark hollows of the tree trunk.

Now paint dots of Titanium White onto the eyes to make them appear as if they are peering downward toward the fire.

We will be using the same technique to define the remnants of the campfire. Use your round brush 0 for this step as follows.

First, use a thick mixture of Yellow Ochre, and highlight the upper edge of the sticks.

Use the same color to paint embers flying out of the sticks.

Then use Gamboge + Titanium White to further glow some of those embers.

Step 8

Let's draw in the smoke. Here we are going to use a Glacier Blue color pencil. If you don't have the exact color, you can also use any light-blue pencil. Color pencils are great to pair with watercolor mediums, allowing for more precision, definition, and texture.

Lightly draw swirls of smoke spiraling out of the firewood. Make sure to draw the pencil lines over the dark areas of the paint, so the smoke is visible.

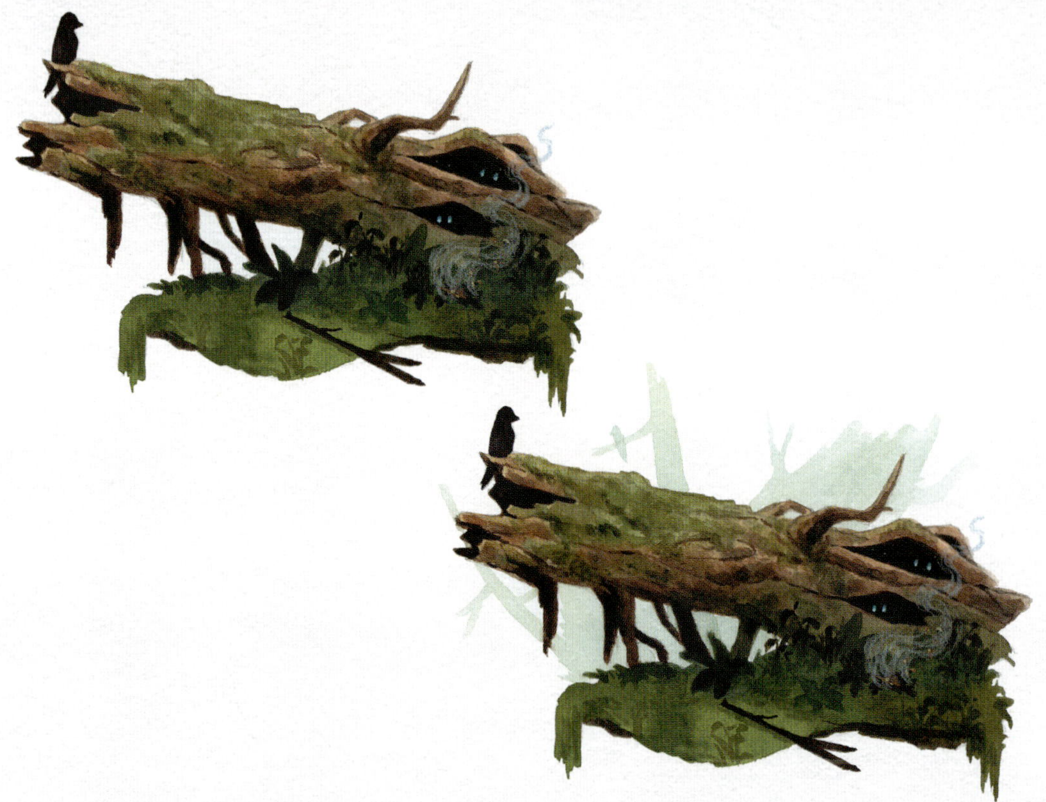

Step 9

Finally, the last thing we need to do is add some finishing details. Use Sap Green + Ultramarine Blue with your round brush 2 to paint more silhouette details in the grass. (You can refer to page 20, Common Shapes and Color Combos, for references for these foliage shapes.) Make sure to include variation in the shapes as well.

Use Ultramarine Blue to deepen the lines and textures on the bark, the branch's shadow, and the falling roots.

Step 10

As a bonus, let's finish this illustration with distant details. After all, this scene is part of a larger forest dimension.

Use your round brush 2, dabbed in a lot of water, and mix Gamboge + Cerulean Blue. These details should look far away, so ensure this layer is quite transparent. Paint branches curving outward behind the main scene. Use more Cerulean Blue in your watery mixture as you paint the bottom.

Now use your round brush 0 to paint birds in the distance. The general shape of the bird is a circular head, with a triangular tail and beak.

Let the layer dry.

The scene is complete! I can clearly imagine a visitor cooking a warm meal here. Congratulations, fellow wizard! In one stroke of magic, you conjured smoke, birds, and lush foliage. You are one unstoppable sorcerer.

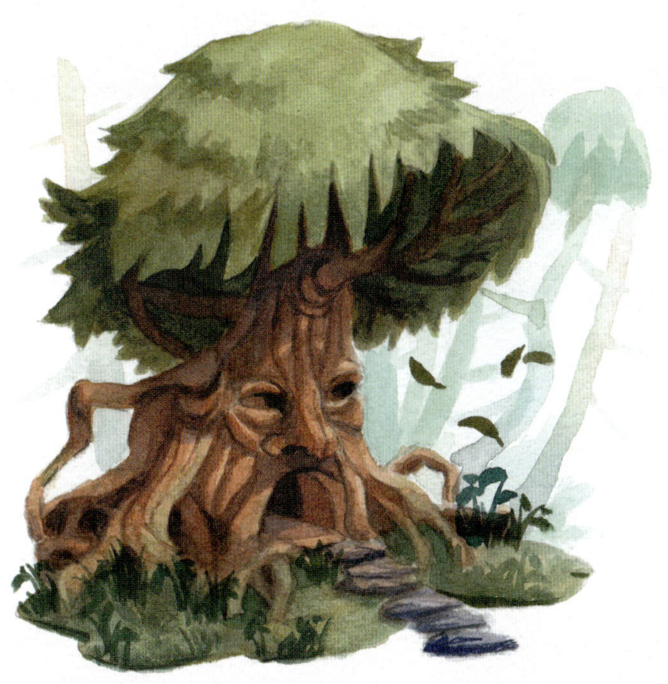

The Talking Leafhead Tree

have you ever come across a tree so huge and so old, it makes you wonder what it could have possibly witnessed? What tales could it share of heroes and villains alike, if only it had a mouth to speak those tales aloud?

Fortunately for us wizards, we can create a tree with a face—a tree that could speak to our visitors and confuse them with riddles. In this tutorial, we're going to paint an ancient tree that is hundreds of years old—one that is eager to share a conversation with any bold adventurer.

Brushes

Round brush 10, 2, 0

Colors

Gamboge

Cerulean Blue

Violet

Sap Green

Crimson Lake Red

Burnt Sienna

Ultramarine Blue

Yellow Ochre

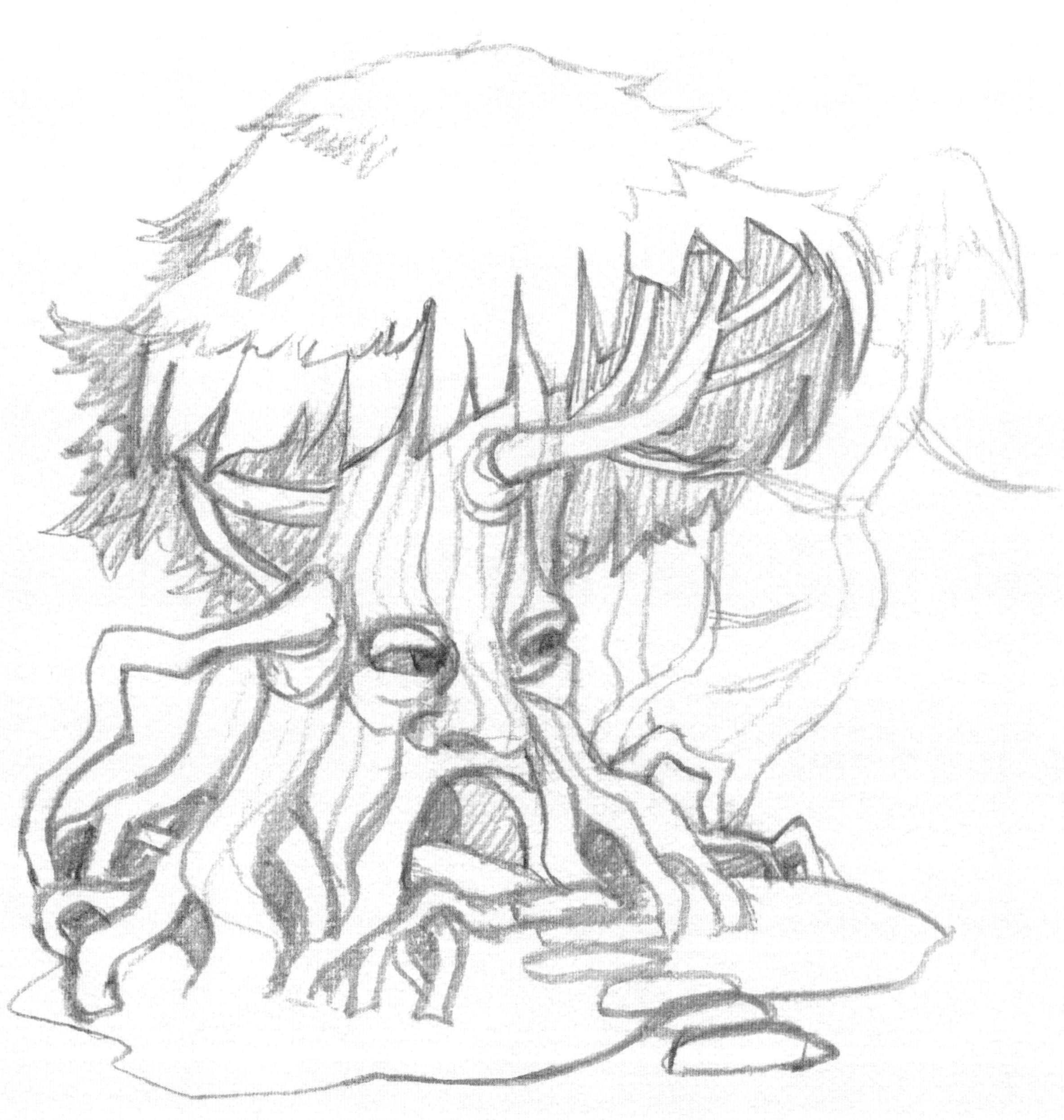

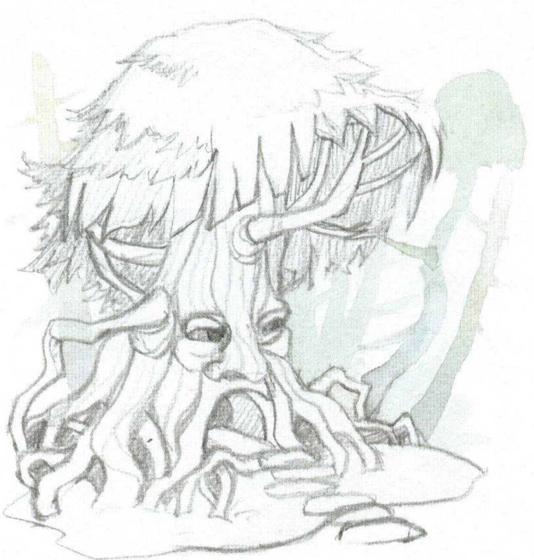 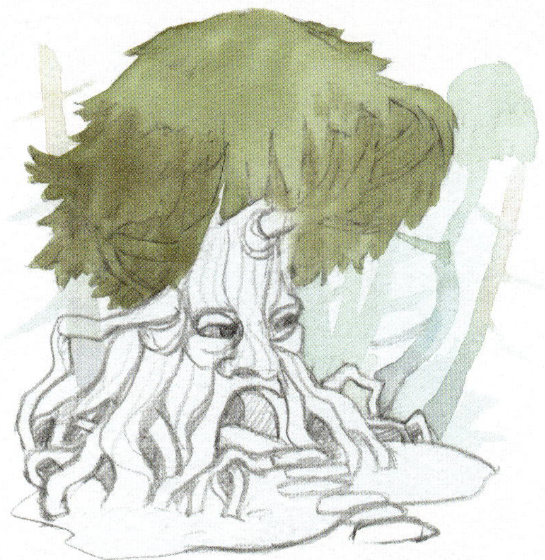

Step 1

Draw the sketch onto your watercolor paper. For this talking tree, the key shapes are—of course—his eyes and nose, and the giant leafy canopy swinging above.

Erase any dark lines as needed before painting.

Step 2

Let's begin with the background trees. Since they are in the distance, we'll paint minimal detail on them, focusing more on the gradient. Raise your sketchbook at a slight angle (as described in *The Bead Method* in Chapter 1 on page 15), and use your round brush 10 dipped in a fair amount of water.

Begin with Gamboge + Cerulean Blue and a lot of water for the top of a leafhead tree in the background. Let the water run down the page in a curve, so the shape of the tree trunk is sprouting from the ground.

While the paint is still wet, dab more Cerulean Blue as you work your way down. Further down, dab Violet.

Repeat the same technique and colors for more background trees and blades of grass.

Step 3

Once the previous layer is completely dry, use *The Wet-on-Wet Technique* described in Chapter 1 (page 16): Dip your round brush 10 into water, and use it to wet the paper in the leafy area of the tree. Mix Sap Green + Crimson Lake Red + a touch of Gamboge, and apply it to the wet page. The paint will spread around with the water, creating natural textures that will later translate to the tree.

While the paint is wet, mix more Crimson Lake Red in your Sap Green, and add it to the shadowy parts of the tree (mainly the underside of the leafhead). It's okay to cover the branches, since they are in shadow and we can paint over this later.

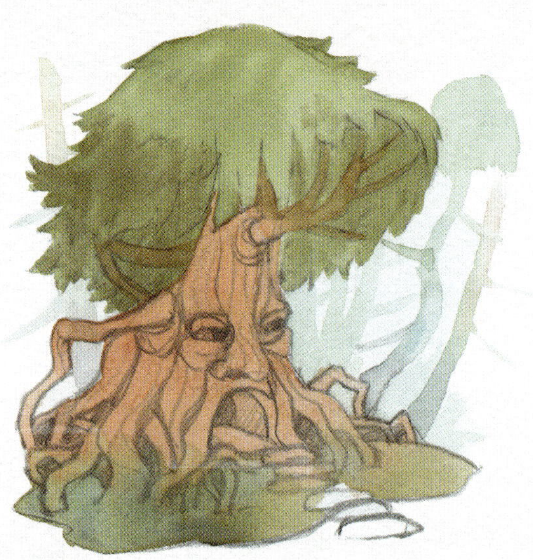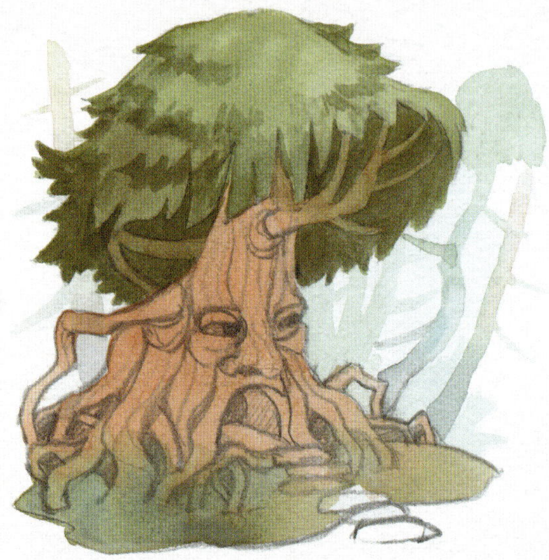

Step 4

Switch to your round brush 2. Use Burnt Sienna, diluted to a watery consistency, and start applying this color as a base for the bark of the leafhead.

Then mix Sap Green + a touch of Crimson Lake Red for the base color of the grassy ground. Let the green blend with some of the Burnt Sienna on the roots.

Step 5

Continue working with your round brush 2. Mix Sap Green + Crimson Red Lake to create a dark-green color for defining the leafy shadows on the tree canopy.

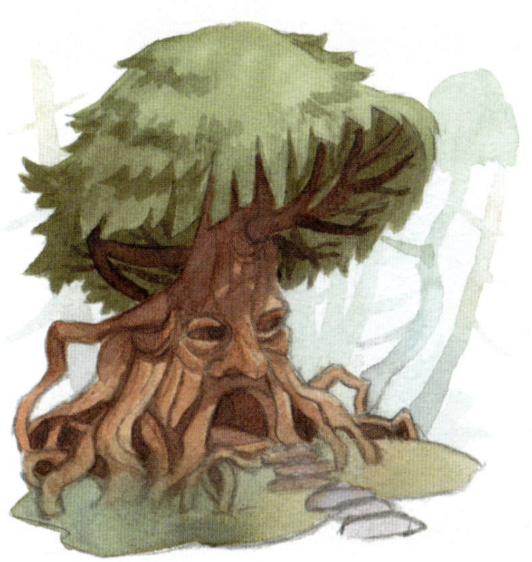 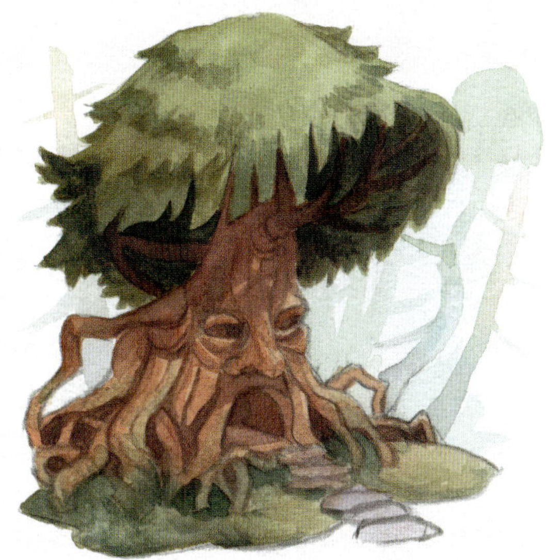

Step 6

Mix Burnt Sienna + Violet with a fair amount of water, and apply this color to the darkest areas, starting from the branches under the canopy. Paint diagonally to imply that the leaves are casting a shadow across the trunk, leaving some spots of light.

Paint a thin wash of Violet on the stepping stones. Let these layers dry.

Step 7

Still using your round brush 2, mix a darker green with Sap Green + Crimson Lake Red + Ultramarine Blue, and apply this color on the underside of the leaf canopy, defining its shape more clearly.

Use Sap Green + Ultramarine Blue for dark shadows on the grass where the tree roots curl.

Then use Sap Green + a lot of water to dab some spots on the roots or bark where moss would be growing.

Add Yellow Ochre to the Sap Green, and apply this color to random areas on the tree canopy and grass, to create more interest and variation to the greenery.

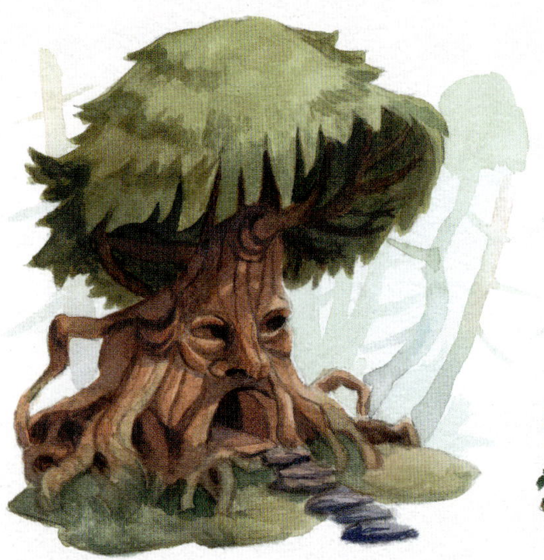 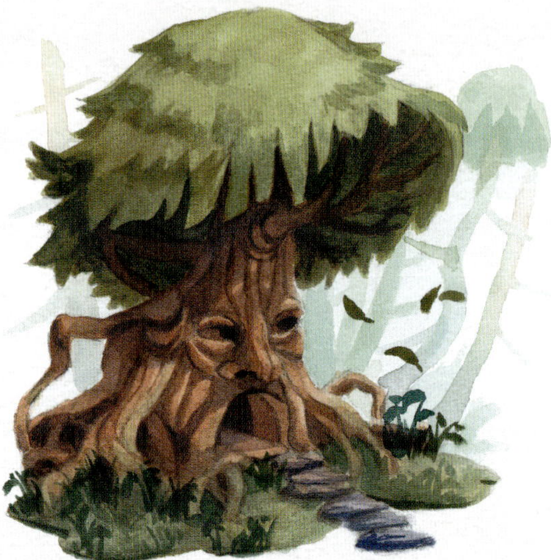

Step 8

Switch to your round brush 0 for this step. Let's begin defining the lines and shadows more. First, mix Ultramarine Blue + Crimson Lake Red to create a dark-purple (almost black) color. Apply this to the shadow under the roots, the eyes, the opening of the mouth, and the stepping stones.

Then use Violet for the shadow directly beneath the canopy on the tree trunk, as well as beneath the nose. Also apply this color at an angle inside the mouth.

Next, mix Burnt Sienna into the Ultramarine Blue + Crimson Lake mixture to create a dark-brown color, and darken the linework on the tree trunk.

Erase any pencil lines that are still visible.

Step 9

Use your round brush 2 for these finishing details. Create a dark-green color by mixing Sap Green + Crimson Lake Red + a touch of Ultramarine Blue, and paint the silhouettes of leaves and grass blades on the ground.

Using the same dark-green color, paint some falling leaves swirling away in the wind.

Then switch to your round brush 0, and dip it into Burnt Sienna, with a bit of water. Use this color to define the tree trunk, applying shadow where the lines on the bark are.

Finally, let's give a little bit of definition to the leafhead tree in the background. Using a round brush 2, mix Cerulean Blue + Gamboge with a lot of water, and glaze the underside of the leafy canopy.

When the paint is dry, we've successfully completed another unique feature of our dimension. Now, a visitor can wander down a path and have a conversation with our talking tree.

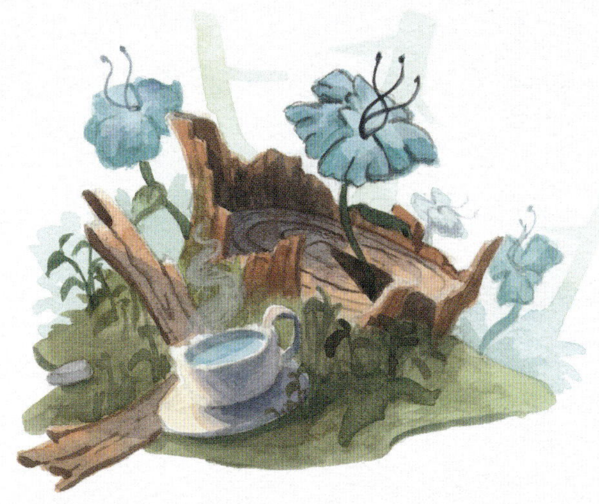

Fresh Flowers for the Homesick

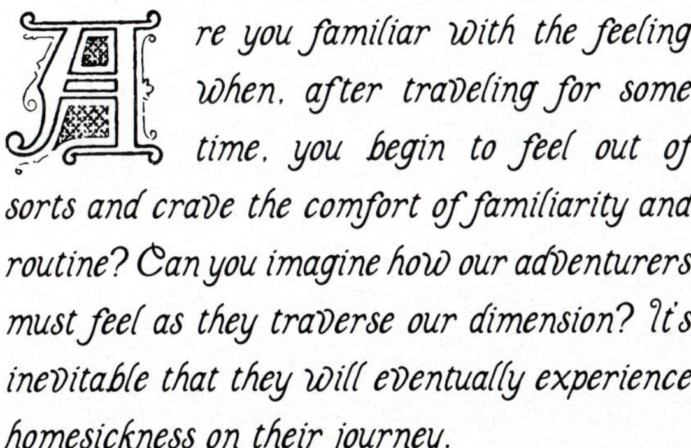

Are you familiar with the feeling when, after traveling for some time, you begin to feel out of sorts and crave the comfort of familiarity and routine? Can you imagine how our adventurers must feel as they traverse our dimension? It's inevitable that they will eventually experience homesickness on their journey.

So in this tutorial, we're going to paint some beautiful flowers that can be brewed into tea, and provide warm comfort. There is some fine print, of course . . . but we can't be held liable for any side effects of the tea (hallucinatory or otherwise).

Brushes

Round brush 10, 2, 0

Colors

Cerulean Blue

Gamboge

Yellow Ochre

Sap Green

Crimson Lake Red

Violet

Ultramarine Blue

Burnt Sienna

Color Pencil

White

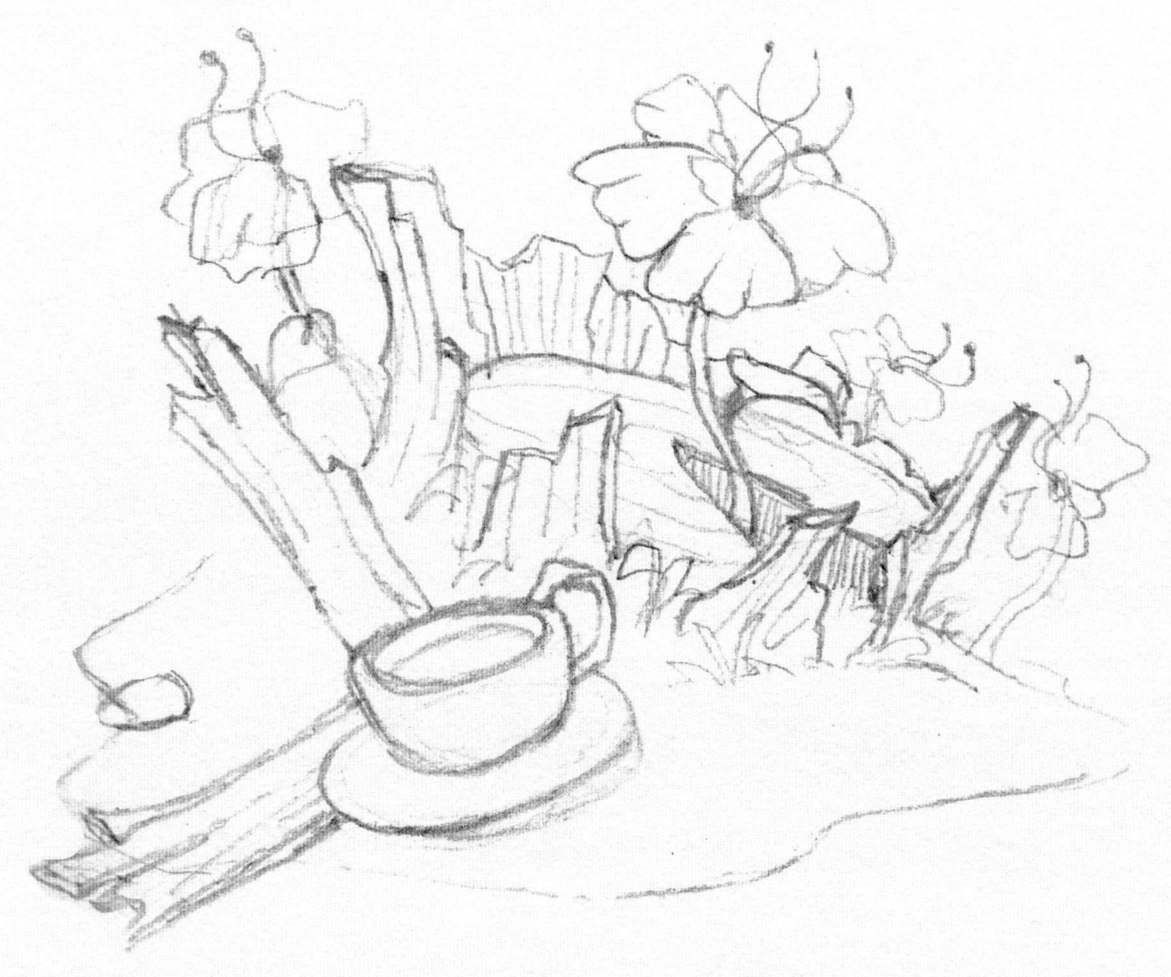

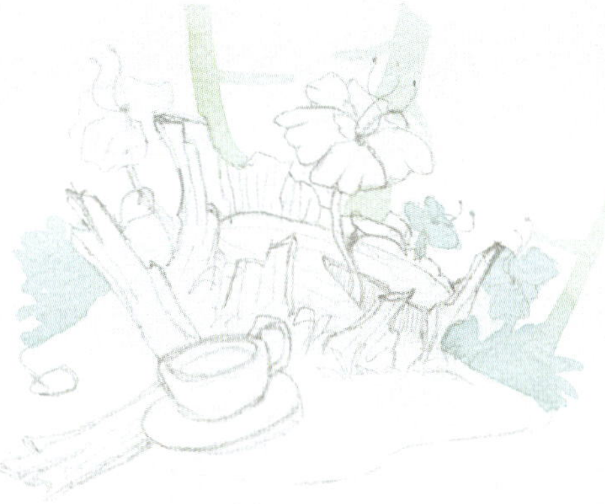

Step 1

Draw the sketch onto your watercolor paper. Focus on drawing clear shapes for the teacup and the delicate flowers sprouting out of the stump.

Step 2

Let's begin with a wet layer, and paint the distant trees and flowers that will be pushed to the background. Use your round brush 10, dipped well in water, and mix Cerulean Blue + Gamboge with plenty of water.

Raise your sketchbook at a slight angle as described in *The Bead Method* in Chapter 1 (see page 15). Paint the top of the distant trees. Let the water run down the page with gravity. As you reach the bottom, dab some diluted Cerulean Blue, and use this color to paint the silhouettes of flowers and grass blades in the background.

Let this layer dry thoroughly before moving to the next step.

Step 3

Use your round brush 10, a slightly raised sketchbook, and a fair amount of water for this step. Start by painting the wooden areas with a wet layer of Yellow Ochre. Let the paint run down the page. While it's still wet, mix Sap Green + a touch of Crimson Lake Red, and paint the grassy ground. On the right-most side of the grass, mix Sap Green + Gamboge for highlights on the ground, and let the water mix the colors together naturally.

Let this layer dry before moving to the next step.

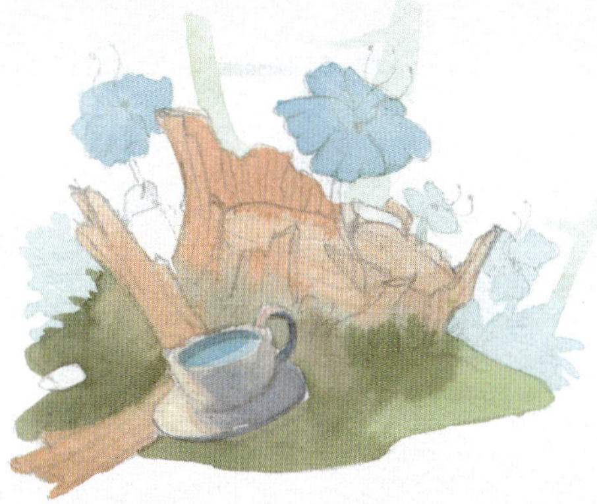

Step 4

Switch to your round brush 2. Use Cerulean Blue with an equal amount of water to paint the blue flowers. While the paint is still wet, dry your brush. Then, using *The Lifting Technique* described in Chapter 1 (see page 18), lift the paint from the center of the flowers, creating the beginning of a glow.

Now paint the inside of the teacup with Cerulean Blue. Then use Gamboge, watered down, and apply it to the whole teacup. While the layer is still wet, mix Violet + Ultramarine Blue with a lot of water, and dab that color in the shadow areas of the teacup. Keep in mind that the light is striking from the upper left. Next, glaze another layer of Cerulean Blue inside the teacup. (See *The Glazing Method* in Chapter 1, page 16.) This creates more depth, with an angular shadow on the tea.

The tea is the same color as the flowers because we want to indicate that they are linked.

Step 5

Continue painting with your round brush 2. Mix Burnt Sienna + Ultramarine Blue, and paint the inside of the broken stump. Make sure to leave some areas of the wood unpainted, so the Yellow Ochre from the previous layer shows through and creates the form of the planks. As the stump turns to face the light side, clean your brush, and paint the wood with diluted Burnt Sienna. Use the same color to glaze the outside of the broken stump.

Paint the other wooden planks with a wet layer of Burnt Sienna. While the paint is wet, add dabs of Burnt Sienna + Ultramarine Blue. When these shades mix together and dry, they will create interesting wooden textures.

Paint the lone rock on the left with Violet + Ultramarine Blue.

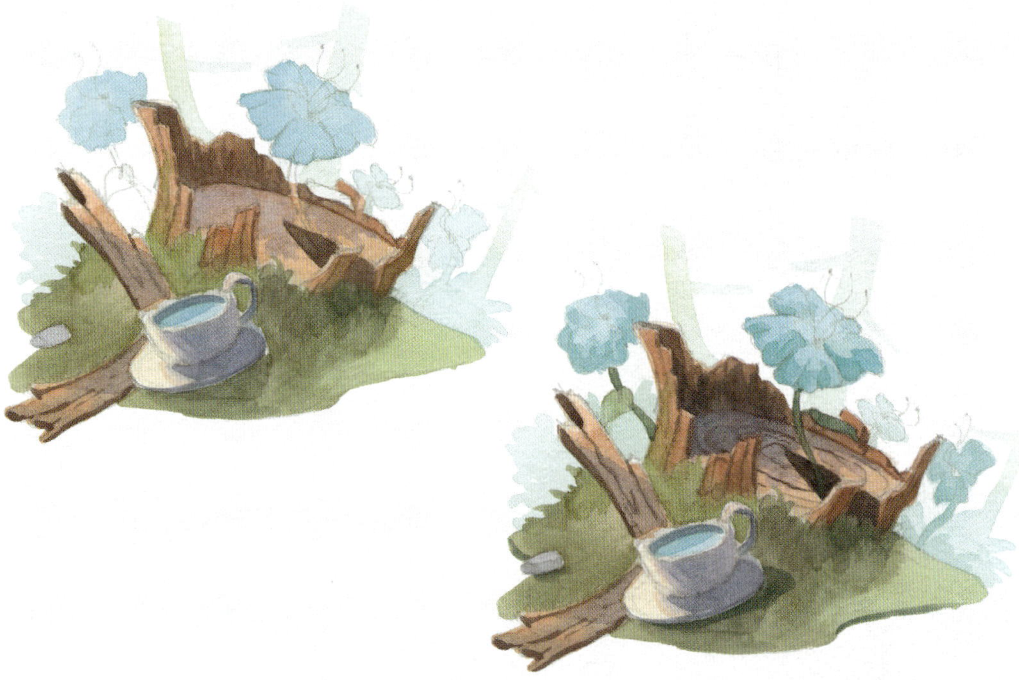

Step 6

Use your round brush 2 to start painting the shadows. Mix Violet + a touch of Ultramarine Blue with an equal amount of water, and apply this shadow color diagonally across the wooden planks.

Apply the same shadow color to the inside of the tree stump where the broken planks would be casting a shadow.

Also apply the shadow around the back of the teacup and saucer.

Step 7

Use your round brush 2 and Ultramarine Blue with *The Glazing Method* from Chapter 1 (page 16) to deepen the shadows inside the broken tree stump. Apply this color to the bottom of the rock on the left.

Then use a watery mixture of Cerulean Blue to paint shadow shapes on the flowers where the petals curl downward, away from the light source.

Next, switch to your round brush 0. Mix Ultramarine Blue + Burnt Sienna, and paint the lines on the wooden stump and planks.

Then mix Sap Green + Ultramarine Blue, and paint the flower stems.

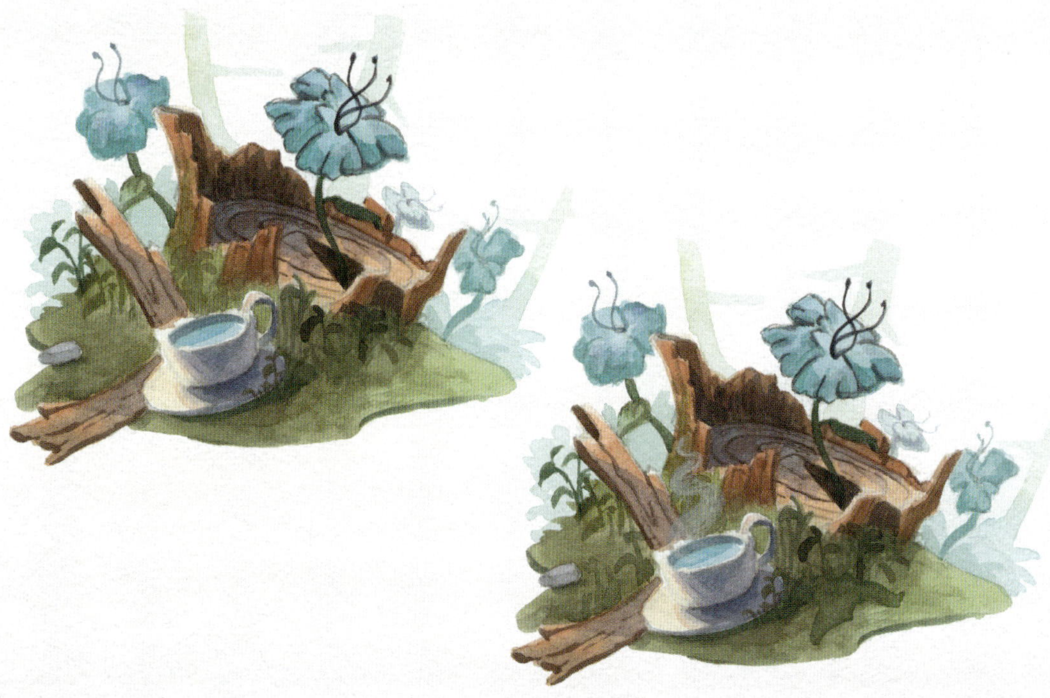

Step 8

Use your round brush 0 for this step. First, use diluted Violet, and apply this color to the shadow areas of the central flower.

Next mix a dark color, almost black, with Crimson Lake Red + Ultramarine Blue + Burnt Sienna, and paint the delicate seeds spiraling out of the flower.

Then create a dark-green color by mixing Sap Green + Ultramarine Blue, and paint the silhouettes of leaves, stems, and grass blades across the ground. Use *The Dry Brush Technique* from Chapter 1 (page 19) to create texture on the ground, with the dry dark-green color still on the brush.

Erase any pencil lines that are still visible.

Step 9

Now we can add the final details. Use a round brush 2 and Sap Green + Ultramarine Blue to paint more silhouettes of leaves and foliage on the ground.

Use a white pencil, and draw curves of steam spiraling out of the teacup. This detail always adds a touch of coziness in my opinion, perfect for luring any adventurer—no matter how tough they think they are.

With that, we are done with this illustration! Great job, wizard. Now we can patiently wait for those homesick adventurers to stumble upon our scene . . .

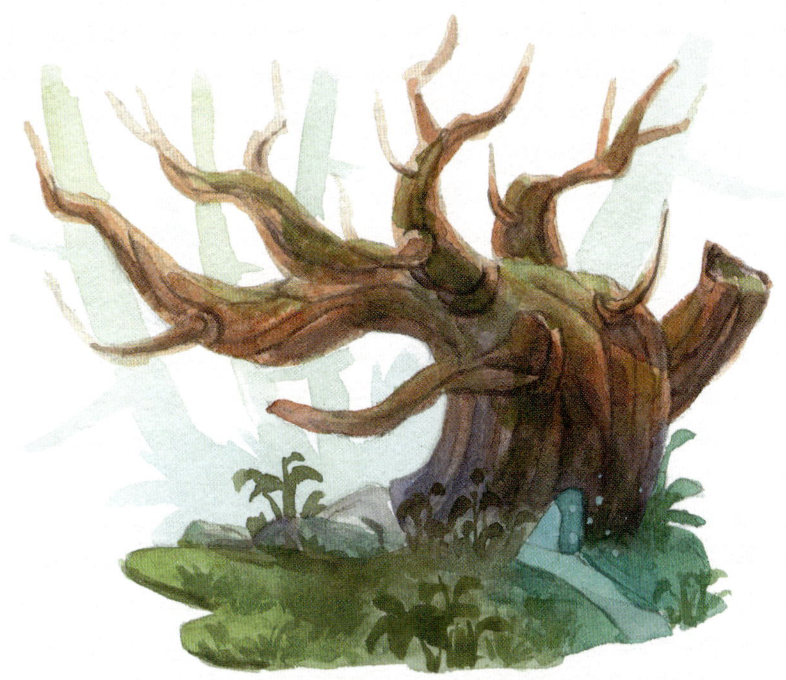

Portal to the Unknown

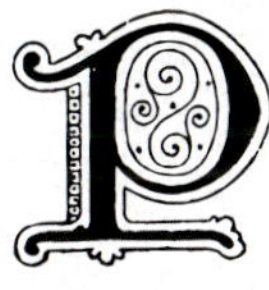

ortals. Doorways. Gateways to other worlds. And a wizard's best friend.

In this tutorial, we're going to paint a tree portal: a pulsing blue doorway embedded in a leafless tree. Our adventurers may step through, of course, but there are no instructions or manuals on what they should expect beyond it.

Brushes

Round brush 10, 2, 0

Colors

Gamboge

Cerulean Blue

Yellow Ochre

Burnt Sienna

Violet

Sap Green

Crimson Lake Red

Ultramarine Blue

Titanium White

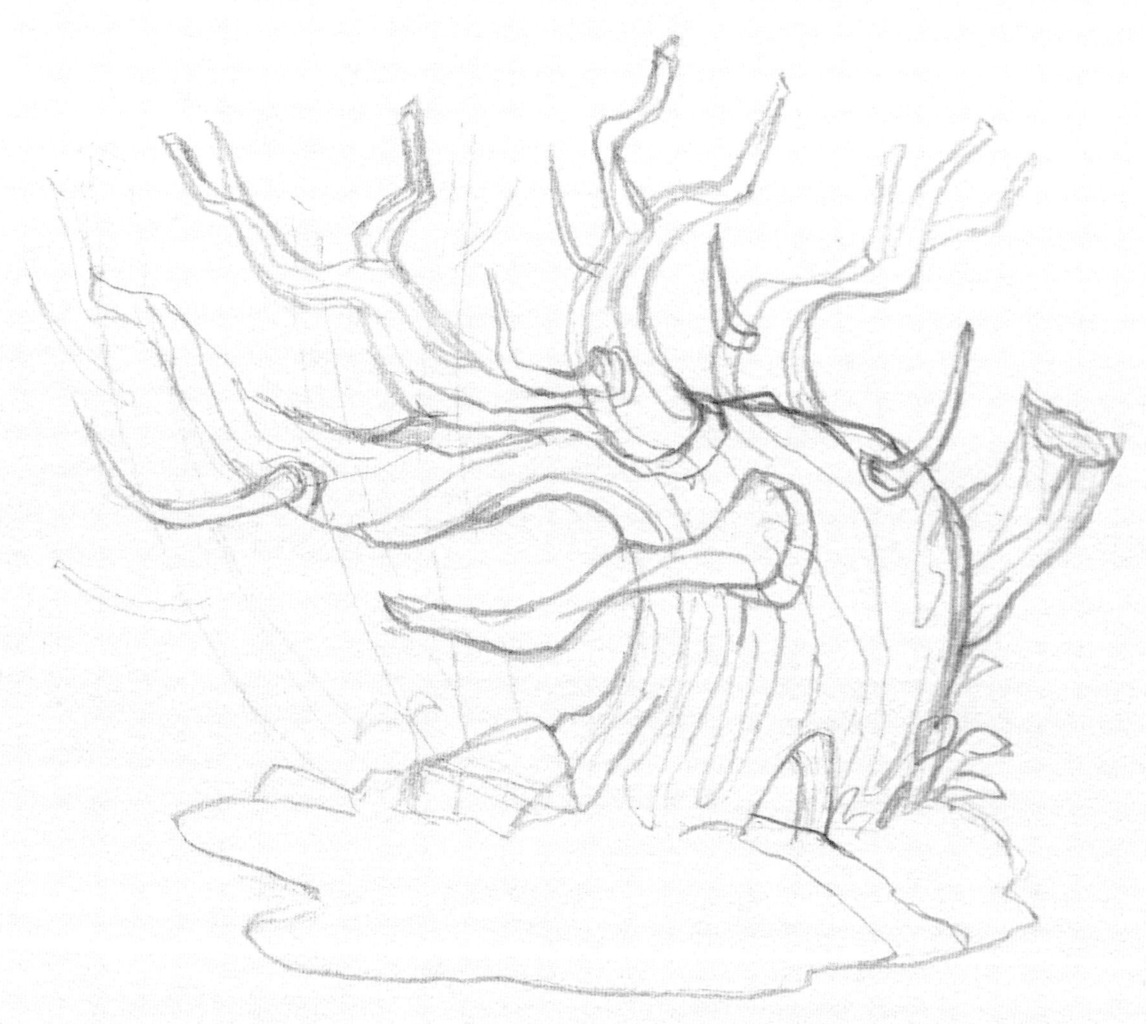

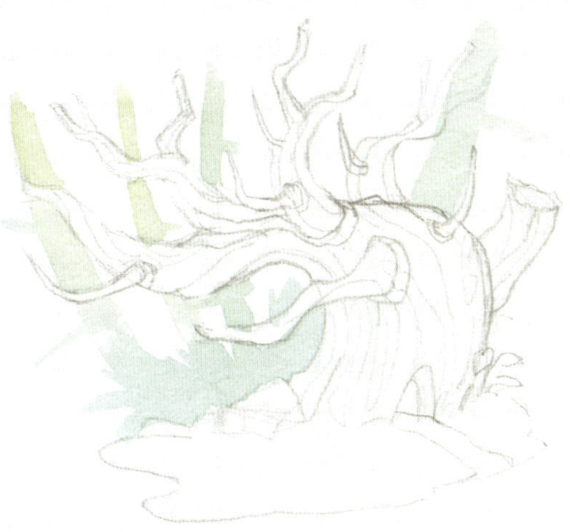

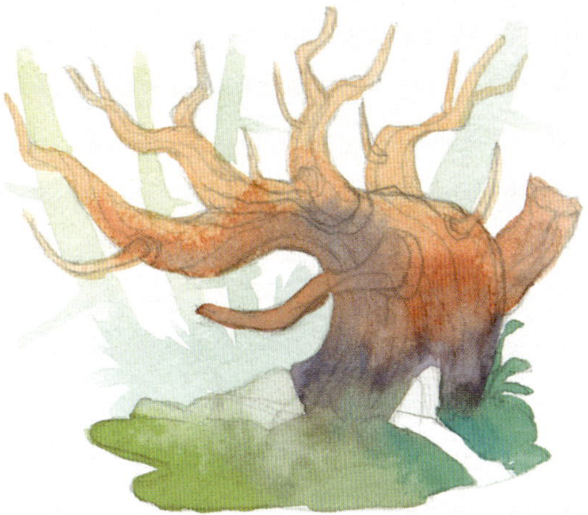

Step 1

Draw the sketch onto your watercolor paper. The key shapes to focus on are the large curving trunk of the tree, with the branches sprouting vertically, and the small portal nestled on the bottom.

Step 2

Use *The Bead Method* for this step, as described in Chapter 1 (see page 15). Raise your sketchbook at a slight angle, and wet your round brush 10 with a fair amount of water. Then use Gamboge dipped in a lot of water, and begin painting the top of the trees growing in the distance.

As you paint farther down the tree, add more Cerulean Blue. Repeat this shape and technique for more trees and grass and leaves at the bottom.

Step 3

Work quickly on a wet layer for this step. Wet your round brush 10 with a fair amount of water, and start with Yellow Ochre on the top of the tree branches. While the paint is still wet and spreading across the page, add wet Burnt Sienna to the tree. Keep in mind where the curves and shadows would be.

Next add Violet to the bottom of the tree. Let the paint granulate and create delicious textures.

Continue working while the paint is wet. Add Sap Green + Cerulean Blue to paint the grass closest to the portal. As you paint outward, use Sap Green + Crimson Lake Red to paint the grass. And on the furthest left where the light would be striking the grass, use Sap Green + Gamboge.

For the stones and rocks, use Violet, and let the green from the grass spill and mix with it.

Let this wet layer dry thoroughly.

Step 4

Switch to your round brush 2. Use Cerulean Blue mixed with an equal amount of water to color in the portal. For the pathway leading up to the portal, use Cerulean Blue + a touch of Sap Green.

Step 5

Continue painting with your round brush 2. Start with diluted Burnt Sienna, and paint texture details onto the bark of the tree where the shadows would form below the upward-curving branches.

Next, use Violet to deepen the shadows that are closer to the right and downward.

Then glaze another layer of Cerulean Blue on the outer layer of the portal.

As the final touch for this step, use the Sap Green + Cerulean Blue mixture for the shadow of the rocks, and use diluted Violet for the upper parts of the rock.

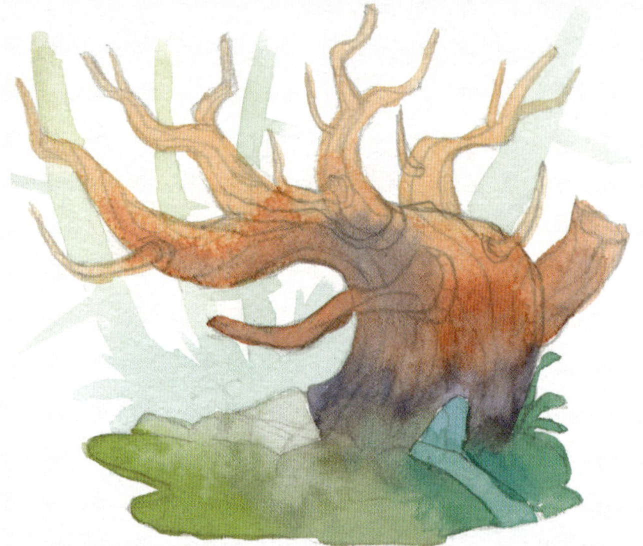

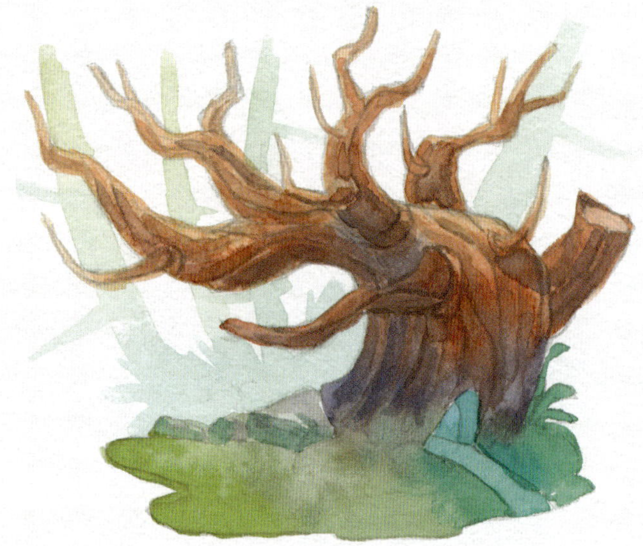

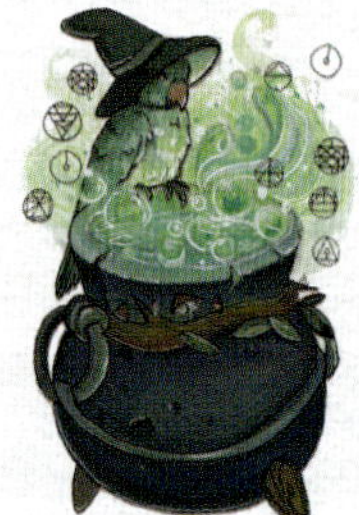

Apprentice Notes:

Let the watercolor do its thing. Notice how the paint and water move across the page, react with other colors, granulate, and dry with different textures. The more textures the better, especially on the wooden tree.

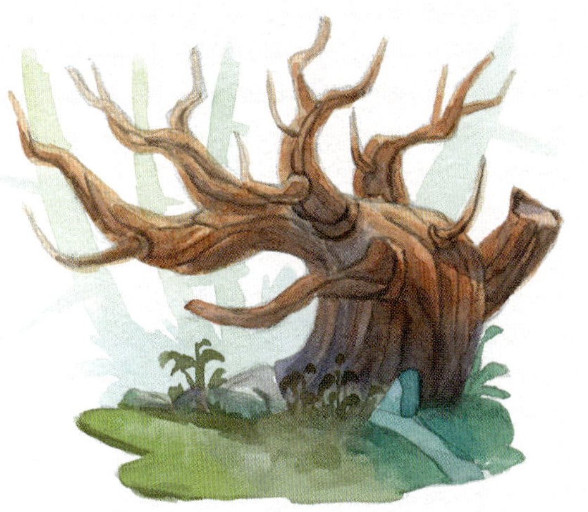 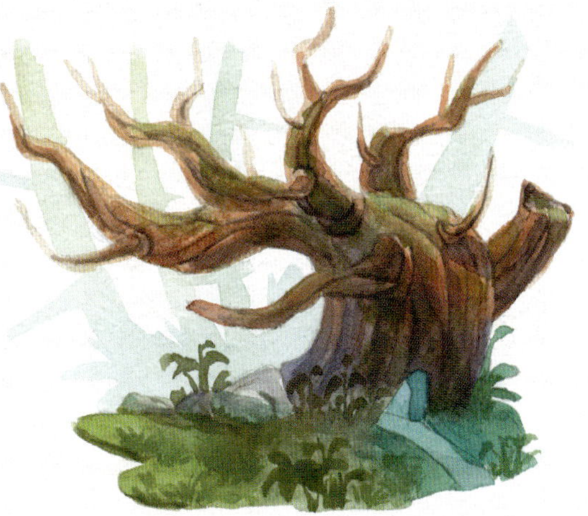

Step 6

Let's start defining the illustration more. Mix Sap Green + Ultramarine Blue, and paint the silhouettes of leaves, stems, and grass blades near the bottom of the tree. Add some of that color to the bottom of the rocks for shadow.

Next, use Violet to paint an angular shadow across the stump on the right, and on the bottom of the pathway where the ground curves away from the portal.

Glaze another layer of Cerulean Blue on the inside arch of the portal.

Step 7

Let's paint the final details. Use your round brush 2, and mix Sap Green + Crimson Lake Red to paint more details of leaves and grass on the ground. Use the same color for the moss on the tree trunk. As the moss moves toward the light areas of the bark, mix Sap Green + Gamboge to create a sense of highlights on the moss.

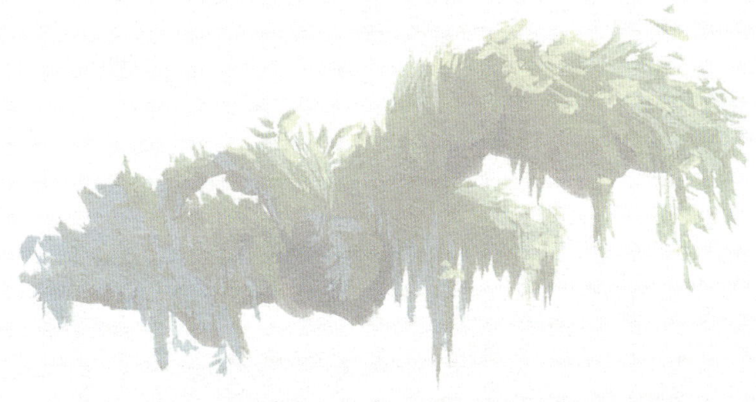

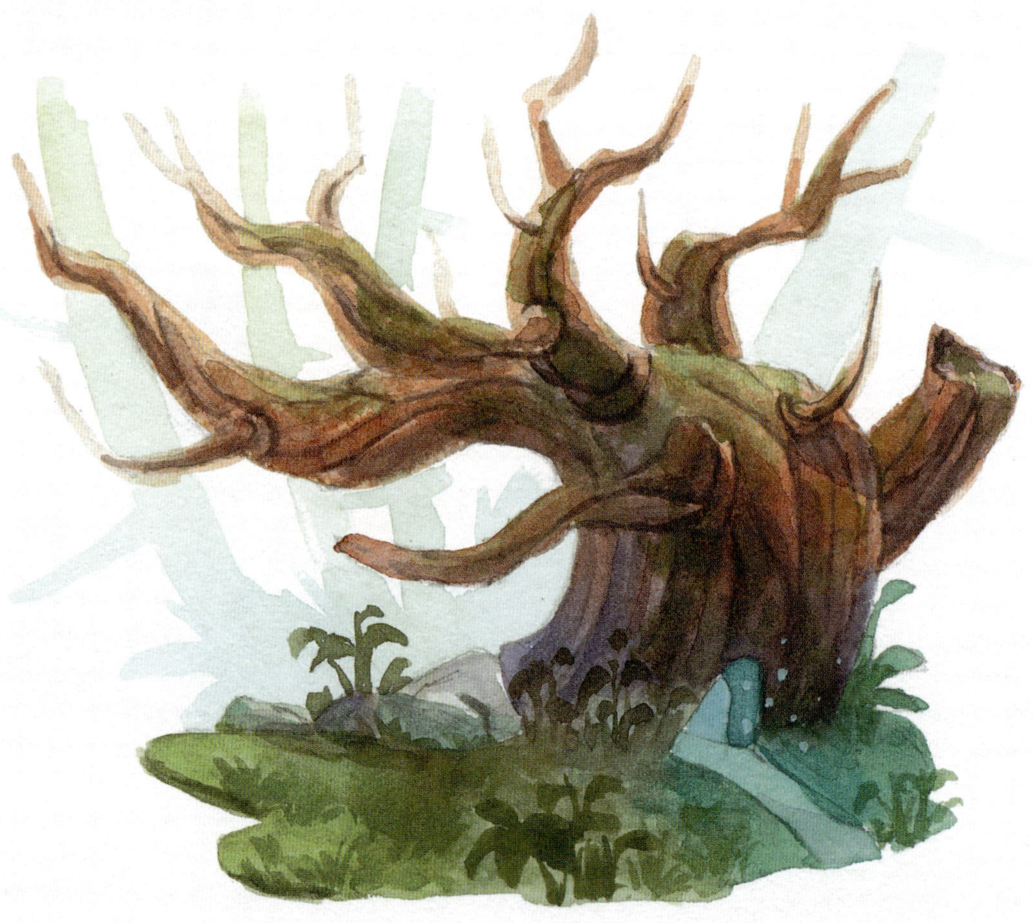

Step 8

Switch to your round brush 0. Mix a thick light-blue color with Cerulean Blue + Titanium White. Carefully, paint dots wafting out of the portal. This is the final detail of our portal, which hypnotizes any wanderers nearby and leads them into this gateway.

With that, we have successfully installed our first—but definitely not our last—portal to the unknown. Your magic is slowly increasing in power as you paint more and more elements of this enchanted world.

The Grove of Wonders

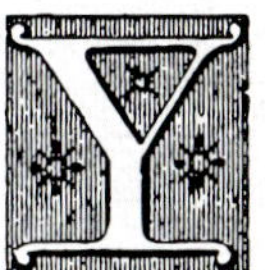 ou might find yourself one day asking this question: *What makes a group of trees so special? Well, the answer is this: Nothing, really. A bunch of trees growing together really slowly, roots connected so they can share nutrients (and the latest gossip) with each other, performing microscopic miracles daily in each leaf . . . there's absolutely nothing special about it.*

But what if this specific group of trees . . . was *floating?*

In this tutorial, we're going to enchant a plot of land so that it floats, and the grove of trees growing on it will hover above our wanderers, making them look skyward in awe and wonder. These trees will appear like little planets, only much closer. And they can fall at any time, crushing anybody beneath them. I'm not saying they will, but they certainly could—based on their own devious impulses.

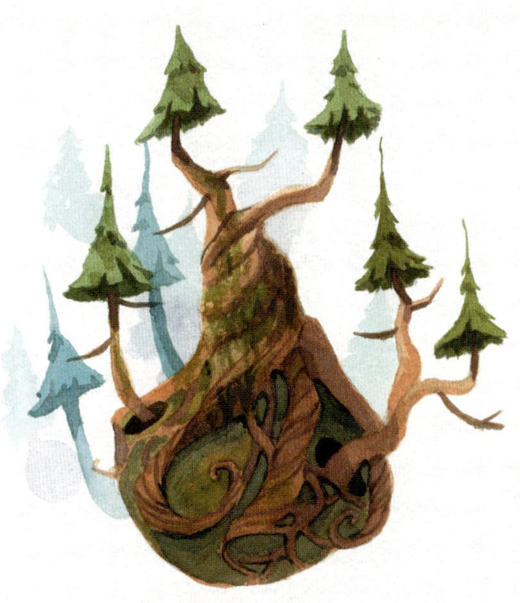

Brushes

Round brush 2, 10, 0

Colors

Violet

Cerulean Blue

Yellow Ochre

Burnt Sienna

Sap Green

Gamboge

Crimson Lake Red

Ultramarine Blue

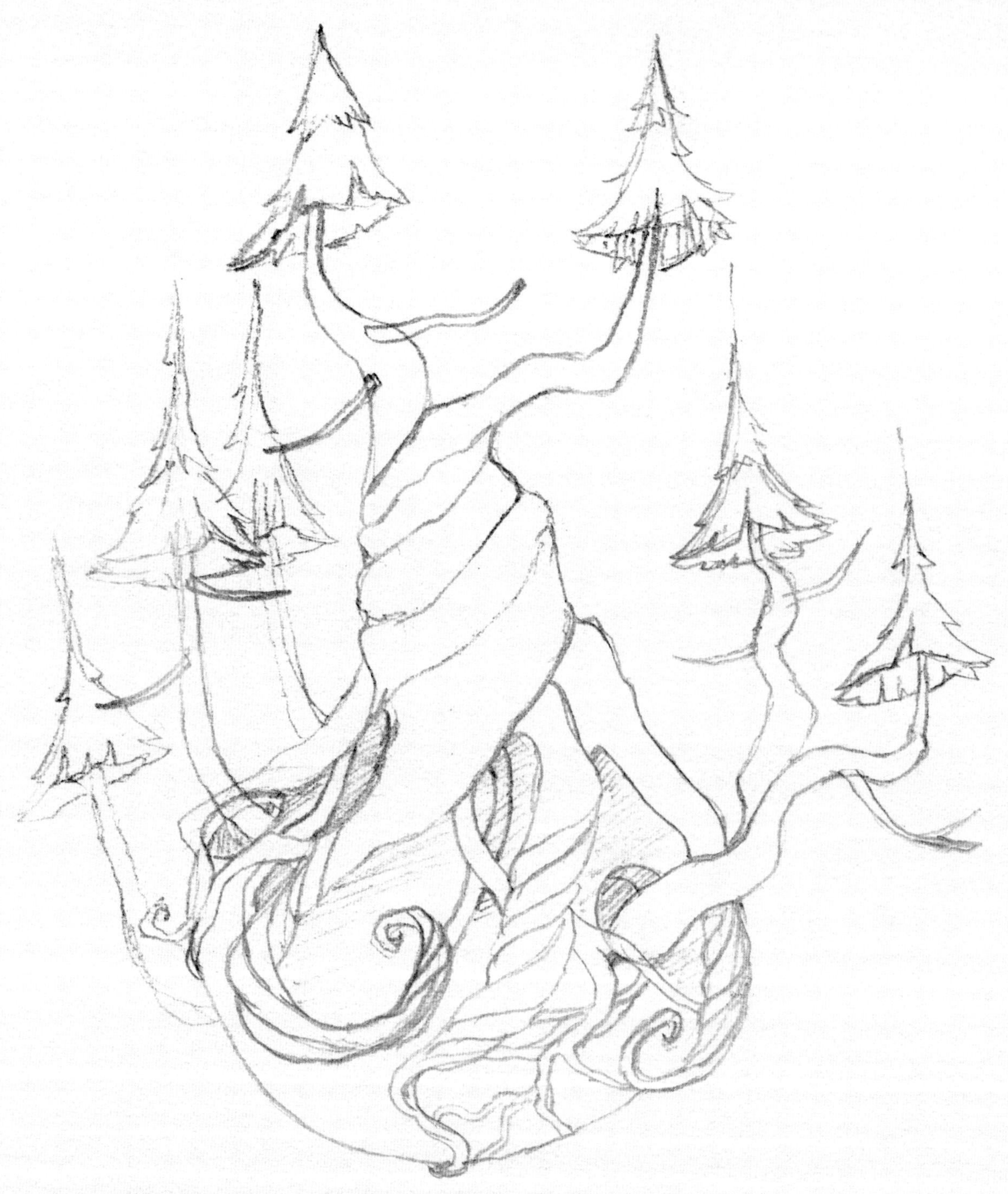

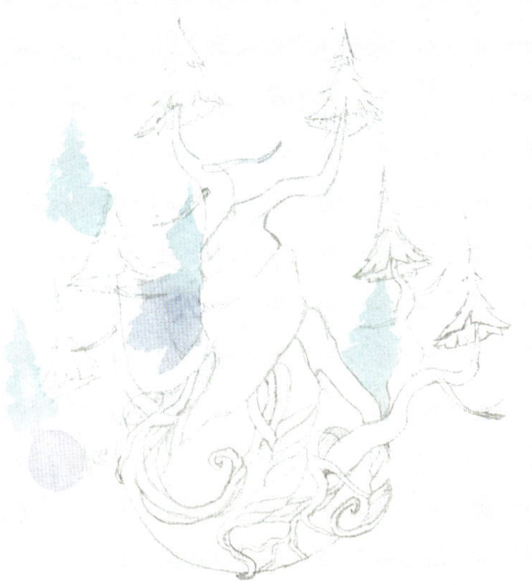

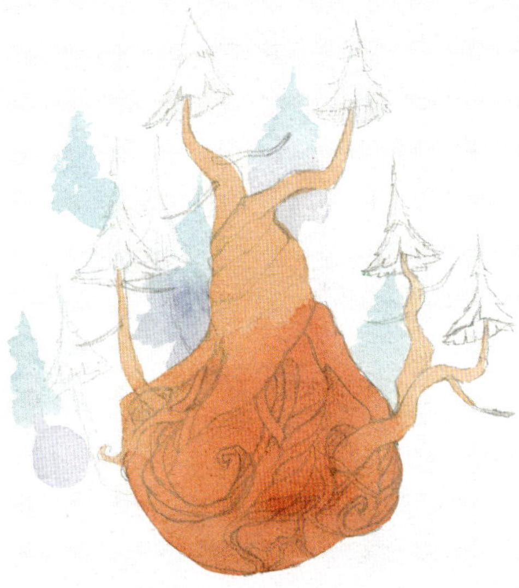

Step 1

Draw the sketch onto your watercolor paper. The key shapes to focus on are the pointed trees and the round sphere from which they sprout.

Step 2

As usual, let's start with the furthermost background elements. Use a round brush 2 for this, and a fair amount of water.

Paint little circles of Violet, and the silhouette of Cerulean Blue pine trees sprouting out. Let this layer dry completely.

Step 3

Switch to your round brush 10 for this step. Raise your sketchbook at an angle, applying *The Bead Method* described in Chapter 1 (see page 15). Then begin painting the bark and branches of the trees with a watery wash of Yellow Ochre. Let this wash fall across the page naturally.

Toward the bottom, add a wash of Burnt Sienna. Let this layer dry.

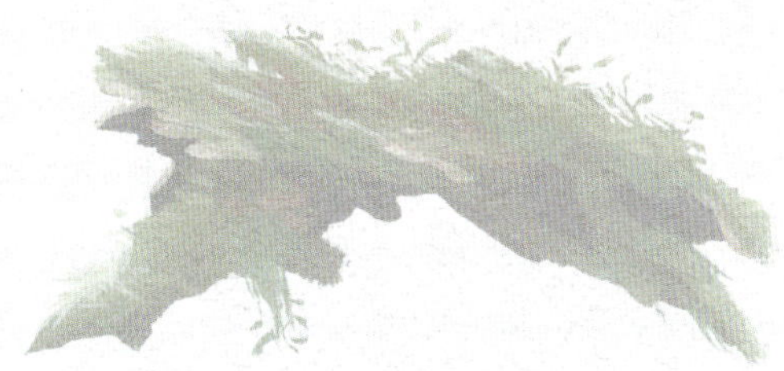

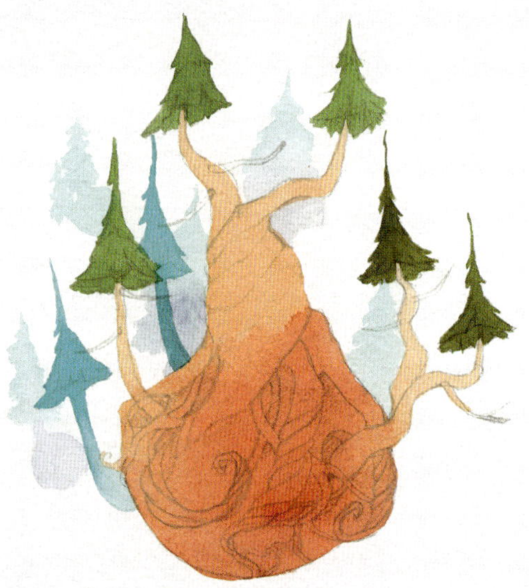

Step 4

Switch to your round brush 2. Use Cerulean Blue with an equal part of water, and cover the trees in the middle ground on the left side.

Then, mix Sap Green + Gamboge + a hint of Crimson Lake Red, and paint the leafy canopy on all the little trees.

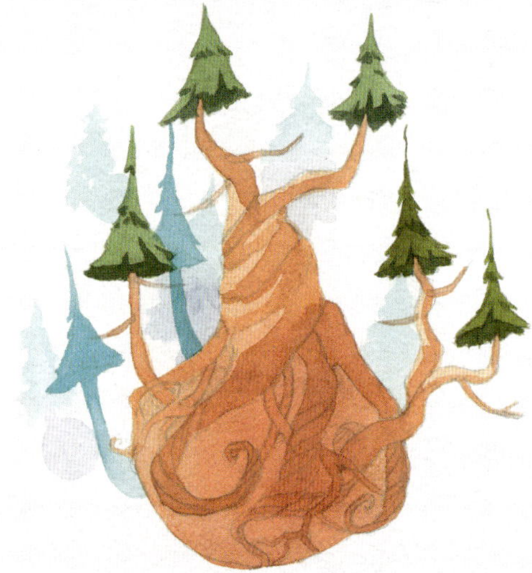

Step 5

Now that the base colors are established for this illustration, we can begin defining the shadows and form. With a wet round brush 2, apply Burnt Sienna to the bark of the trees and all the spiraling roots, leaving some of the Yellow Ochre from Step 3 unpainted on the left side of the branches, because that's where our light source is striking from.

Then mix Sap Green + Crimson Lake Red + a touch of Ultramarine Blue, and paint the underside and shadows of the tree canopies.

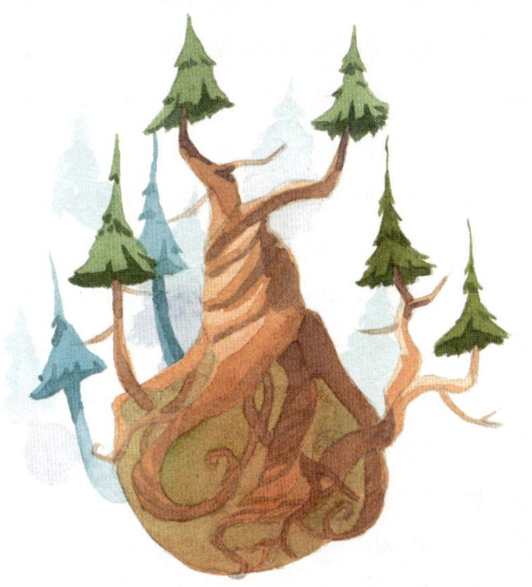

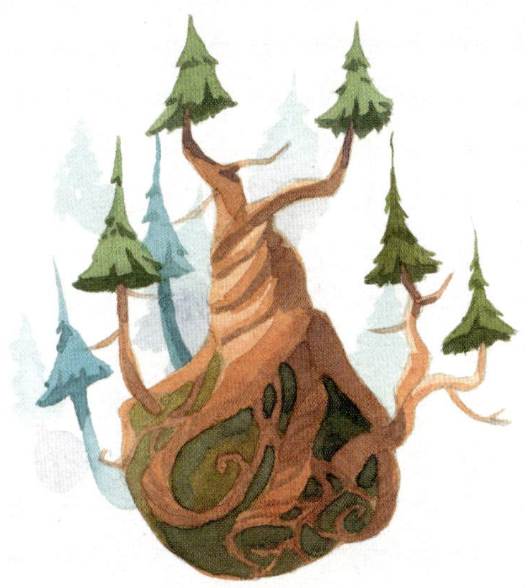

Step 6

Mix Violet + a touch of Burnt Sienna for the shadow on the branches, trunk, and roots. Apply this color more on the right side of the trunk, and cover the roots where the shadows would fall.

Then use a watery wash of Sap Green to paint the sphere, being careful to avoid the brown roots.

Finally, apply another layer of Cerulean Blue to darken the underside of the background trees on the left.

Step 7

Continue painting with your round brush 2. We can now begin to detail this illustration. Start with another layer of Sap Green + Gamboge over the left side of the sphere. As you move toward the right of the sphere, use Sap Green + Ultramarine Blue with a fair amount of water.

While that layer is still wet, dab spots of Ultramarine Blue in the wet paint at all the intersections of the roots on the right side, applying *The Wet-on-Wet Technique* described in Chapter 1 (see page 16). With this simple brushstroke, we can create texture and shadow, which will define the tree more.

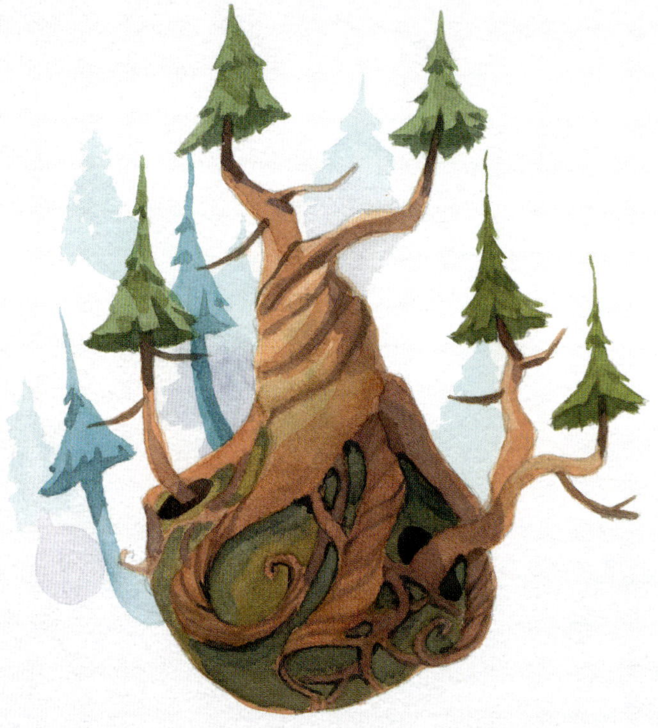

Step 8

We're almost done with this illustration—the final one for this chapter! Switch to a round brush 0. Use Ultramarine Blue + Crimson Lake Red + Burnt Sienna, and repeat the instructions from Step 7 to deepen the shadows on the roots, where they intersect. Use this same dark color to paint the circle portholes where the branches are sprouting out of the sphere, and paint over the lines on the roots and trunk and angular tree shadow beneath the leaf canopy.

Then, use Violet + Burnt Sienna to paint an angular shadow on the branches of the two trees sprouting from the porthole. Use the same color to deepen the shadow on small roots that curve beneath another root.

Next, use Ultramarine Blue to paint curving shadows below the curling roots.

Finally, use a very wet brush to dab spots of water onto the trunk at the center. Then—quickly while the page is wet—dab spots of Burnt Sienna diluted to a very transparent color. Again, while the colors are wet, dab spots of diluted Sap Green. When this dries, the subtle green shade over the bark will enable us to create a transition into moss.

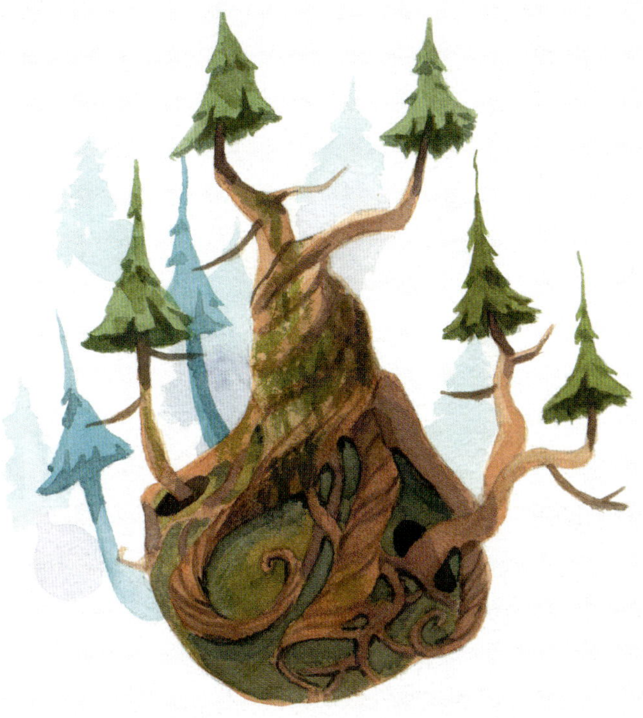

Step 9

For this last step, with a wave of your wand you will be using a round brush 0 and *The Dry Brush Technique* described in Chapter 1 (see page 19). Mix Sap Green + a touch of Crimson Lake Red, and paint the texture of moss with *The Dry Brush Technique*. Slowly add more layers on the right side to create form and shadow. On the left side (the light side), use Sap Green + Gamboge with the same technique.

It might look messy at first, but as you build up layers, the chaotic dry paint will start to look like moss on bark.

When that's dry, you can step back and admire your creation. The Grove of Wonders that you created is sure to spark awe and amazement among our travelers. Well done, fellow wizard!

Now, how vast is your knowledge on mycology?

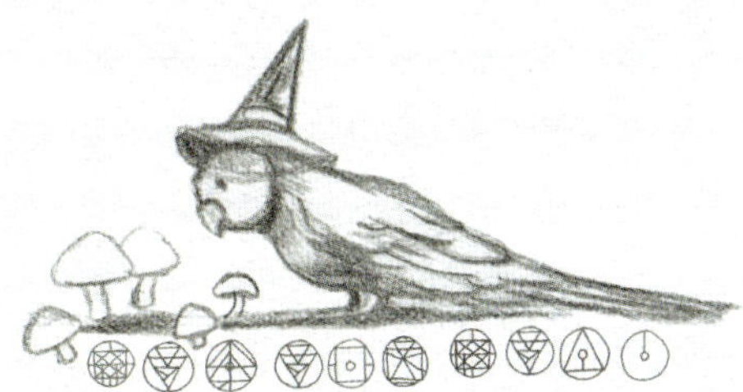

Chapter three
A Dash of Mushrooms

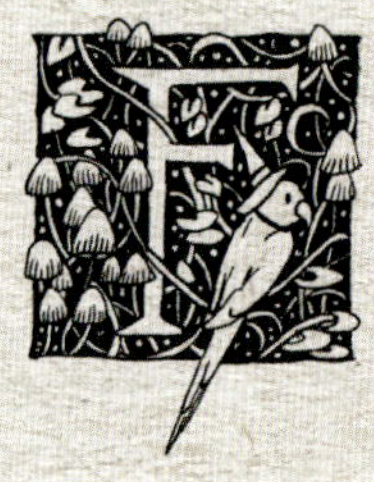ungi are like the darker cousins of plantae. Mushrooms, lichen, toadstools, and the like are all associated with decay, rot, death, and the end of times. Many among wizards also believe that fungi are the key to necromancy.

In this chapter, we're going to delve into the dark, gritty side of nature's magic. As natural as the light and good, the dark side is also a necessary component to our reality, and thus to any other world or dimension we will create.

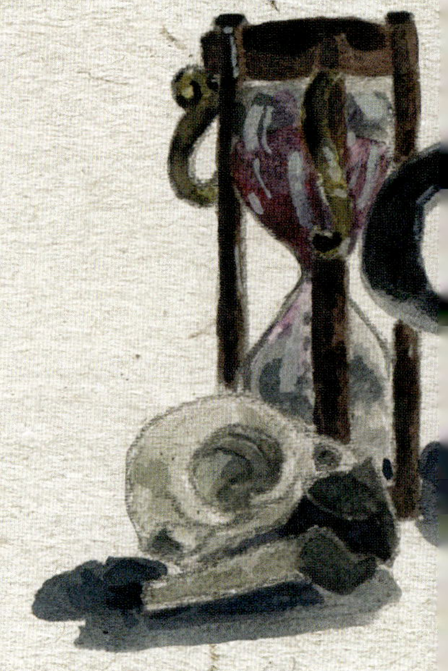

From trickster pixies, to travelling snails, to a secret wizarding order who tether themselves to cursed knowledge, this chapter is for the dangerously curious wizard. Proceed with caution.

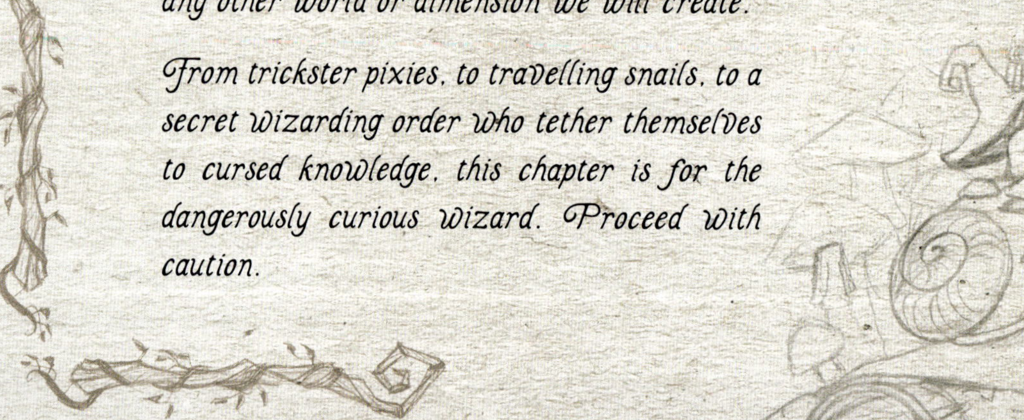

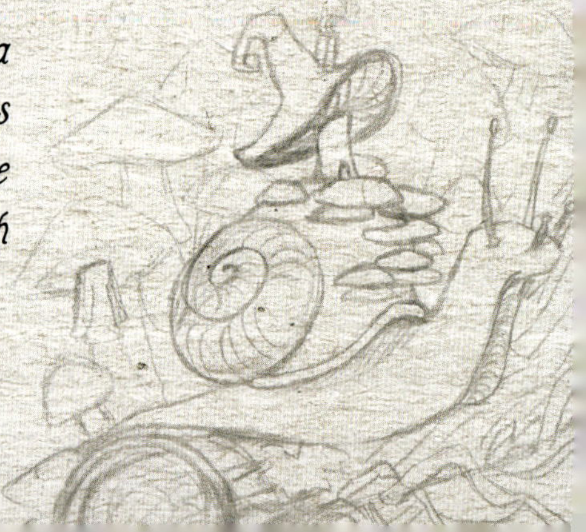

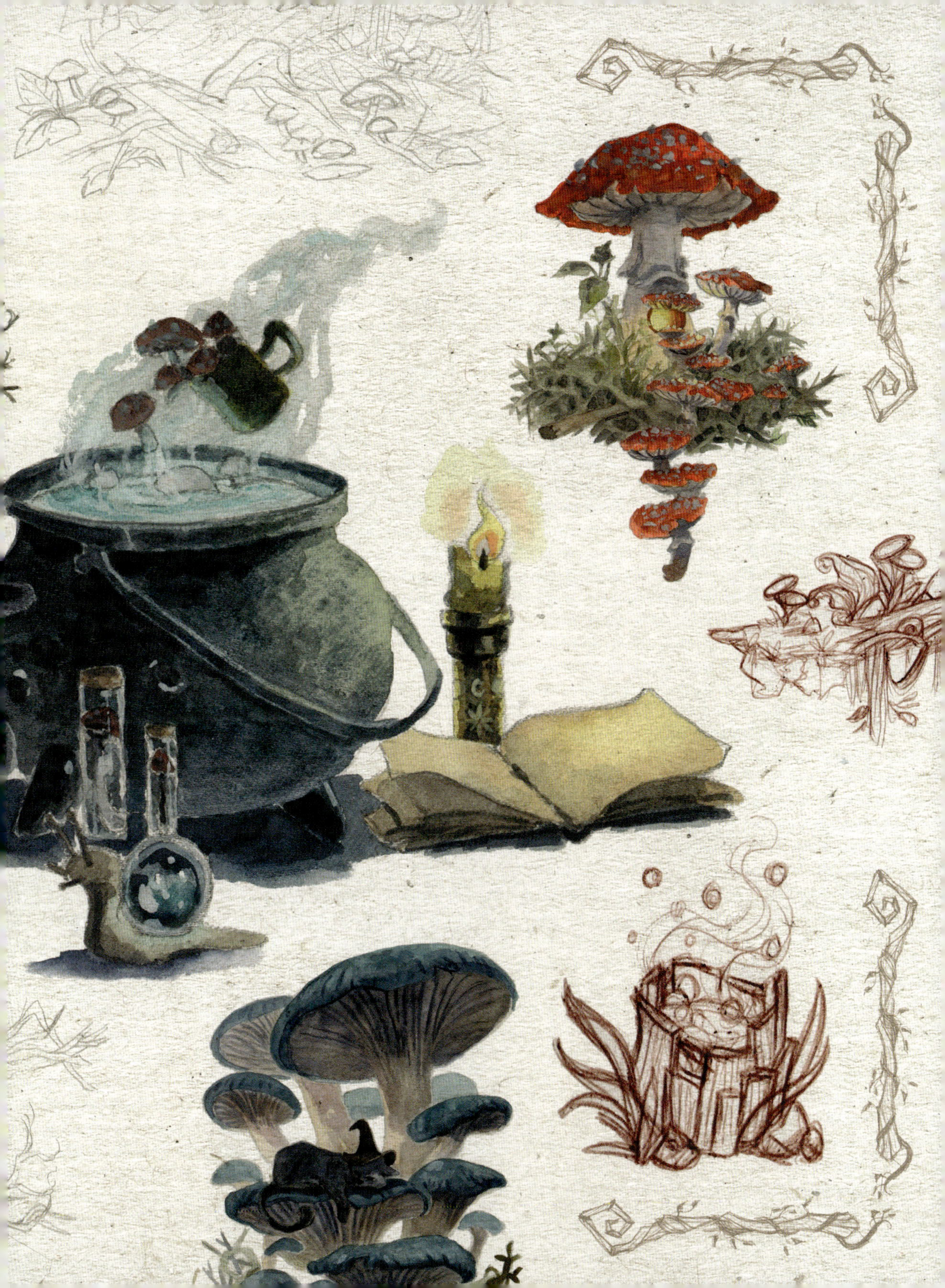

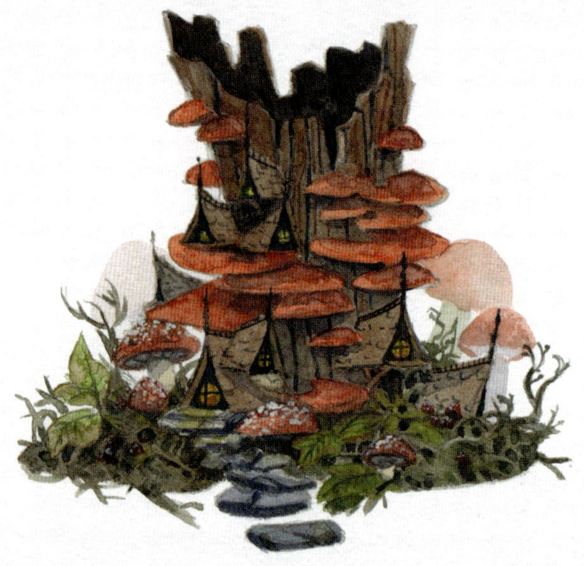

The Pixie Party House

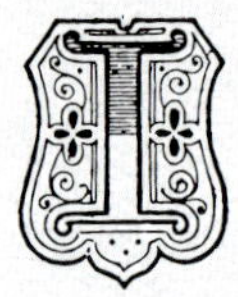
It's a known fact among experienced wizards that if you ever want to spend a few days forgetting your troubles, the best place to go to is a pixie's house. Pixies love to party. And they know all the potions, illusions, and trickery to open up your mind.

In this tutorial, we're going to paint a tree stump covered with lichen and toadstools and tiny little glowing homes that secretly conjoin toward one giant meeting room where the pixies hold all their feasts.

Brushes

Round brush 2, 10, 0

Colors

Vermillion

Crimson Lake Red

Cerulean Blue

Payne's Grey

Burnt Umber

Burnt Sienna

Ultramarine Blue

Sap Green

Lemon Yellow

Deep Blue

Violet

Titanium White

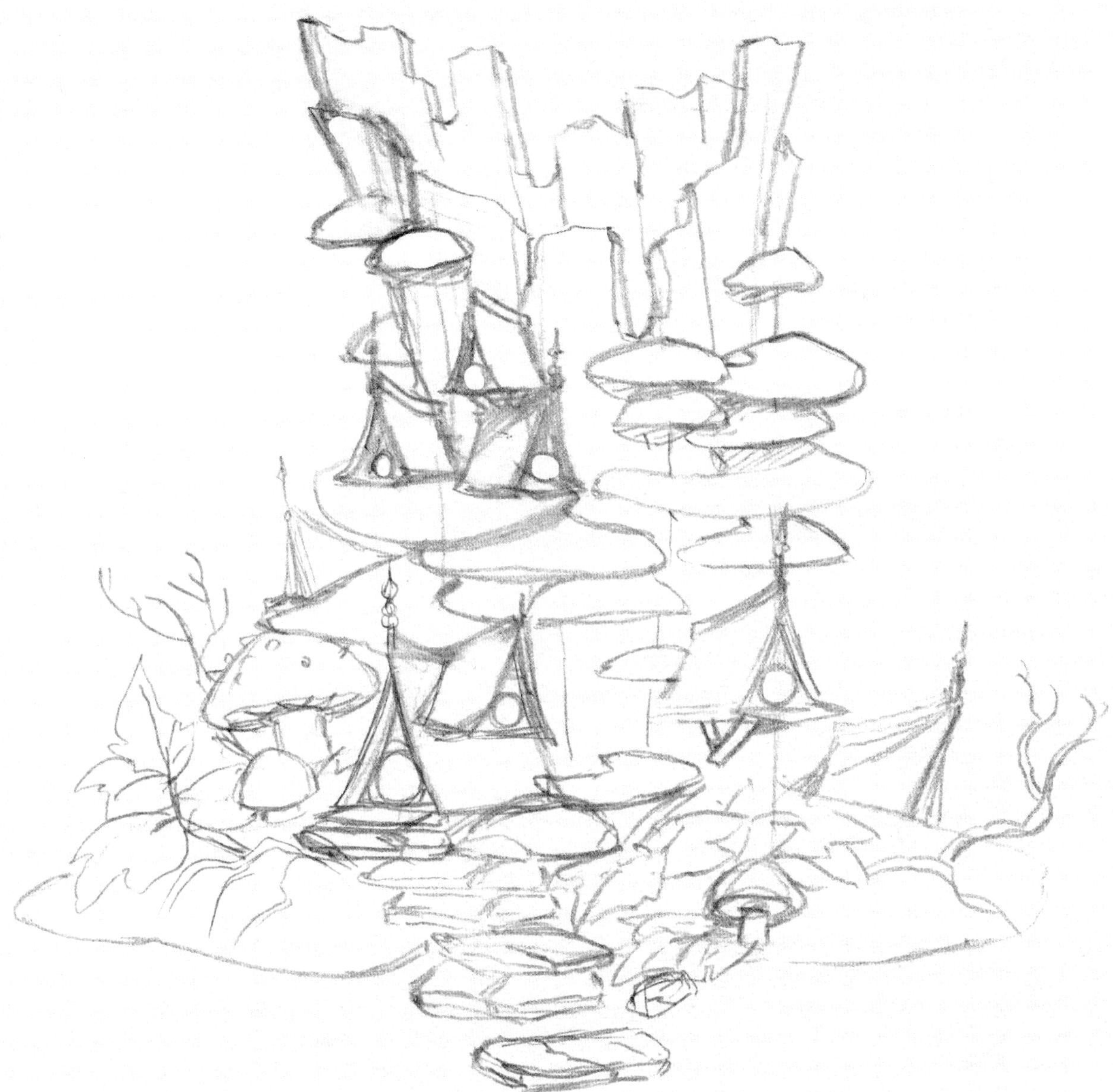

Step 1

Draw the sketch onto your watercolor paper using my drawing as a reference. Feel free to dabble with your own creativity and alter the design how you'd like. The key shapes in the drawing are the round mushrooms and lichen feeding on the tree bark, and the triangular pixie houses.

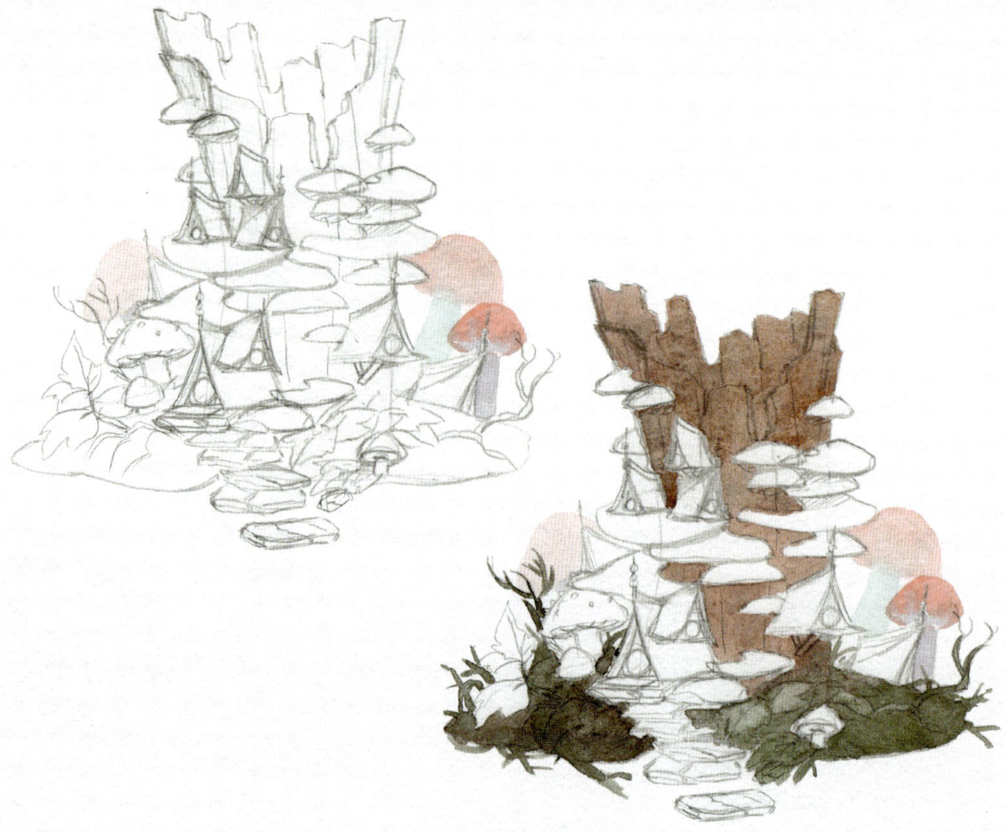

Step 2

Let's begin painting the mushrooms in the background, fading into the distance. Use a wet round brush 2 for this step. Start with Vermillion + a touch of Crimson Lake Red diluted with a lot of water. Paint the curve of the mushroom caps behind the main drawing. For the larger mushroom stem, use Cerulean Blue diluted with plenty of water.

For the middle-ground mushroom, use Vermillion with a bit less water than you used for the mushroom cap. And for this mushroom's stem, use Payne's Grey. Paint the stem while the Vermillion is still wet, so these colors blend together.

Step 3

Switch to your round brush 10, and work quickly using a fairly wet brush. Start with Burnt Umber, and apply it to the entire bark of the tree. For the grassy ground, use Burnt Sienna + Ultramarine Blue + Sap Green for a moody autumn-green color. While painting the ground, create the shapes of numerous branches, twigs, and sticks jumbled on the ground. Be careful to avoid painting over the mushrooms, houses, and stone steps on the path.

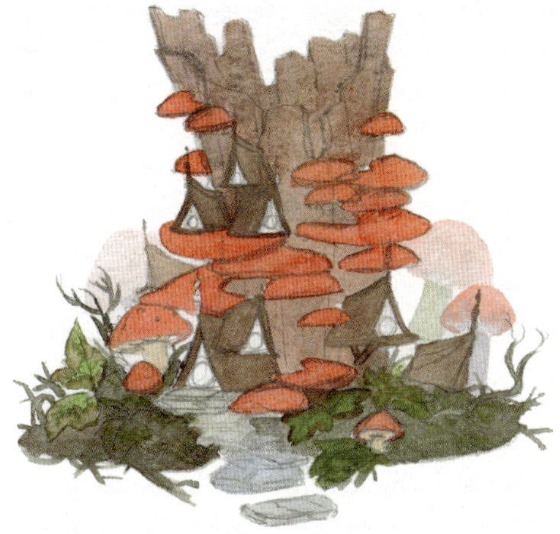 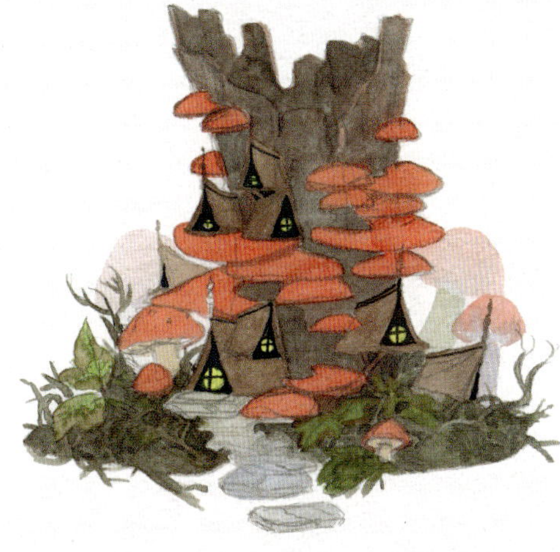

Step 4

It's time to establish the base colors for the rest of the illustration. Use Vermillion + a touch of Crimson Lake Red to paint all the mushroom caps and lichen in the scene.

Then mix Lemon Yellow + Sap Green, and paint the remaining leaves on the ground. While each leaf is still wet, use Burnt Sienna + Ultramarine Blue to carefully paint the *outline* of the leaf. The wet colors will push against each other, naturally and quickly creating the effect of a dried leaf.

Next, use Burnt Sienna + a touch of Vermillion to paint the roofs of the little houses.

Finally, use Deep Blue + Violet to paint the stepping stones. For the stone directly below the bottom house, dab a spot of Lemon Yellow in the wet paint, to indicate the light that we'll paint on the windows later. (See *The Wet-on-Wet Technique* from Chapter 1, page 16.) Use the same color to paint over the Cerulean Blue mushroom stem in the background (the one from Step 2) and the other mushroom stems in the scene.

Step 5

Now we need to define the shapes, light, and shadows. Start by switching to your round brush 0. Using Lemon Yellow, paint all the circular windows in the houses.

Then switch to your round brush 2, and use Deep Blue diluted with water to glaze another layer over the tree bark. Be careful to avoid painting over the red lichen and houses. Use the same color to paint in between the sticks on the ground, outlining their shapes a little more.

Switch back to your round brush 0. Use Deep Blue + Payne's Grey to paint the inside of the house surrounding the window and the window panes.

 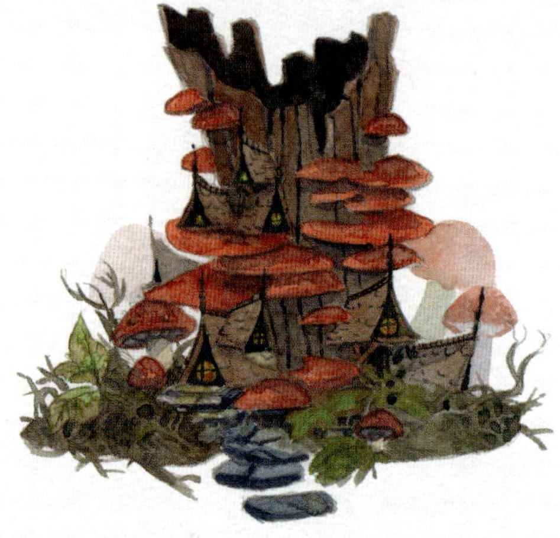

Step 6

Use your round brush 2 for this step. Start by painting another layer of Payne's Grey + Burnt Sienna over the inside of the tree stump.

Then use Payne's Grey to paint shadows on the bark beneath the mushrooms, and beneath mushrooms that overlap one another. Paint angular shadows across the roofs of the houses, the stone steps, and in between the sticks on the ground to further emphasize their form.

Next, mix Crimson Lake Red + a touch of Payne's Grey, and dab this color onto the mushrooms to create texture and variation.

Step 7

Continue painting with your round brush 2 for this step. First, use *The Glazing Method* described in Chapter 1 (page 16) to paint another layer of Vermillion + a touch of Crimson Lake Red for a shadow on the mushroom cap in the background on the right.

Next, glaze another layer of Burnt Sienna over the bark of the tree, emphasizing the front part of the stump to ensure it separates from the bark inside.

Now apply a dot of Lemon Yellow + Crimson Lake Red into the yellow windows to warm up the glow.

Finally, switch to your round brush 0. Use Payne's Grey + a touch of Deep Blue to paint more detail on the pixie houses— short horizontal lines to indicate the roof tiles, and a tall vertical spire sticking out from the front of the house. Use the same color to outline the stepping stones.

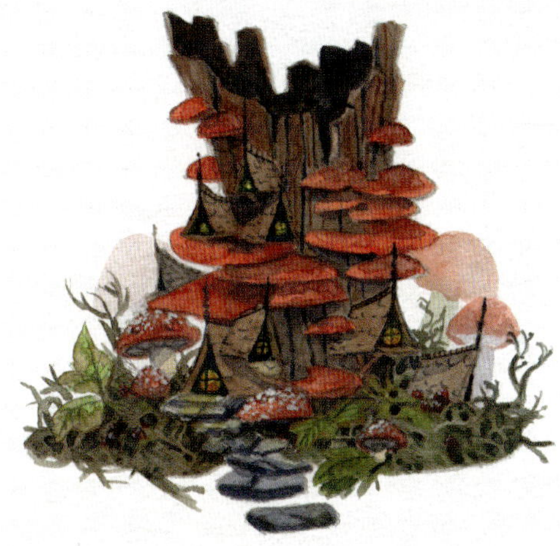

Step 8

Use your round brush 0 for this step. Dip your brush into a thick mixture of Titanium White watercolor. Paint delicate spots on the toadstools on the ground. For the spots in shadow, add a touch of Payne's Grey into the white watercolor.

Then clean your brush, and create a dark-green color by mixing Sap Green + Crimson Lake Red. Paint spots on the ground in between the sticks, branches, and twigs, using *The Inverse Painting Technique* described in Chapter 1 (see page 17). With watercolor, we need to work from light to dark, so imagine where the stick is on the ground, and paint the shadow *around* it. Use the same color to paint the lines on the large leaves.

Step 9

This last step is for cleaning up any loose ends of the illustration. Use your round brush 0 and Vermillion. Paint tiny spots of more toadstools littered on the ground. Then clean your brush, and use Titanium White watercolor to paint the white spots on the cap so they look like mushrooms.

Use Payne's Grey to apply another layer to the angular shadows that got lost in the details of the previous steps.

With those last shadows more pronounced, this illustration is complete! The pixies are ready for their next party—and our adventurers are invited for a night of tingling trickery.

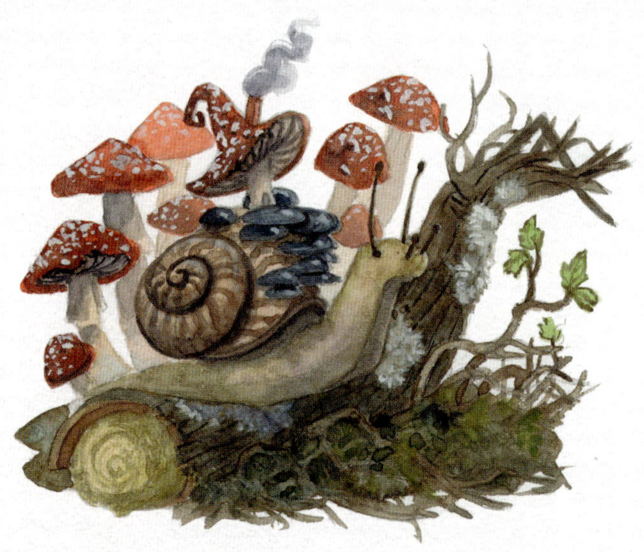

The Mushroom Wizard

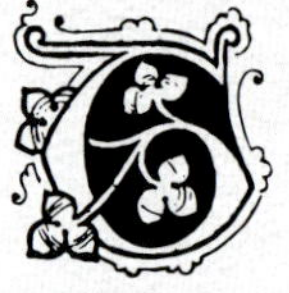 here is a giant traveling snail who visits from town to town, carrying a library of books of alchemy, mycology, and sorcery inside its shell. Just as you never see a snail coming (it's always suddenly just there), this creature mysteriously appears and sets up camp in a new town every week. Its purpose? To spread knowledge, freeing folks from the shackles of their ignorant minds. I happen to know the wizard who runs this scheme. She's a clever, rebellious one who calls herself The Mushroom Wizard.

In this tutorial, we're going to paint this wizard and her abode, inviting her to our dimension momentarily for our visitors to meet.

Brushes

Round brush 2, 10, 0

Colors

Vermillion

Crimson Lake Red

Lemon Yellow

Payne's Grey

Deep Blue

Burnt Sienna

Ultramarine Blue

Sap Green

Yellow Ochre

Titanium White

Burnt Umber

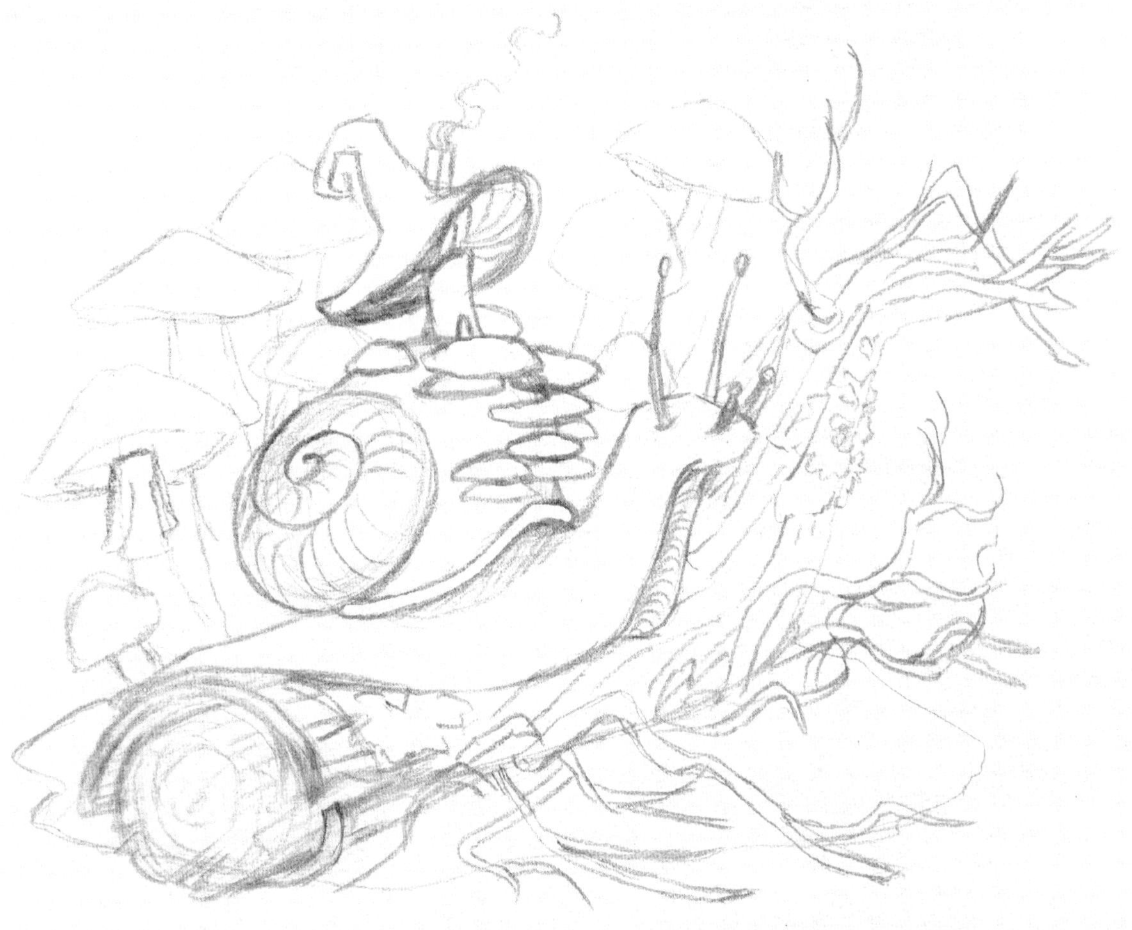

Step 1

Draw the design of this scene using my sketch as a reference. Feel free to change the design according to your imagination. The key shapes are the round snail shell, the mushroom caps, and the pointy jumble of sticks on the ground.

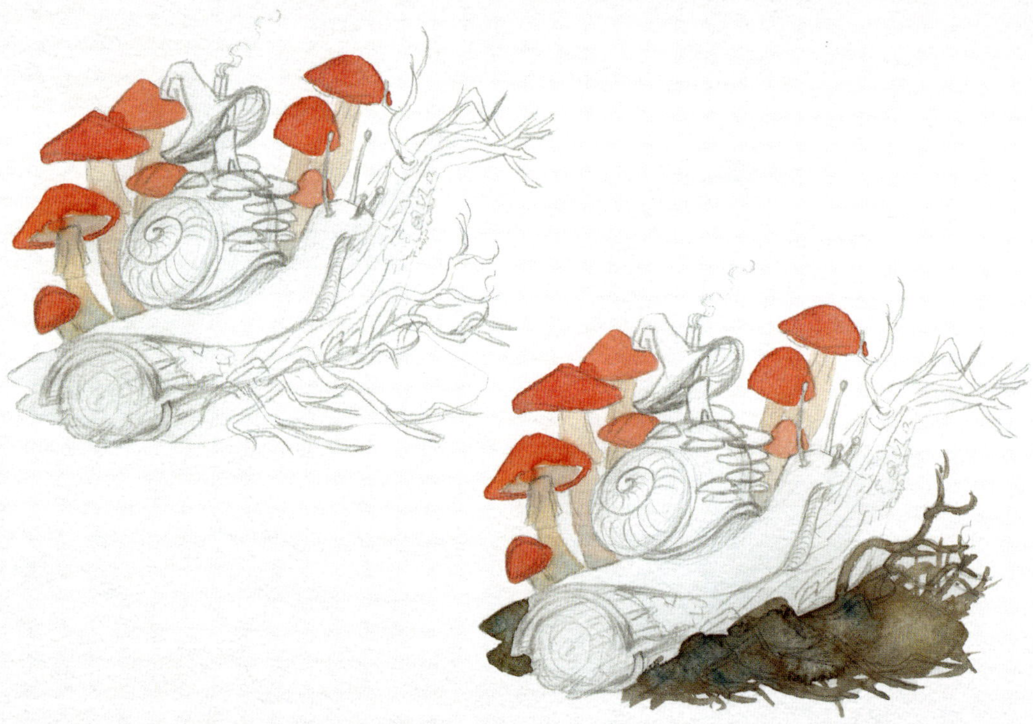

Step 2

Let's begin painting the base colors for the mushrooms in the background of the scene. Use a round brush 2 dipped in a fair amount of water. Mix Vermillion + Crimson Lake Red, and paint the mushroom caps with this color. While the paint is still wet, use *The Wet-on-Wet Technique* (see page 16), and dab Lemon Yellow into the paint, and let them blend together naturally. Make sure the colors for the caps are not too uniform on all of them; use more Crimson Lake Red on the caps closer to the foreground, and more yellow on the caps in the background.

Mix Lemon Yellow + Payne's Grey + a touch of Crimson Lake Red diluted with a lot of water. Use this peachy color to paint the stems of the mushrooms. While the paint is still wet, apply *The Wet-on-Wet Technique* (page 16), and dab spots of Deep Blue, diluted with a lot of water, on the bottom of the stems.

Step 3

Switch to your round brush 10 to begin laying out the colors for the branch-littered ground. Mix Burnt Sienna + Ultramarine Blue + Sap Green for a moody autumn-green color. Work loosely with free and chaotic brushstrokes to mimic sticks, branches, and twigs, all strewn together across and over each other. While the paint is still wet, dab spots of Deep Blue in the areas closest to the main branch and snail.

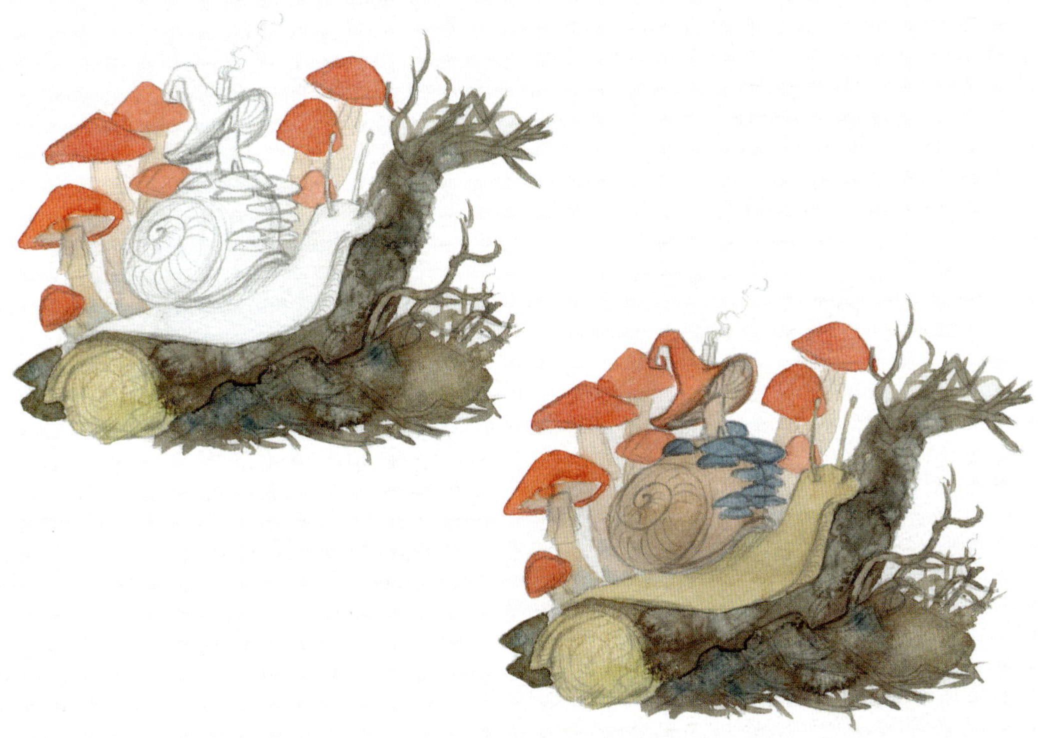

Step 4

Now we're going to lay the base colors for the big branch the snail is crossing over—a blend of multiple colors. Working quickly on a wet layer, use your round brush 10 to create a diluted mixture of Yellow Ochre + a touch of Lemon Yellow, and paint the round end of the branch.

To paint the lichen, we will use *The Wet-on-Wet Technique* as described in Chapter 1 (page 16). Mix Burnt Sienna + Deep Blue, and paint the rest of the main branch. Then dab spots of thick Titanium White into the wet paint of the branch—these will be the grey lichen growing on the wood. Observe how the thick white paint pushes against the brown, creating lichen textures easily.

Let this layer dry thoroughly before continuing to the next step. It might look messy now, but part of painting is trusting the process and understanding that you can sculpt paint into anything.

Step 5

Use your round brush 2 dipped in a fair amount of water. Mix Burnt Umber + Yellow Ochre and paint the shell. Then mix Lemon Yellow + Burnt Umber + a touch of Sap Green, and paint the body of the snail.

Use Deep Blue for the mushrooms on the snail shell and Vermillion + Lemon Yellow for the mushroom cap on the shell.

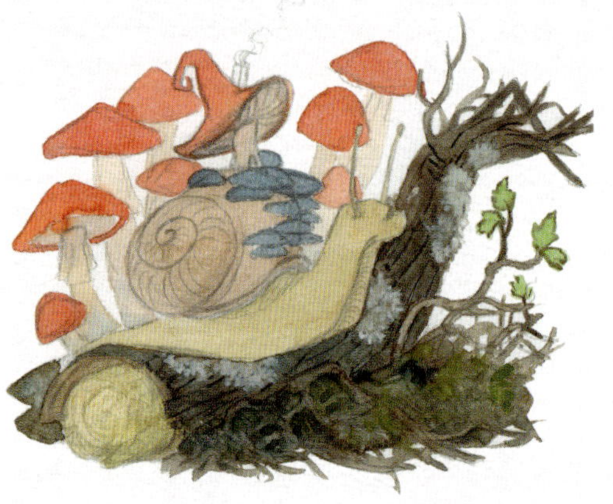 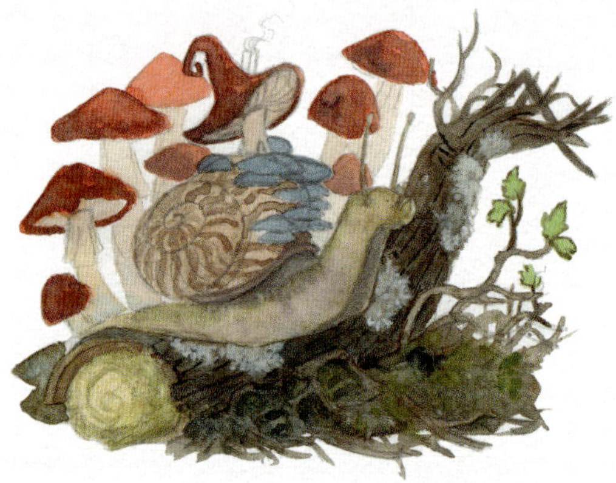

Step 6

Continue using the round brush 2. Glaze another layer of Deep Blue + Burnt Sienna on the main branch, bringing it forward.

Then use Payne's Grey + Sap Green to paint quick spots on the grass. Imagine where the sticks are, and paint the shadows *around* them. (Refer to *The Inverse Painting Technique* from Chapter 1 on page 17 for more information on this.)

Next use Lemon Yellow + Sap Green to paint quick spots of green on the ground to indicate leaves littered among the sticks. Paint a few leaves on the branches that stick out above the ground.

Now switch to your round brush 0 to begin adding the details. First, use a thick mixture of Titanium White watercolor to enhance the little petals of lichen on the bark. Then use Burnt Sienna to outline some of the green leaves, giving the effect of those leaves slowly drying and being about to fall. Finally, use a thick mixture of Payne's Grey + Burnt Sienna to detail the lines on the main bark.

Step 7

With your round brush 2, use Lemon Yellow + Sap Green diluted with water to paint the edges of the body of the snail. Then use diluted Violet to dab spots of this color on the central area of the snail's body. While those colors are still wet, apply a thin wash of Burnt Sienna on the snail, and Payne's Grey for the shadow on its neck and back beneath the shell.

Glaze another layer of Deep Blue on the bark beneath the snail, deepening the shadow and making the snail stand out more.

When that layer is dry, use your round brush 2 to mix Burnt Sienna with an equal part of water, and paint delicate wavy lines across the shell of the snail.

Next, use Crimson Lake Red + a touch of Payne's Grey to glaze another layer over the mushroom caps. Paint this color with free strokes, letting some paint dry in areas and blend in other areas, allowing for interesting textures to happen on the page.

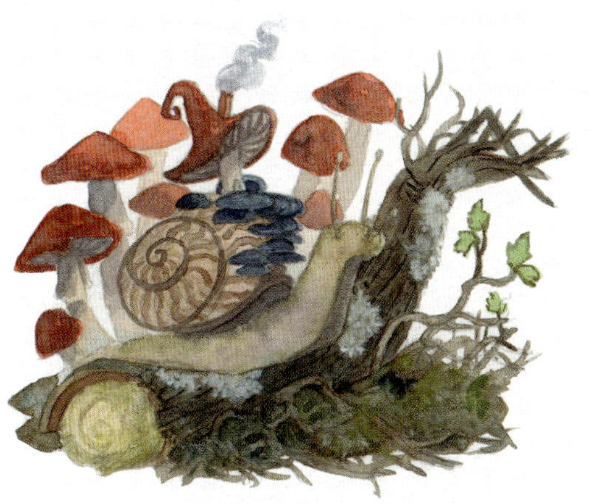 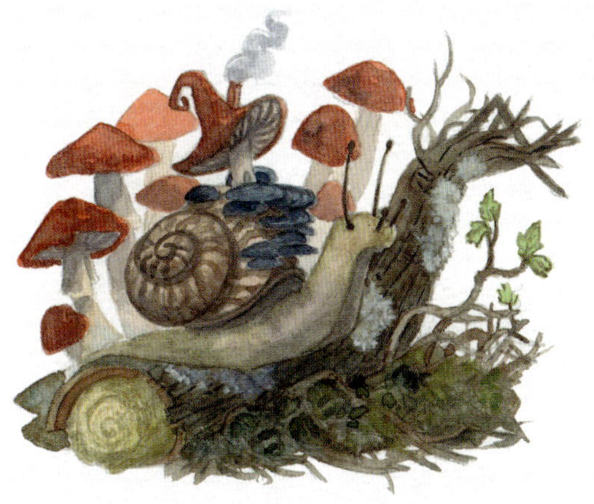

Step 8

Continue painting with your round brush 2. First, use Vermillion to paint the chimney on the main mushroom, and paint the shadow side of the chimney with Crimson Lake Red + a touch of Payne's Grey.

Next, use Payne's Grey to paint the shadows beneath the mushroom cap, the shadows on the stems, and the little curving lines under the mushroom caps. Then, using a fair amount of water, paint the smoke rising from the chimney. To give the effect of smoke, paint the areas close to the chimney more opaquely—more transparently the further away it rises.

Use Payne's Grey + a touch of Deep Blue to paint shadows on the blue mushrooms on the snail shell.

Step 9

We're almost done with this illustration! The last few touches will be painting the shadows on the shell, defining its form a bit more. Use Payne's Grey and your round brush 2. Paint this color in a delicate curve toward the bottom of each round shape on the shell. Also apply this shadow color over the lichen growing beneath the snail, emphasizing the shadow even more.

Next use Sap Green + Payne's Grey to make the snail's form stand out more. Paint this green-grey color on the curve of the snail's body toward the bottom where it's moving over the branch.

Use the same green-grey color to paint circular lines on the inside of the tree branch, the eyes of the snail, and more spots in the ground in the shape of leaves that have fallen in the autumn weather.

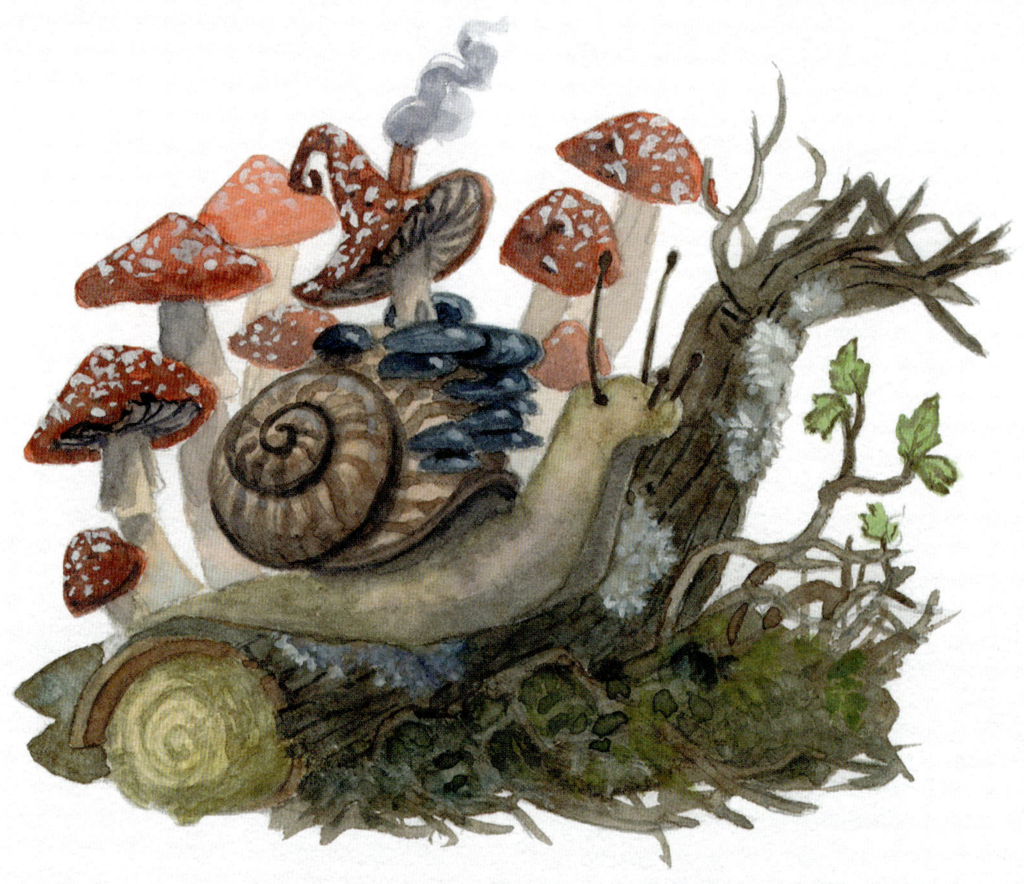

Step 10

Finally, the most delicious part of the painting! Use a thick mixture of Titanium White watercolor paint and your round brush 0 to paint the little white spots over the mushroom caps. Then use Payne's Grey to paint little dots beneath each white spot as a shadow. Also apply some diluted white watercolor as little spots on the blue mushrooms and the snail's shell. There's something so deliciously satisfying about painting the final white highlights on an illustration.

And now The Mushroom Wizard is complete, set on an epic quest over branches and forest floors. Well done, fellow wizard!

The Path of the Toadstool

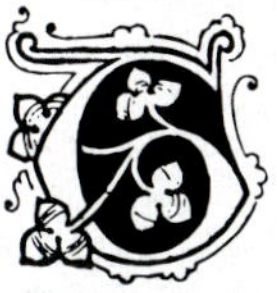

T he Path of the Toadstool is an order of wizards who gather once every ten years to pool together their individual research. It's a secret organization, and their members' identities are kept anonymous. You see, they study a very taboo application of mycology. It's taboo because the general public doesn't like undead things, and they study necromancy.

In this tutorial, we're going to paint the secret meeting place of this organization (a giant toadstool), and the only way to enter is by hopping on a path of tiny toadstools.

Brushes

Round brush 2, 10, 0

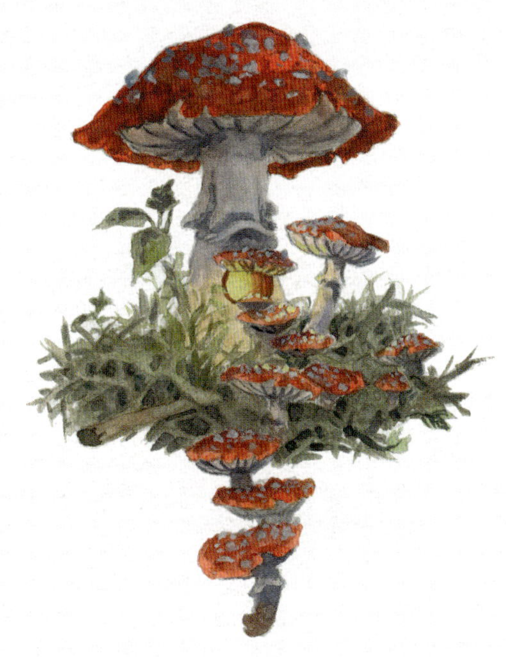

Colors

Gamboge

Vermillion

Crimson Lake Red

Lemon Yellow

Violet

Sap Green

Burnt Sienna

Payne's Grey

Yellow Ochre

Deep Blue

Titanium White

Gouache (optional)

Lemon Yellow

Titanium White

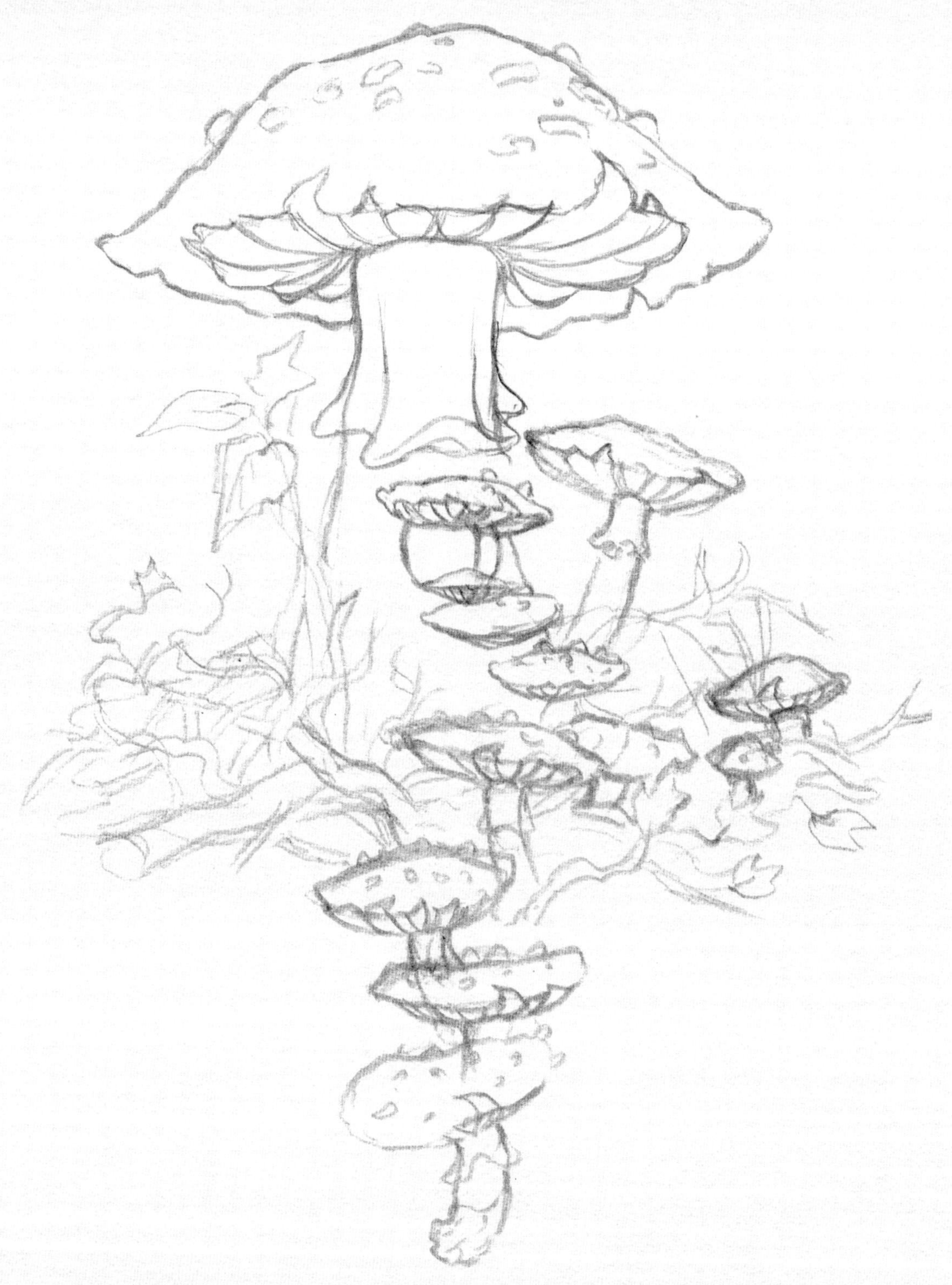

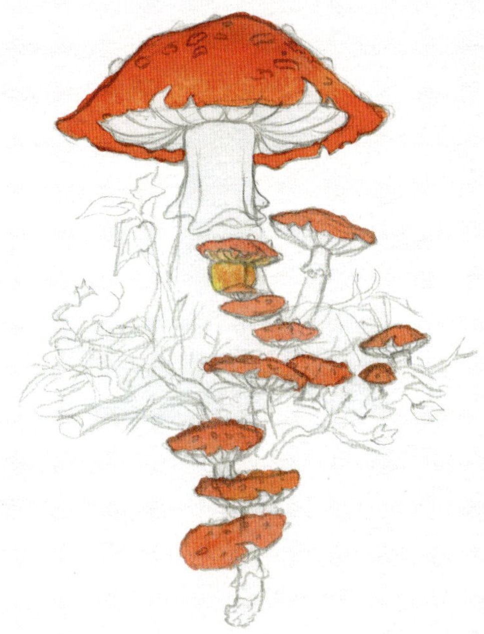

Step 1

Draw the base pencil illustration using my sketch as a reference. As always, you can feel free to change the design according to your imagination. The key shapes to keep in your drawing are the rounded mushroom caps and their stems, and the jumble of sticks on the ground. Also make sure the circular opening in the giant mushroom is clearly visible and blank.

Step 2

First let's establish where our main light source will be coming from: the glowing window nestled in the stem of the giant mushroom. Using Gamboge and a round brush 2, paint the circular opening. Then while the paint is wet, mix a touch of Vermillion into the Gamboge, making a light-orange color. Lightly dab this color into the window frame, and let the colors seep together naturally.

Then use Vermillion + Gamboge to paint the caps of the toadstools that are closest to the glowing window. As you paint the toadstools farther away from the window, use more Vermillion in your mixture.

Then switch to your round brush 10 to paint the large mushroom cap. Use Crimson Lake Red + Vermillion, and start painting from the top of the cap. Add more Gamboge into the mixture when painting toward the bottom of the cap. For the outer rim on the bottom, use Crimson Lake Red + Vermillion again. And while the paint is still wet, dab spots of Lemon Yellow into the paint on the front of the mushroom cap, toward the rim. Let this color seep like tendrils and push the red, creating the texture of a frilly mushroom.

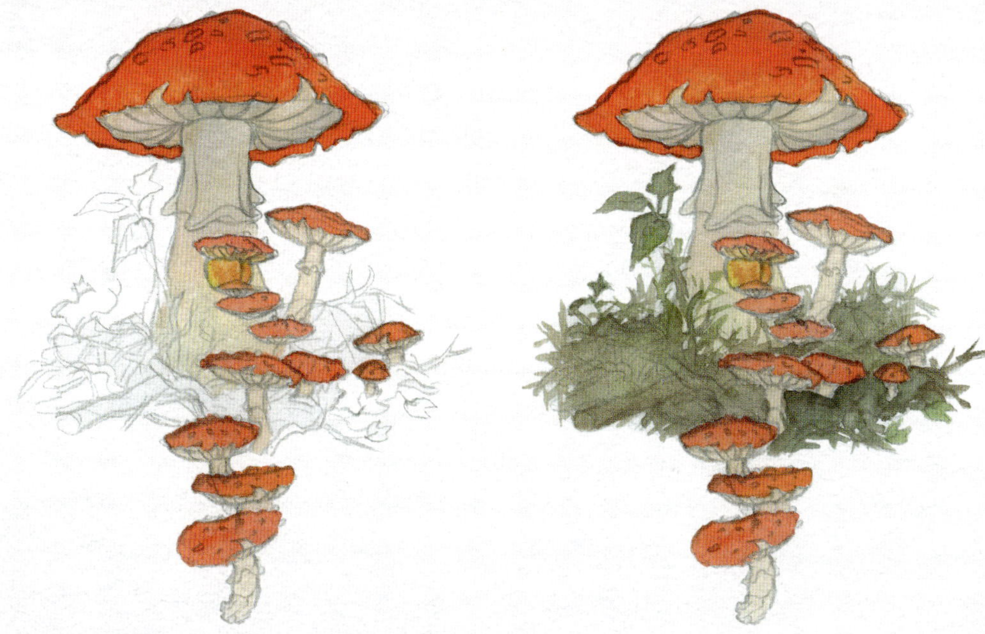

Step 3

Use your round brush 2 for this step. Mix Lemon Yellow + Crimson Lake Red and a lot of water. Apply this color to the stem of all the mushrooms. While the paint is still wet, dab spots of diluted Violet into the stem color where the shadows would be stronger, creating super-subtle transitions in tones. Apply *The Wet-on-Wet Technique* (page 16) once again, and dab spots of Crimson Lake Red diluted with a lot of water. Apply the Crimson Lake Red mainly on the gills of the cap. The resulting colors will be extremely subtle hues on the white mushroom stalk, just visible enough to create beauty.

Step 4

Switch to your round brush 10. In this step, we're going to work quickly on a wet layer, and paint the base colors for the grassy ground. Mix a moody autumn-grey color using Sap Green + Burnt Sienna + a touch of Payne's Grey, with a fair amount of water. Start applying this color to the grassy ground, carefully avoiding the mushrooms. For the grass blades that reach up close to the glowing window, use Sap Green + Lemon Yellow. And for the grass that is under the mushroom's shadow, use more Payne's Grey in the mixture.

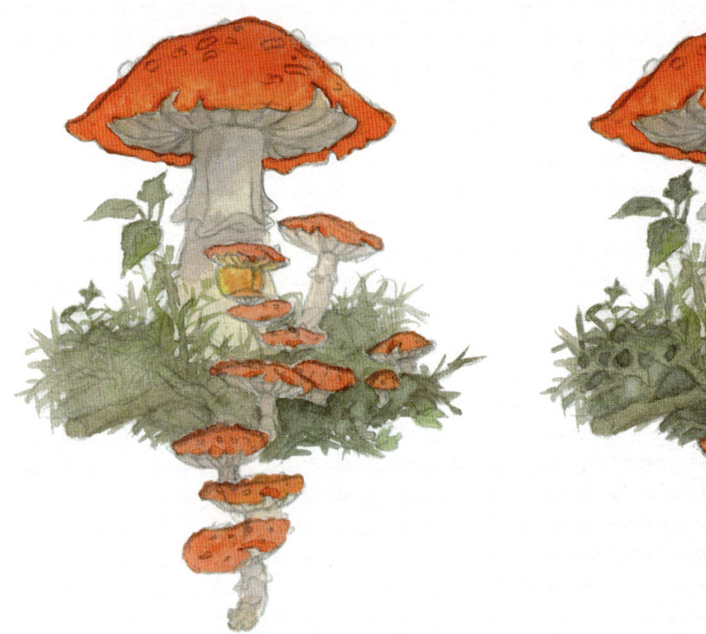

Step 5

Use your round brush 2 dipped in a fair amount of water, with a diluted Violet. Apply this color to the underside of the mushroom caps. Paint a smooth gradient on the gills to indicate light coming from above the scene, and harsher transitions to indicate sharp edges on the inside of the cap.

Then use Crimson Lake Red to deepen the shadow on the mushroom cap where the groove is.

When the Violet layer is dry, use Yellow Ochre, diluted, to randomly paint spots on the underside of the giant mushroom cap, further enhancing the decaying effect that mushrooms represent.

Step 6

Continue painting with your round brush 2. Use Payne's Grey with an equal part of water, and begin defining the sticks, twigs, and branch-littered forest floor. Remember *The Inverse Painting Technique* described in Chapter 1 (page 17)? The technique is to imagine where a stick would be and then paint the shadow *around* it, working from light to dark, and painting the negative space. Do this across the ground, and watch how the sticks come to life.

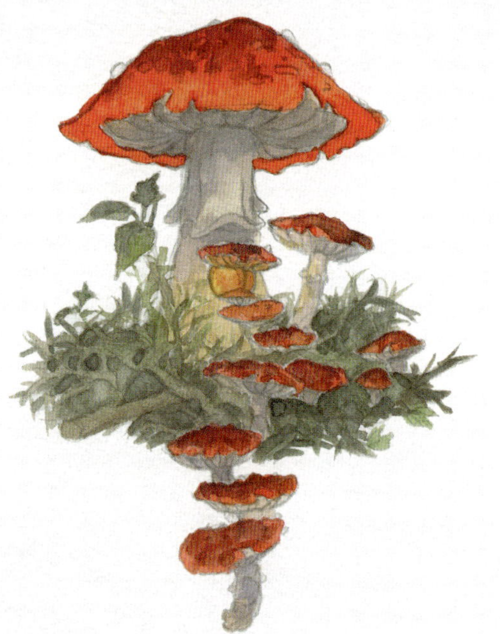
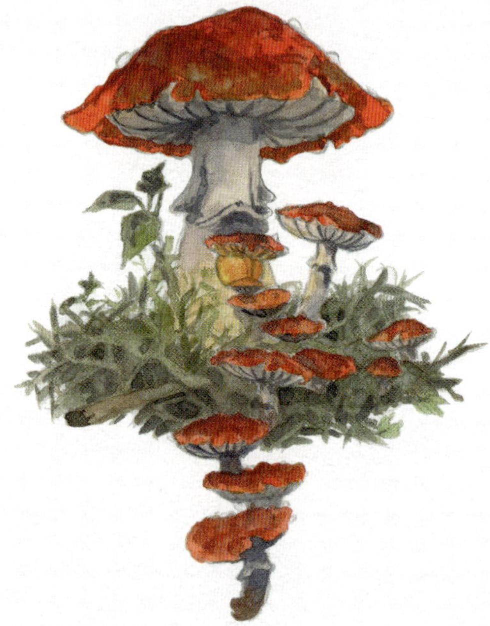

Step 7

In this step, we can begin to define the shapes we've laid out so far in this illustration. This entails deepening the shadows using *The Glazing Method* from Chapter 1 (see page 16), making the light stand out more and glow.

First, use your round brush 2 and Crimson Lake Red + Payne's Grey to paint the top of the mushroom cap, using quick brushstrokes. Apply this same color to the other mushroom caps on their shadow side (away from the glowing window).

Then clean your brush, and use Lemon Yellow to apply a layer of glow on the mushroom caps, stems, and blades of grass that are the closest to the window.

Next, use Violet + Payne's Grey to deepen the shadow on the mushroom caps.

Step 8

Mix Deep Blue + Sap Green, and deepen the shadows on the sticks, twigs, and branches using *The Glazing Method*. Then use Payne's Grey and a delicate touch to outline the gills beneath the mushroom caps. Use the same color on the small fallen log to outline its shadowy hollow.

Then use Lemon Yellow + Sap Green to paint more suggestions of leaves and grass blades catching the glowing light from the window.

Finally, apply a watery glaze of Payne's Grey onto the giant mushroom cap. This will react with the Lemon Yellow, creating a decaying green effect on the mushroom.

Step 9

We're almost done with this illustration! For the final details, use a round brush 0 and Titanium White + Payne's Grey to paint the little spots on the toadstools that are in shadow. As they come into the light, use Titanium White + Lemon Yellow, enhancing the glow even more.

Then use Violet to deepen the final touches of the shadows on the mushroom stems and cap. While the Violet is still wet, use diluted Crimson Lake Red to get a light-pink color, and apply this to the underside of the giant mushroom cap, warming that shadow just a little.

Finally, use Deep Blue + Sap Green to deepen some of the shadows beneath the sticks on the ground, applying this color mostly to the shadows *away* from the glowing window. Then use Burnt Sienna + Deep Blue to paint a small rim around the window.

Wait a few minutes for the paint to dry thoroughly. Then erase any pencil lines that are still visible.

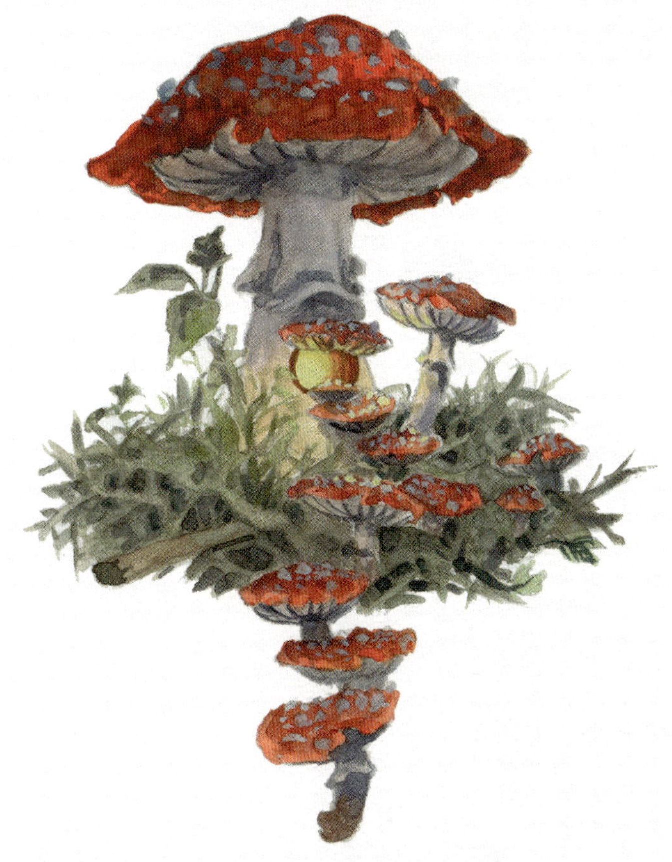

Apprentice Notes:

As a bonus, you can also adjust the glow in your painting, using Lemon Yellow and Titanium White gouache. Use the same color for highlights on the white spots on the mushroom caps. These are fine and delicate details, but they can really wrap up a piece and make it feel complete.

With that, *The Path of the Toadstool* is complete! Now our adventurers can follow the glow, hopping from one toadstool to another, until they enter the organization's secret lair and discover cursed knowledge.

A Fungivore in the Underbrush

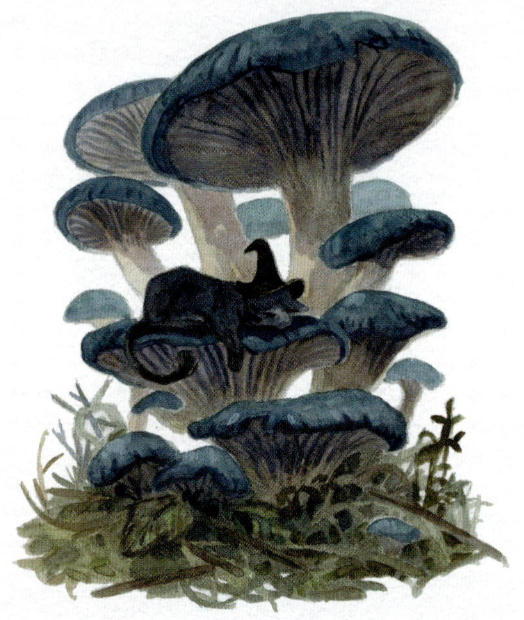

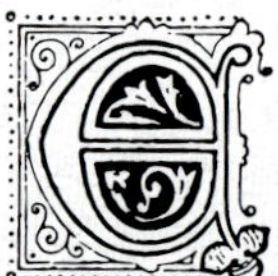 very dimension worth its salt has a mysterious, slightly terrifying–yet alluring–cat. Think of the Cheshire Cat of Alice's Wonderland. Our dimension will need to live up to this standard. Thankfully, I know just the wizard to invite for this task. And he happens to live solely on a diet of fungi.

In this tutorial, we're going to paint my good friend Kryptid the Cat Wyzard. Although parrots and cats don't necessarily get along, magical parrots and cats can sometimes tolerate each other.

Brushes

Round brush 10, 2, 0

Colors

Deep Blue

Deep Green

Payne's Grey

Yellow Ochre

Vermillion

Sap Green

Burnt Sienna

Lemon Yellow

Carbon Black

Violet

Crimson Lake Red

Titanium White

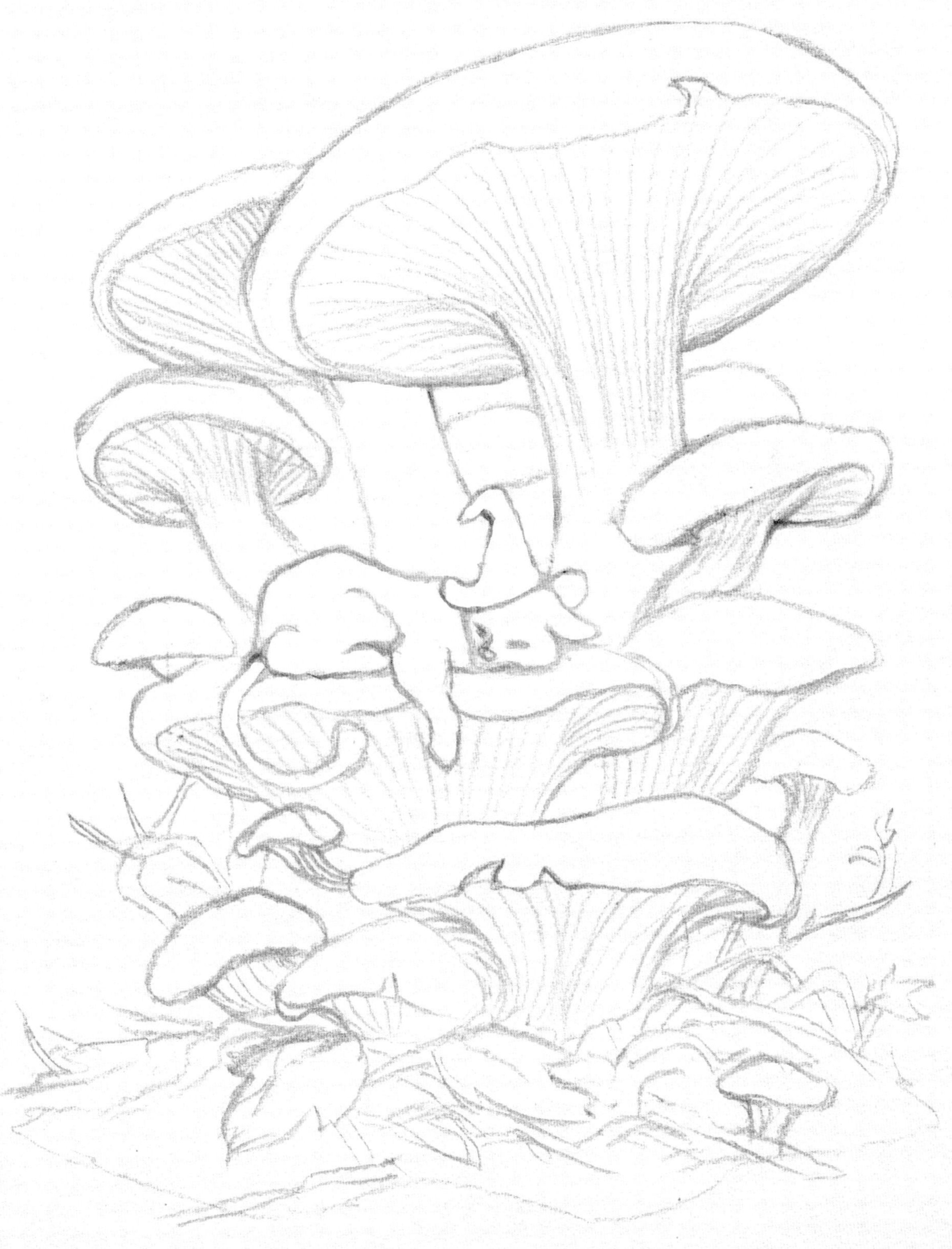

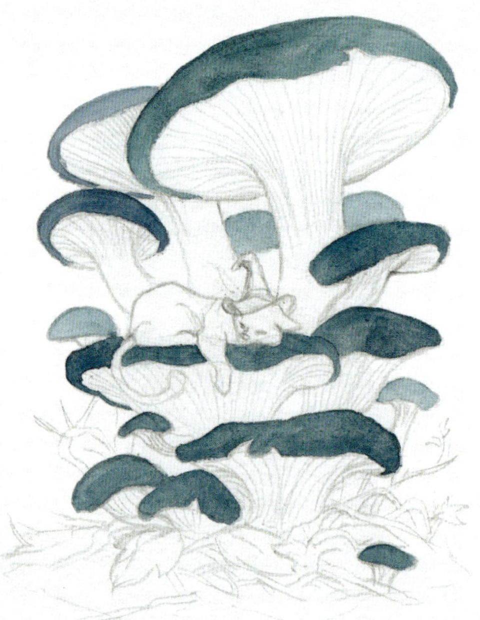 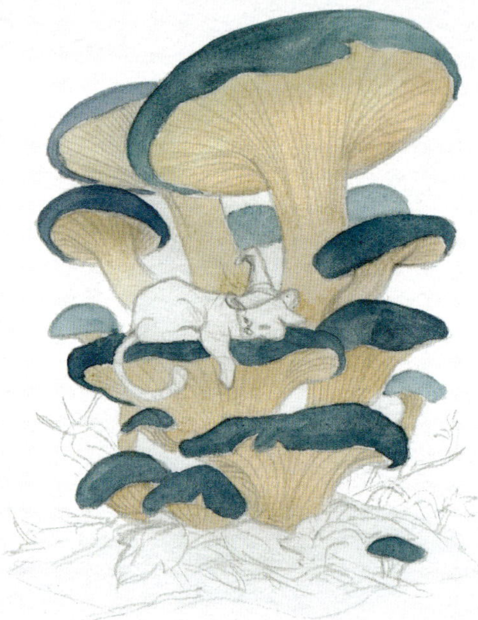

Step 1

Draw the base sketch onto watercolor paper, using my drawing as a reference. Simplify the cat into basic shapes: a triangle for the head, and a circle for the body and paws. Ensure that the mushroom it's resting on is larger than the cat.

Step 2

Using a round brush 10, begin painting the mushroom caps with a diluted mixture of Deep Blue + Deep Green + a touch of Payne's Grey. Create subtle variation in the tones of these colors by using more blue on some caps, more green on others, and more water on the caps in the background.

Step 3

Since we are still painting the base colors for this illustration, continue painting with your round brush 10 and a watery consistency of paint. Using Yellow Ochre + a touch of Vermillion + a lot of water, paint all the mushroom stems in the scene. Later we will add more variation, depth, and texture.

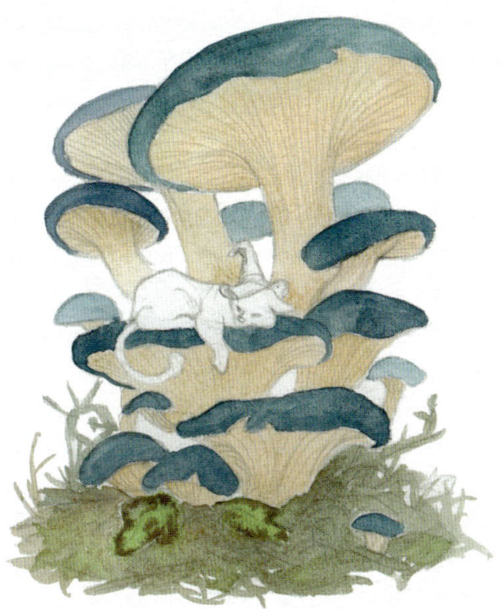

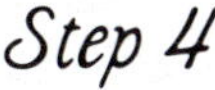

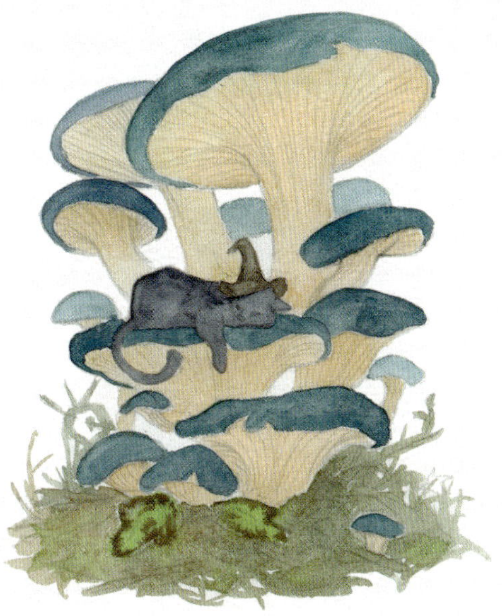

Step 4

With your round brush 10 dipped in a fair amount of water, mix Sap Green + Burnt Sienna + a touch of Payne's Grey, and paint this color on the ground area. Quickly dab spots of Deep Blue in the shadow areas of the ground beneath the mushroom caps, applying *The Wet-on-Wet Technique* from Chapter 1 (see page 16). Use quick and sudden brushstrokes to paint the silhouettes of the jumble of twigs, branches, and sticks littered across the forest floor. Be careful to avoid the large leaf shapes at this stage.

Then, while the paint is still wet, mix Sap Green + Lemon Yellow, and dab spots of this color randomly into the wet paint, suggesting more fallen leaves.

Switch to your round brush 2, and use the same mixture of Sap Green + Lemon Yellow to paint the large fallen leaves. While the green is still wet, use Burnt Sienna + Deep Blue to paint the edges, and let the colors seep into each other, creating the effect of a drying leaf.

Let this layer dry thoroughly before continuing to the next step.

Step 5

Use your round brush 2 with a delicate hand for this step. Mix Payne's Grey + Deep Blue + Carbon Black, and cover the shapes of the sleeping cat, carefully avoiding the mushroom itself.

Then mix Burnt Sienna + Deep Blue to paint the wizard hat on the cat.

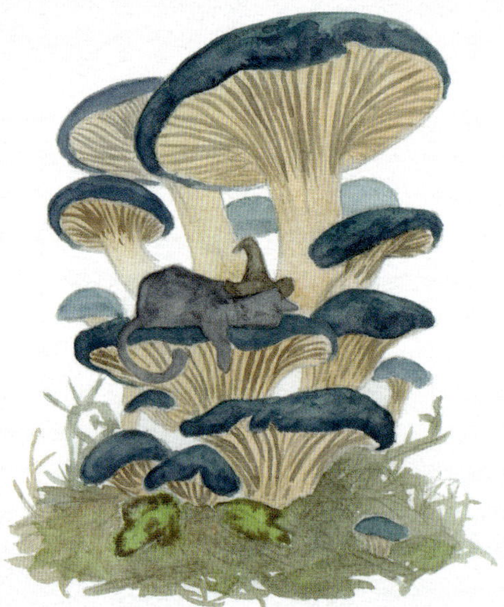 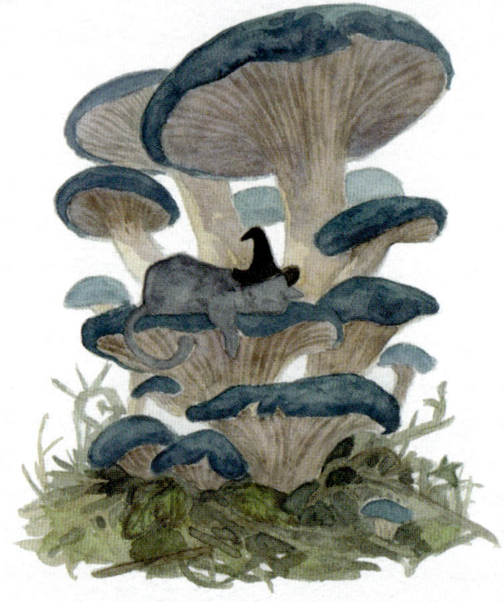

Step 6

For this step, use your round brush 2. Mix Burnt Sienna + Payne's Grey to get a grey-brown color. Paint the careful curves under each of the mushroom caps, painting the shadows of the gills.

Next, mix Deep Blue + Payne's Grey, and glaze another layer on the mushroom caps around the curve.

Step 7

Now that the base colors are established, we can begin painting shadows, emphasizing light and creating depth and interest in the illustration. Start by using your round brush 2 dipped in a fair amount of water, and apply Violet under the mushroom cap gills as a shadow color and in scattered spots on the stem, leaving some of the yellow peeking from below to create highlights.

Then use Payne's Grey + Sap Green to bring out the details of the sticks and branches on the forest floor, applying *The Inverse Painting Technique* described in Chapter 1 (see page 17). Also use Burnt Sienna to glaze over the brown in the fallen sticks, creating variation in color among the greens.

Finally, mix a thick consistency of Burnt Sienna + Payne's Grey to glaze another layer on the cat's hat, darkening the color.

Let these layers dry.

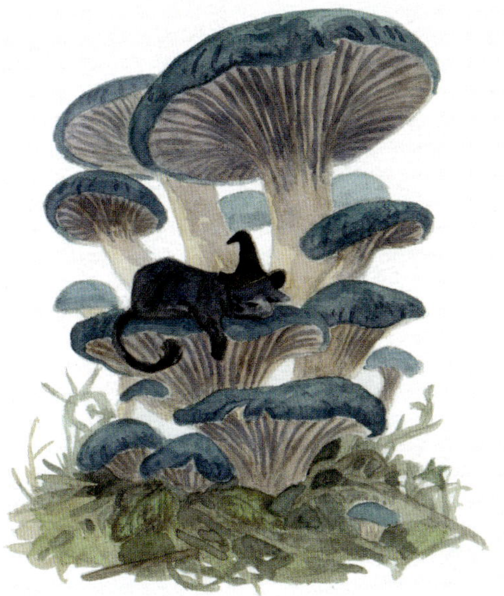 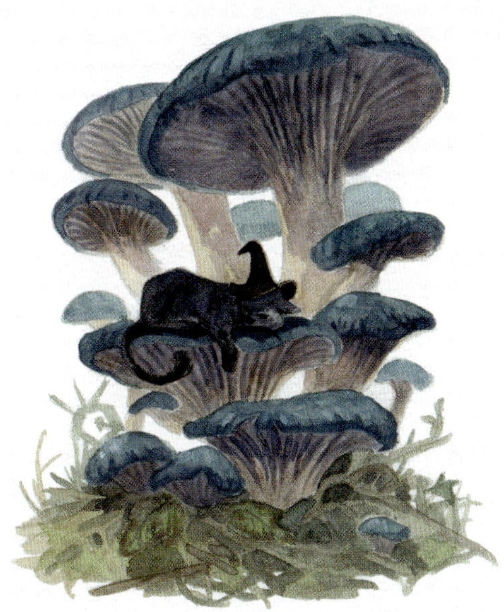

Step 8

With your round brush 2, use Payne's Grey with an equal part of water to glaze over the lines under the gills of the mushroom caps, bringing them forward again. Then mix a touch of Deep Blue into your Payne's Grey, and paint curves across the mushroom caps, creating the beginnings of texture.

Now switch to your round brush 0, and use Payne's Grey + Carbon Black to paint the form of the cat. Add shadows to the curve on the cat's tail, its round belly, and the paw falling off the mushroom. Also use Carbon Black to outline the figure, and paint a shadow on the inside of the hat.

Step 9

With your round brush 2, glaze another layer of Payne's Grey as a shadow beneath the mushroom caps and the cat. Then use Crimson Lake Red, diluted to a watery consistency, to paint the shadow on the stems of the mushrooms. This will warm the illustration just a little bit.

Now clean your brush. Then, using Titanium White watercolor, paint spots of white highlights on the mushroom caps.

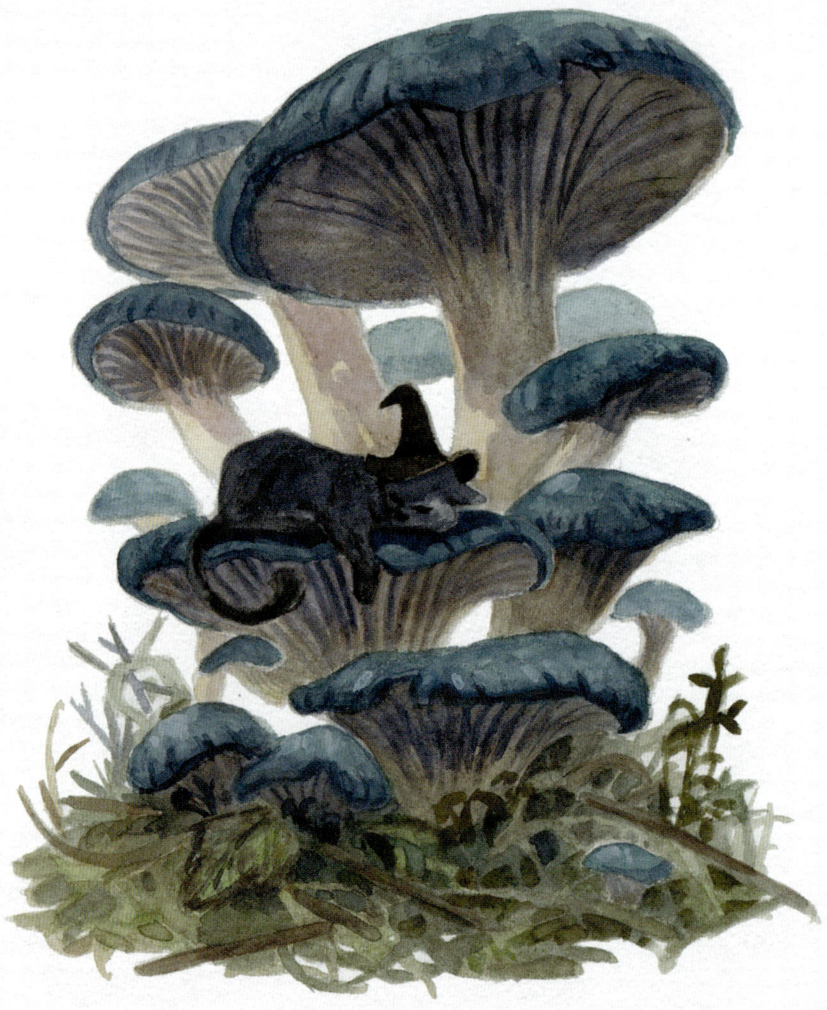

Step 10

In this final step, we're going to clean up the illustration by defining the grassy ground and the outlines of certain shapes.

First, use Sap Green + Burnt Sienna to paint more shadows of the sticks on the ground, using *The Inverse Painting Technique* from Chapter 1 (page 17). Then use Payne's Grey to paint the outlines of the mushroom caps and the gills, defining any shapes that are disappearing from the composition.

And that marks the end of this illustration! Mischievous Kryptid the Cat Wyzard, in deep sleep. When he awakes, he'll find himself surrounded by edible mushrooms— and a party of adventurers who are curious about him.

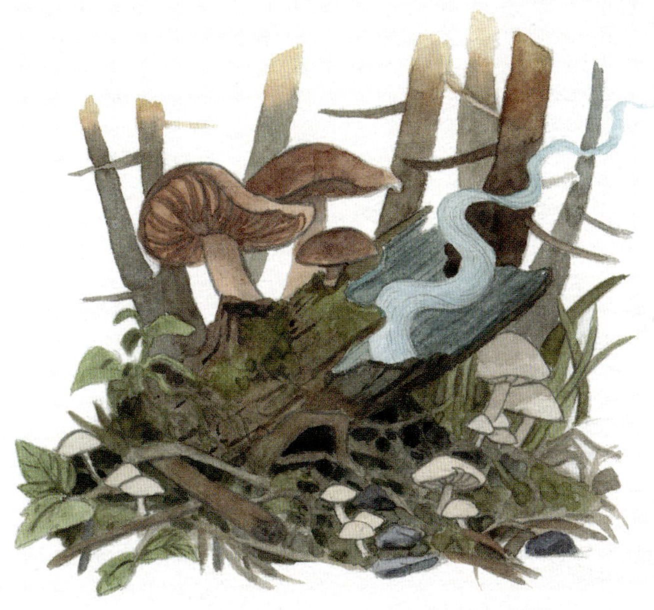

Secrets of the Spores

Fungi are a strange kingdom. They are the only ones who get their food from dead matter, helping in the process of decay. But did you know that when they absorb nutrients from dead wood, for example, they also absorb its secrets?

In this tutorial, we're going to paint the secrets these mushrooms hold in the form of blue mist, so that any adventurer might hear strange voices and follow them into a trap.

Brushes

Round brush 2

Colors

Cerulean Blue

Titanium White

Payne's Grey

Burnt Sienna

Sap Green

Crimson Lake Red

Deep Blue

Lemon Yellow

Yellow Ochre

Ultramarine Blue

Vermillion

Gouache

Titanium White

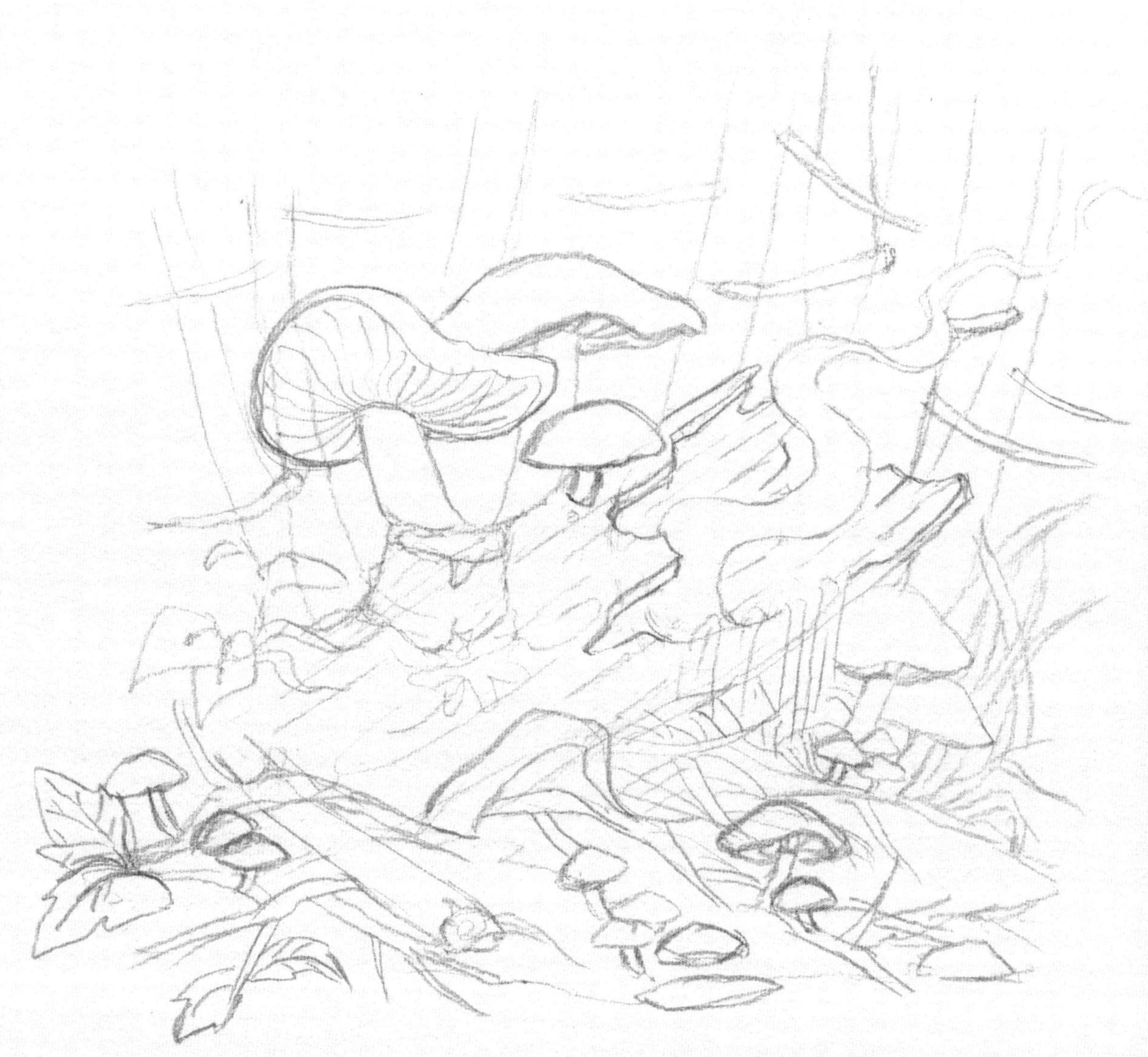

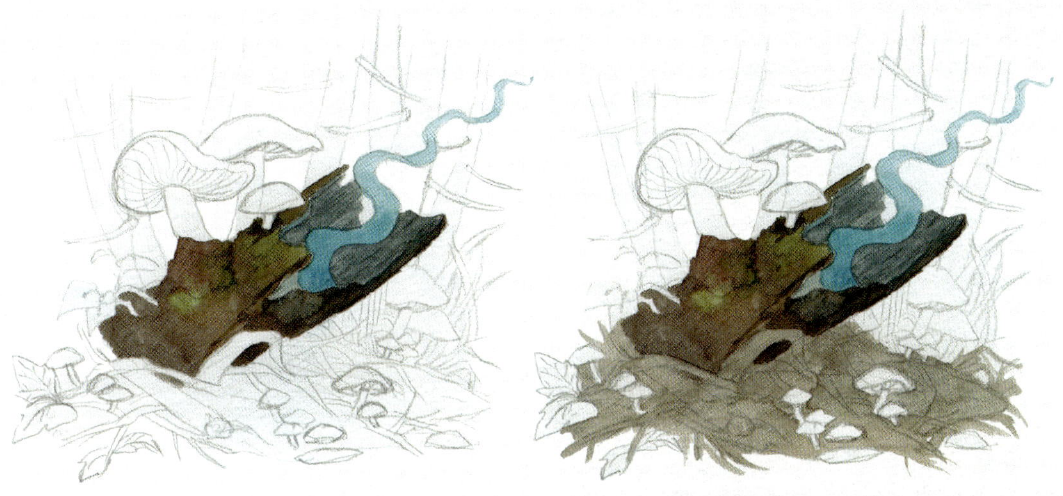

Step 1

Draw the base sketch, using my drawing as a reference. Feel free to change the design according to your imagination. The key shapes to keep in the drawing are the log and the curling wisps of smoke rising out of it. All the mushrooms, twigs, and leaf details can be changed according to how you prefer.

Step 2

You will be using your round brush 2 to begin laying the base colors of the illustration. First, use Cerulean Blue + Titanium White with an equal part of water to paint the curling smoke.

Then mix Cerulean Blue + Payne's Grey + a touch of Burnt Sienna to paint the inside of the log, which will receive some of the reflected blue light from the smoke.

Next, work quickly on a wet layer to paint the outside of the log, using *The Wet-on-Wet Technique* described in Chapter 1 (see page 16). Use Burnt Sienna + Payne's Grey to start painting the wood. While the paint is wet, dab spots of Sap Green + a touch of Crimson Lake Red into the paint for suggestions of moss. For the bottom part of the log, create a dark-brown color by mixing Burnt Sienna + Payne's Grey + a touch of Deep Blue.

Let this layer dry before moving to the next step.

Step 3

Continue painting with your round brush 2. Work with a fair amount of water to paint the twig-littered floor. Mix Burnt Sienna + Deep Blue + Sap Green for a moody autumn-green color, and apply this as a base layer for the grassy ground. Be careful to avoid the mushrooms, stones, and leaves.

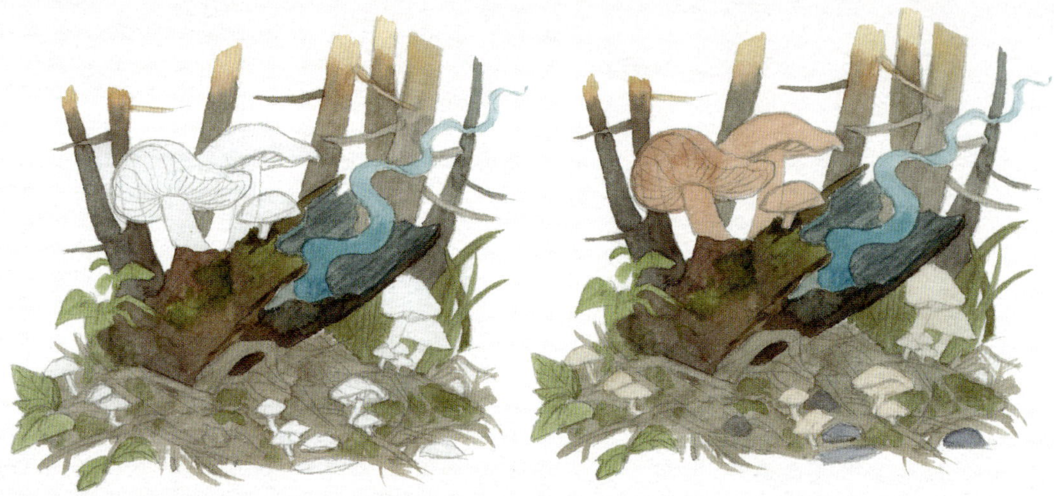

Step 4

Use Sap Green + Lemon Yellow + a touch of Crimson Lake Red to desaturate the green, and paint spots of leaves on the ground, as well as the moss and vines wrapping the log.

Paint the grass in the background with Sap Green + Crimson Lake Red. Don't worry about creating variation and shadows for now; we will do that in later steps after the base colors are established.

Next, using a fairly wet round brush 2, paint the trees in the background. Imagine the glow of a warm sunrise just peeking over the horizon. The light would first touch the upper parts of the trees. So, mimicking that light, use *The Bead Method* from Chapter 1 (page 15) to blend the following colors: Yellow Ochre, at the top of the tree; then Burnt Sienna; and then, for the bottom, blend the color into Burnt Sienna + Ultramarine Blue.

Step 5

Let's fill in the base colors for the rest of the illustration. Start with mixing a dull orange-brown color with Burnt Sienna + Vermillion + Yellow Ochre, diluted with a fair amount of water. Apply this color to the big mushrooms on the log.

Next, mix a pale yellow with Yellow Ochre + a touch of Payne's Grey diluted with a lot of water, and paint the rest of the smaller mushrooms scattered on the ground.

Use Payne's Grey for the small pebbles among the mushrooms.

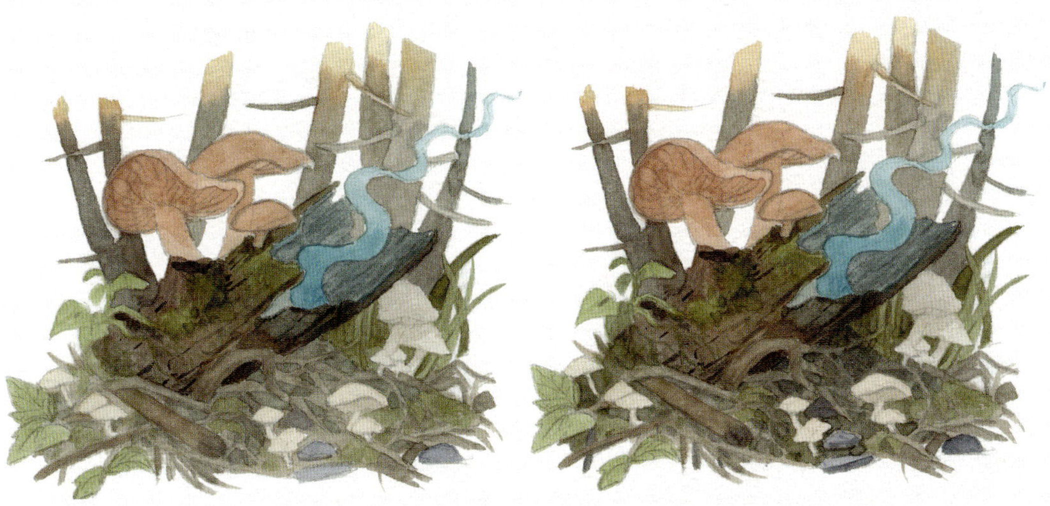

Step 6

Now we can begin the fun part: defining the shadows, light, and form of the base we've established in the previous steps.

Use your round brush 2 to mix Payne's Grey + Sap Green, and paint the shadows between the sticks and branches on the floor. Imagine where a stick would be, and paint the shadow around it. (See *The Inverse Painting Technique* from Chapter 1 on page 17.)

Then apply another layer of Burnt Sienna to the larger branches that are above the thicket. Mix Burnt Sienna + Ultramarine Blue, and paint the lines across the log in quick strokes, as well as the inside of the second stump. Also glaze another layer of the same brown-orange color you used on the big mushrooms to paint the shadow on its gills.

Finally, mix Sap Green + Crimson Lake Red, and paint the strands of grass that are behind the others. Use the same color to dab spots of moss on the log.

Step 7

Apply a watery wash of Payne's Grey over the sticks directly below the log where it would cast a shadow. Using a simple brush-stroke to indicate some form, use the same color to paint the shadow of the little pebbles.

Then mix Sap Green + Payne's Grey, and use *The Inverse Painting Technique* from Chapter 1 (see page 17) to deepen the shadows of the sticks and branches, especially around the mushrooms so they stand out among the dark colors. Remember that with watercolor we work from light to dark, so to bring forward a leaf or a stick, you have to darken the color around it.

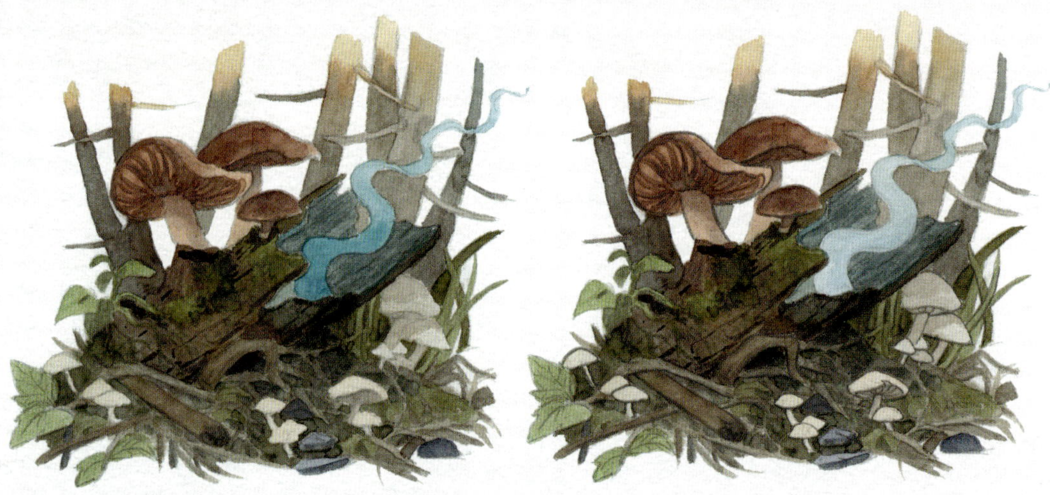

Step 8

In this step, we're going to define the larger mushrooms more. When a lot of objects are bundled together, they can get lost and overlap each other easily. The key to make each object stand out is to overlap light over dark, and dark over light where the edges of two mushrooms meet.

Mix Burnt Sienna + Payne's Grey, and paint over the outline of the gills under the cap of the front mushroom. This mushroom's cap will be light, and the one directly behind it will be dark. Add more Payne's Grey to the mixture to create a darker brown color.

Use pure Payne's Grey diluted with a fair amount of water for an angular shadow across the stem of the mushroom furthest behind. The stem of this mushroom will be light, and the cap of the mushroom directly in front of it will be dark.

Use the same technique for the mushrooms on the floor. Mix Payne's Grey + Yellow Ochre diluted with a lot of water, and paint the shadows on those caps.

Step 9

Watercolor is a forgiving medium, which means we can change the color of something by painting over it with gouache. Now that the illustration is almost complete, we can see that the color of the smoke is not standing out as much as it should. So for this step, use Titanium White gouache and your round brush 2, and paint over the color of the smoke. The gouache will react with the blue underneath, making a light, eerie blue.

While that's drying, use a sharp pencil and outline the little white mushrooms on the forest floor with clean lines, just to make them stand out from the other colors. Also outline the giant mushrooms on the log, and some of the sticks that are on top of the pile.

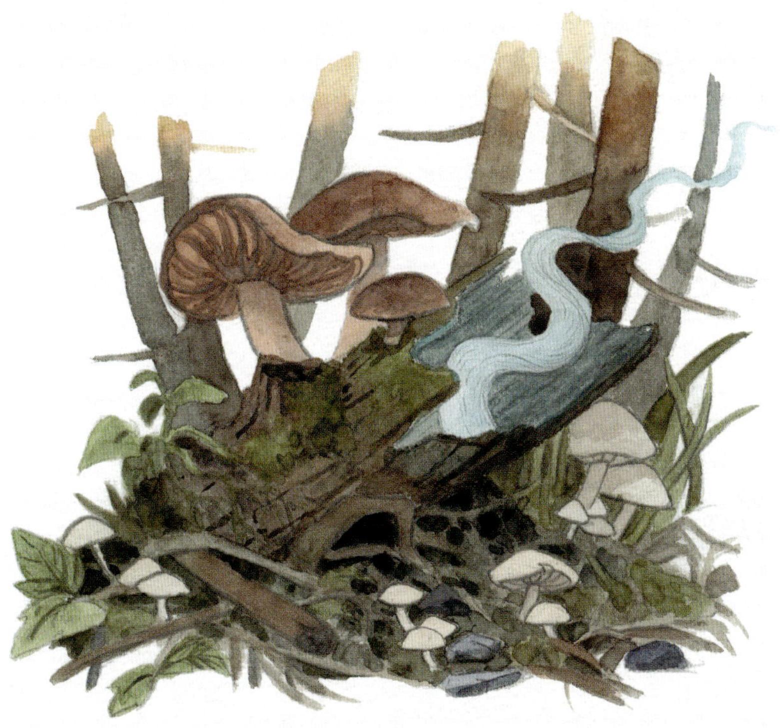

Step 10

For the final details, use your round brush 2. Paint another layer of Burnt Sienna + Ultramarine Blue plus an equal part of water over the tree directly behind the smoke. This layer will be dark, enhancing the shape of the smoke. Use the same color to darken the shadows on the log.

Then use Payne's Grey to glaze the shadows on the ground directly beneath the log. Use Sap Green + Crimson Lake Red + a touch of Ultramarine Blue to darken the green leaves and spots of moss.

Finally, use a sharp pencil to outline the curves on the smoke. Erase any unwanted pencil lines that are still visible once the paint is thoroughly dry.

With that, this illustration is done! The blue mist will carry whispers of secrets into the wild unknown.

Apprentice Notes:

We've explored the kingdoms of plantae and their darker cousins, fungi. What's next? Well, dear wizard, how familiar are you with the formation of the very Earth?

Chapter Four
A Handful of Rocks

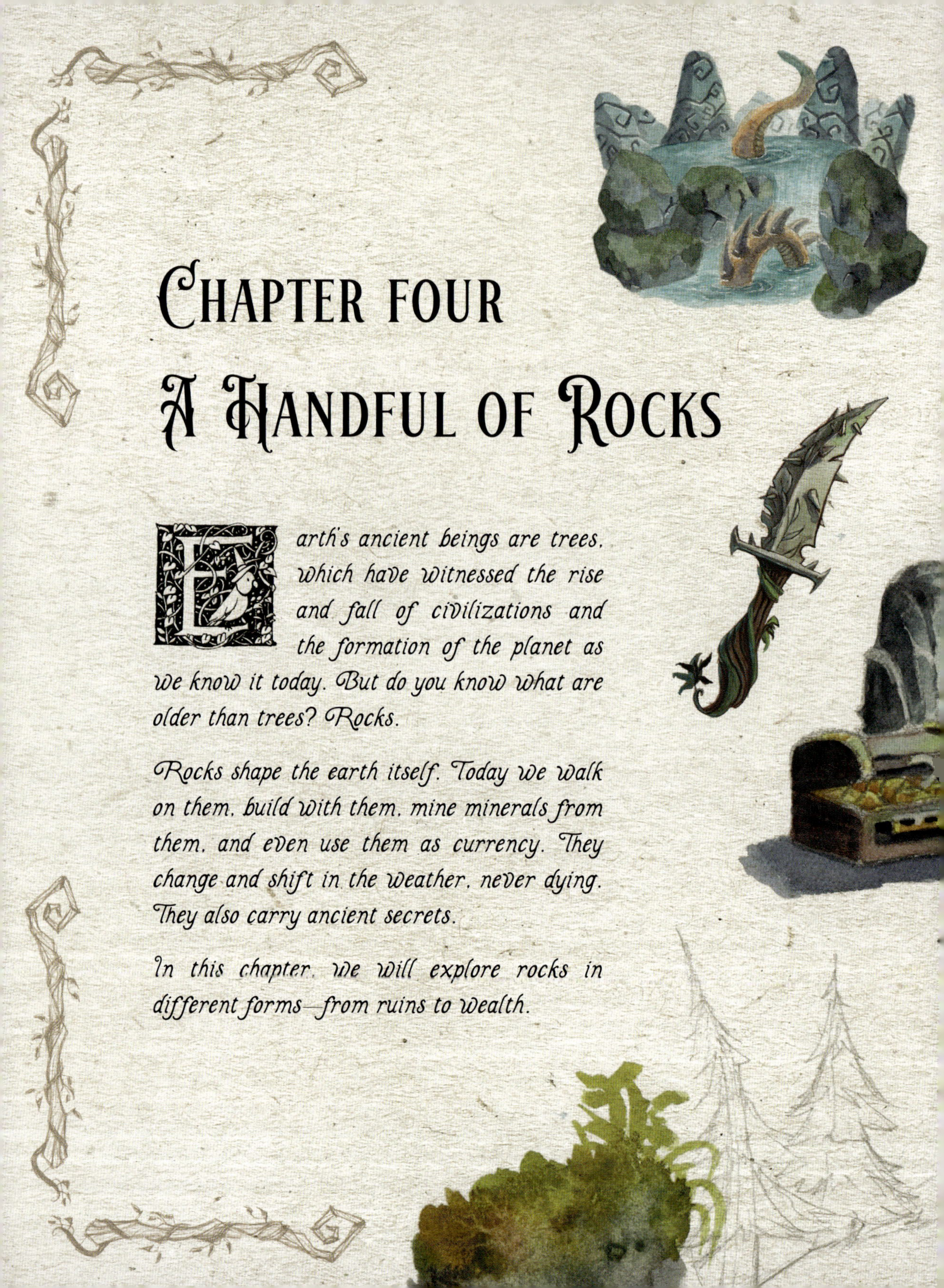

Earth's ancient beings are trees, which have witnessed the rise and fall of civilizations and the formation of the planet as we know it today. But do you know what are older than trees? Rocks.

Rocks shape the earth itself. Today we walk on them, build with them, mine minerals from them, and even use them as currency. They change and shift in the weather, never dying. They also carry ancient secrets.

In this chapter, we will explore rocks in different forms—from ruins to wealth.

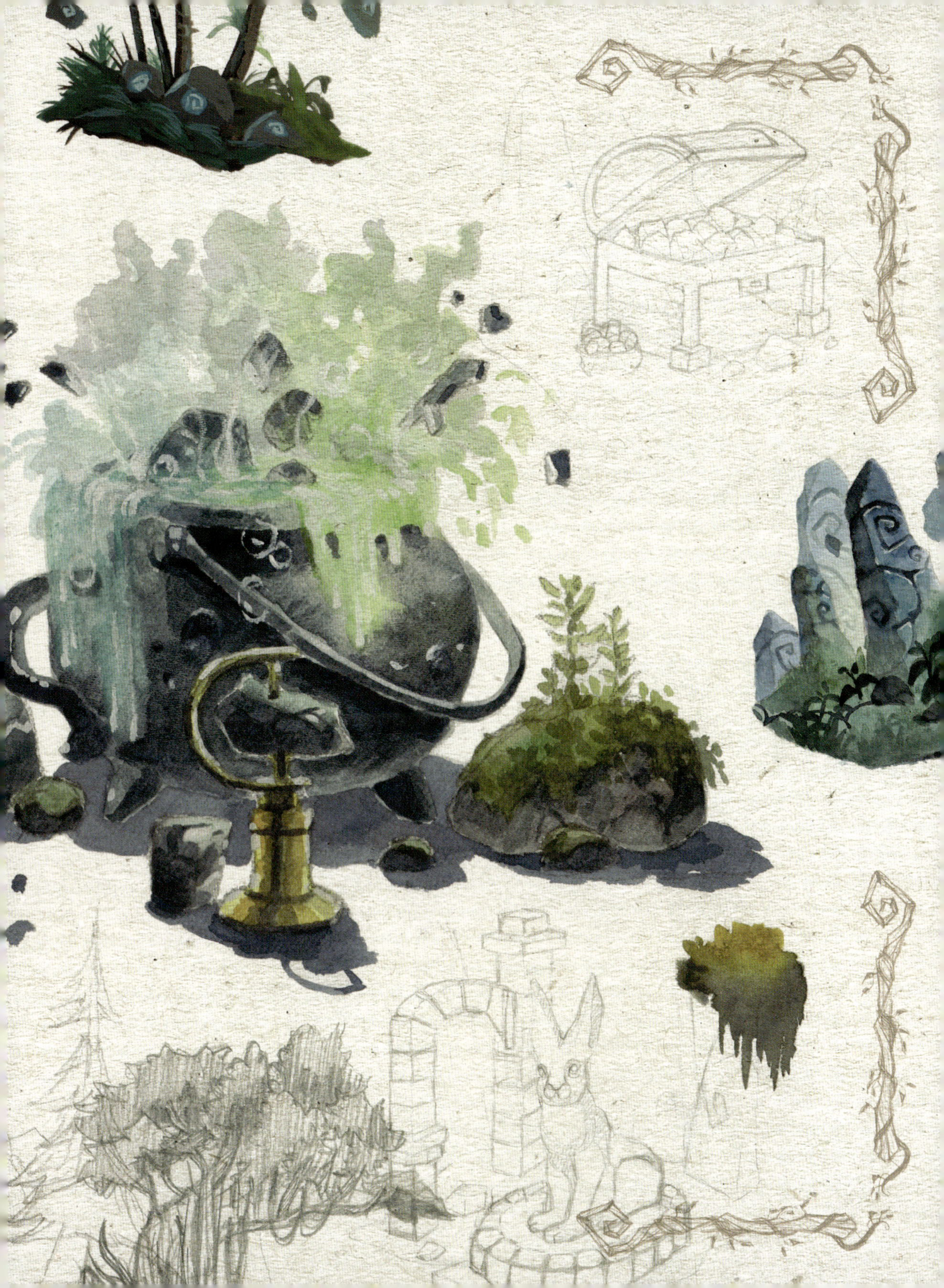

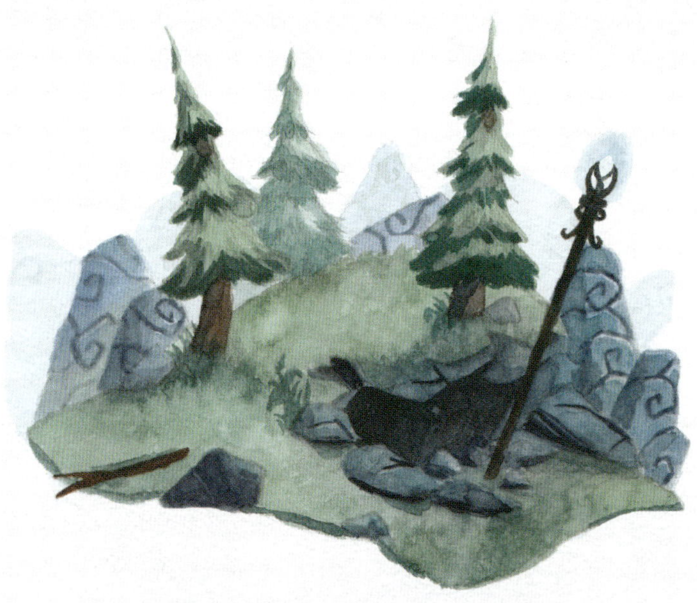

The Caves of Cadmus the Uncanny

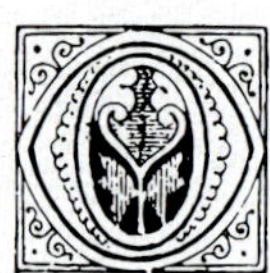ld Cadmus was an uncanny guy. There's nothing much else to say about him. Except he did love a good rock, and one of his many sorcerer quirks was that he rolled around a lot, where other people would simply walk. He also dedicated his life to studying rocks—that's how much he loved them. What happened to him, you ask? Well, he disappeared. Some say he died, a large boulder having smashed him.

Other rumors say he was driven mad. You see, he had this powerful staff with a white gemstone on it, and he often talked to the thing . . .

In this tutorial, we're going to paint the last place Cadmus the Uncanny is rumored to have been spotted: an abode hidden deep within a cave. This cave may appear small on the outside, but the inside contains a vast cavern of corridors.

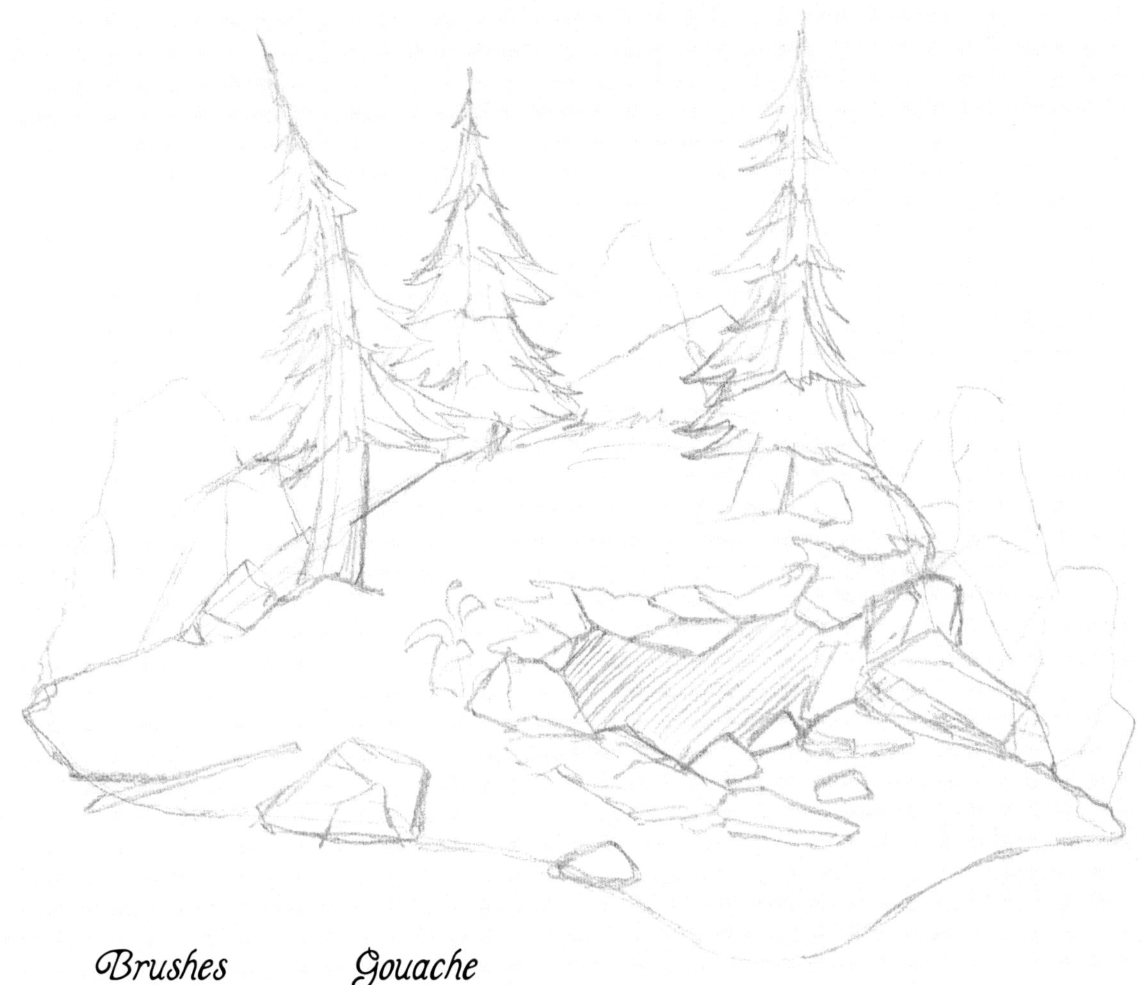

Brushes

Round brush 10, 2, 0

Colors

Deep Blue

Deep Green

Gamboge

Crimson Lake Red

Payne's Grey

Burnt Sienna

Ultramarine Blue

Violet

Gouache

Titanium White

Step 1

Draw the sketch onto your watercolor paper with an HB pencil, using my drawing as a reference. As with all the tutorials, feel free to alter the design of this environment according to your imagination; perhaps you'd like to add more rocks or trees to the scene. The key shapes to transfer are the opening of the cave and the surrounding boulders.

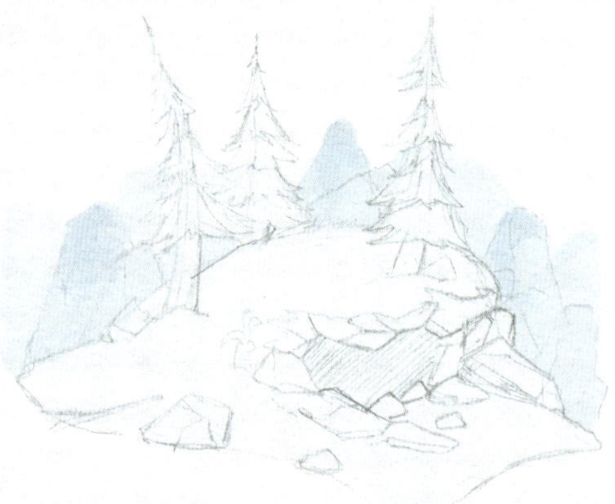

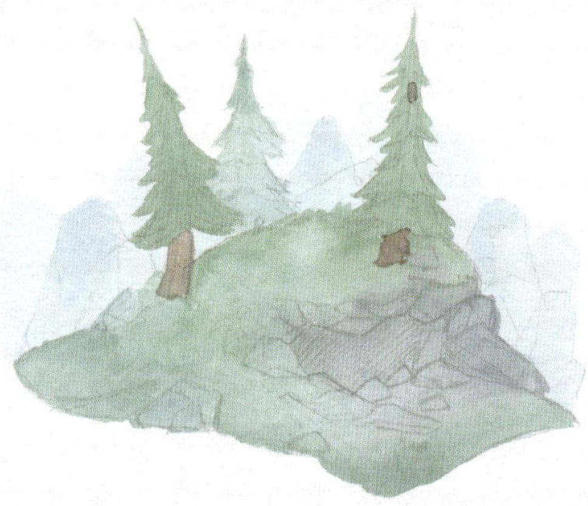

Step 2

Use your round brush 10 dipped in a fair amount of water. Start painting the background rock structures with diluted Deep Blue, working transparently so these colors disappear into the distance. While the paint is still wet, apply *The Wet-on-Wet Technique* described in Chapter 1 (see page 16) to dab more Deep Blue at the top of the rocks, letting it granulate in the water. Add more of these structures outside the pencil lines, using roughly the same shape of the rocks and much more water.

Step 3

For this step, work quickly on a wet layer with a wet brush. Start by mixing Deep Green + Gamboge with a touch of Crimson Lake Red. Paint the tree leaves with this color, as well as the top of the ground. Then, while the paint is still wet, mix a touch of Deep Blue into the green mixture, and apply that to the left side of the grassy ground. For the cave itself and the surrounding rocks, wipe your brush lightly, and then use a watery Payne's Grey. Let the colors transition into each other naturally with the water.

Paint the background tree lightly using Deep Green + Crimson Lake Red at the top. Clean your brush, and create a fade into Deep Blue for the bottom of the tree.

For the tree trunks, apply Burnt Sienna + Ultramarine Blue.

Let this layer dry thoroughly.

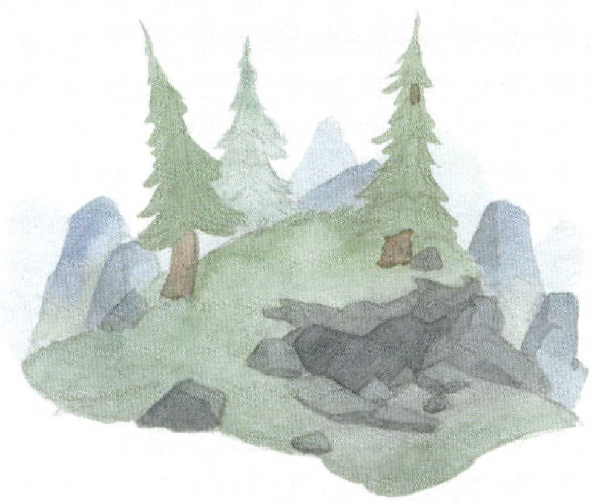 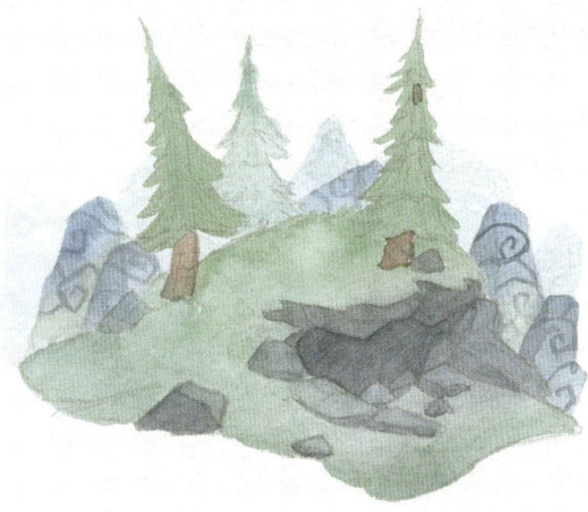

Step 4

Switch to your round brush 2. Mix Deep Blue + a touch of Violet with a fair amount of water, and glaze over the background rocks to bring them a little bit more to the forefront. (See *The Glazing Method* from Chapter 1, page 16.) Create a gradient into Gamboge by cleaning your brush, adding some water onto the page, and dabbing some spots of the yellow color into the water.

Then use Payne's Grey to accentuate the shadows on the right side of the rocks. Glaze another layer of Payne's Grey on the cave itself and the shadow parts of the surrounding rocks.

Step 5

Switch to your round brush 0 for this step. Mix Payne's Grey + Deep Blue, and start painting the spiral rune patterns on the rocks in the background. Add more water to the mixture to paint over the light areas where the rock fades away.

For the rocks in the furthermost background, use Deep Blue + a touch of Gamboge for a green-grey color, and use a lot of water to work transparently.

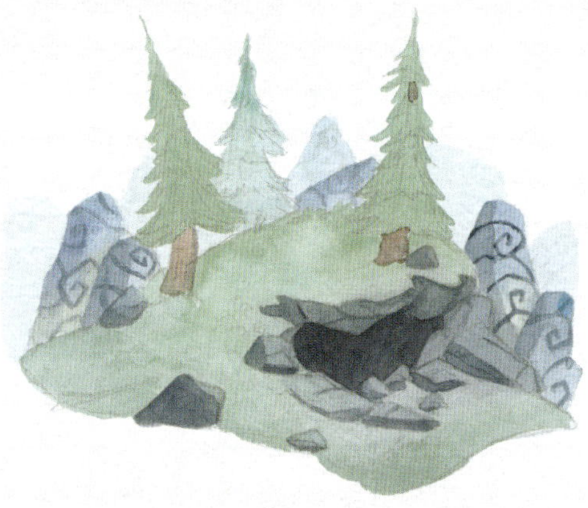 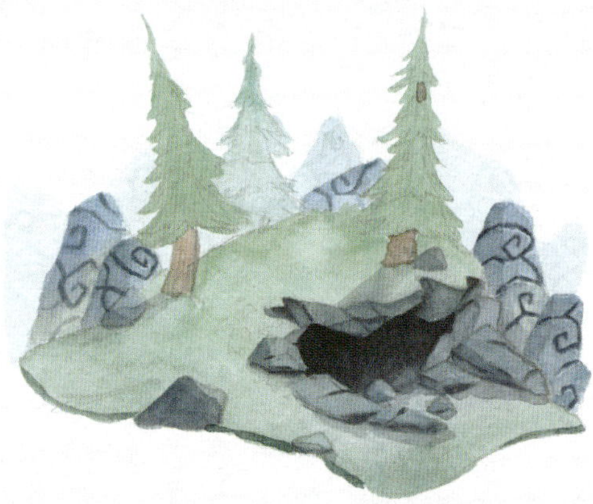

Step 6

Switch back to your round brush 2. Glaze another layer of Payne's Grey over the shadow side of the rocks in the background and the shadows on the rocks around the cave. Add a little detail on the cave rocks—hints of lines and cracks.

Then create a dark color by mixing Crimson Lake Red + Ultramarine Blue + Burnt Sienna, and paint the opening of the cave. While that's drying, use Payne's Grey to deepen the rune engravings using *The Glazing Method* (page 16).

Step 7

Use your round brush 2 dipped in a fair amount of water for this step. Paint the background rocks with diluted Deep Blue, leaving blank spaces on the "lip" of the engravings. This creates more form and depth on the rocks.

While that's drying, paint another layer of Crimson Lake Red + Ultramarine Blue + Burnt Sienna for the inside of the cave. Use the same color to paint quick strokes of lines on the rocks.

Then clean your brush, and paint shadows on the grass beneath the rocks using Deep Green + Deep Blue + a touch of Payne's Grey. Apply this shadow color to the grass beneath the trees as well, and to the lining on the bottom of the curving ground.

Finally, use your round brush 0 again, and glaze another layer of Payne's Grey on the engravings to deepen their color.

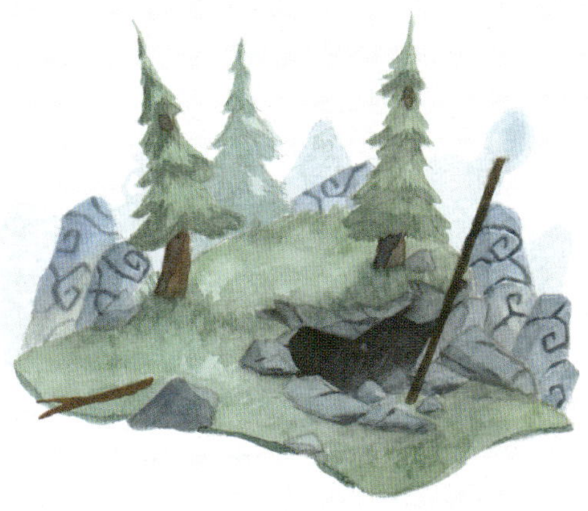 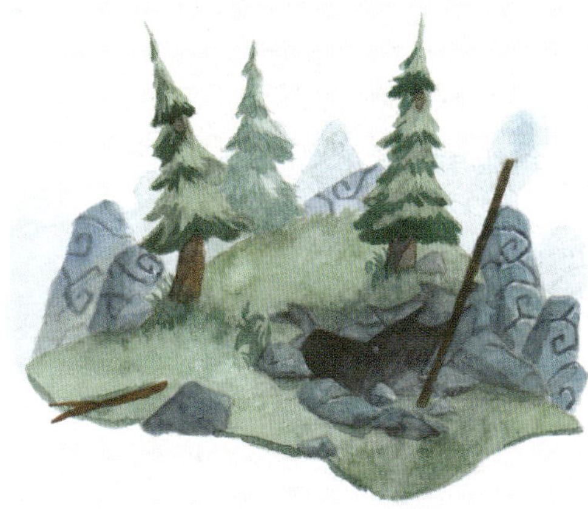

Step 8

Continue painting with your round brush 2 for this step. Let's define the greenery a bit more. Use Deep Green + Gamboge + a touch of Crimson Lake Red, and begin painting the grass ground in short, quick movements, letting the paint dry in some areas to create spots and granulations. This technique quickly creates a variety of shades in an area so that the illustration doesn't look too uniform.

For the greenery on the trees, use Deep Green + a touch of Crimson Lake Red to glaze the areas where the leaves cast a shadow on each other. For the tree in the background, use more water in the mixture + a touch of Deep Blue.

Then mix Burnt Sienna + a touch of Ultramarine Blue, and paint over the bark of the trees. When the Burnt Sienna is semi-dry, paint an angular shadow with Payne's Grey.

Now switch to your round brush 0. Use the same dark-brown color (Burnt Sienna + Ultramarine Blue + Payne's Grey) with

very little water. Paint the fallen twig on the ground, and another long stick in front of the cave. This is the staff of Cadmus the Uncanny. Use Deep Blue to create a circular gradient at the top of the staff handle.

Step 9

Use your round brush 2 for this step. We're nearing the completion of this illustration—there are just a few more brushstrokes to add. First, create a dark-green color by mixing Deep Green + a touch of Crimson Lake Red, and darken the shadow areas of the trees. For the background tree, add more water and Deep Blue.

Use the same color to paint silhouettes of leaves and grass blades on the grass.

To define the rocks in the background more, use Deep Blue and repeat the technique, leaving the space on the "lip" of the engravings unpainted. Use some of this Deep Blue to glaze over the other rocks around the cave.

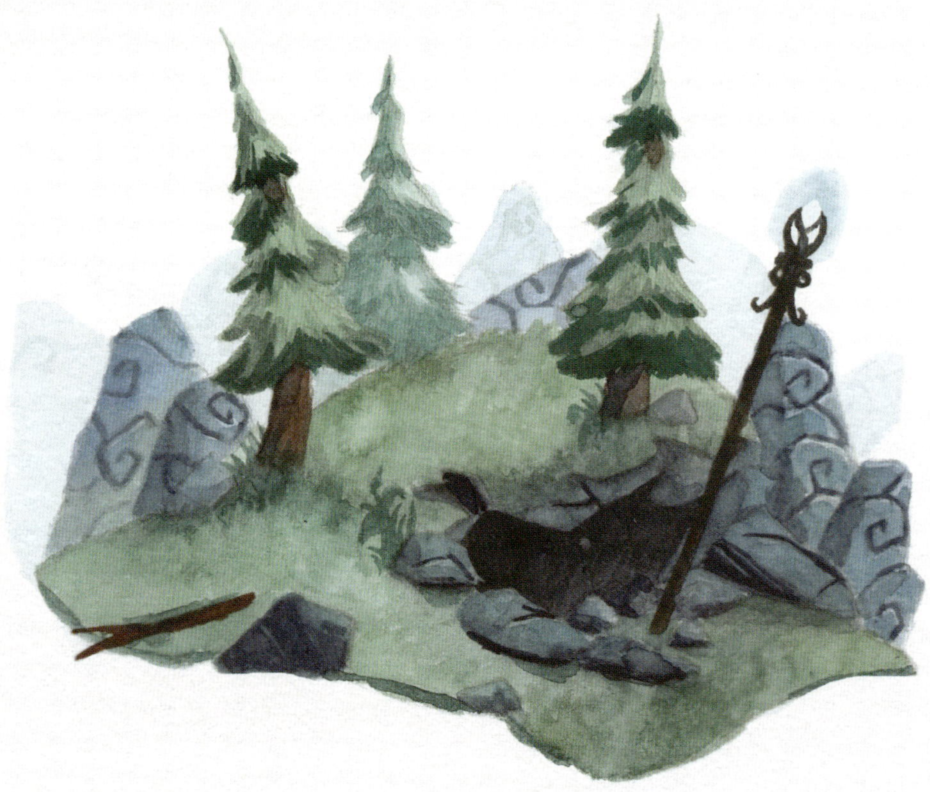

Step 10

Let's finish off our illustration with a few more lines. First, use Titanium White gouache to paint an oval-shaped gemstone at the stop of the staff.

While that's drying, use a round brush 0 to darken the outlines on the rocks, defining it a bit more using *The Glazing Method* (page 16).

Once the gemstone is dry, use the round brush 0 and the dark-brown color you created for the staff in Step 8 (Burnt Sienna + Ultramarine Blue + Payne's Grey) to paint the wood wrapping around the gemstone. Paint swirling patterns on the handle— Cadmus really liked those.

And with that, the cave is complete! Our adventurers can shelter from a storm here, set up a campfire, and quench their curiosity for wizardry. By adding this cave to our dimension, I hope some adventurer will eventually find dear lost Cadmus.

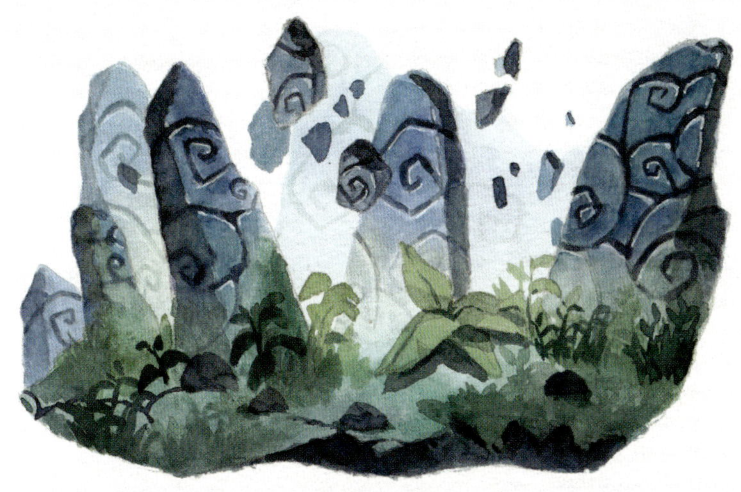

Rune Magic and Rock Rituals

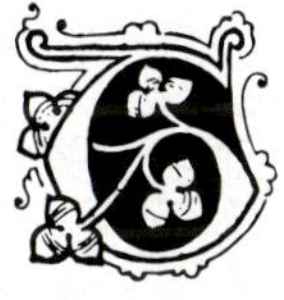

here's one inherent trait that wizards and goblins share: We both love a good rock. Throughout the ages, wizards have engraved secret messages encrypted in complex ciphers, runes, and sacred geometric symbols on stone. These engravings have powerful magic imbued in them, as timeless as the stone itself.

In this tutorial, we're going to paint a circle of stones with rune markings, locked in ritual.

Brushes

Round brush 10, 2, 0

Colors

Deep Blue

Violet

Gamboge

Crimson Lake Red

Deep Green

Payne's Grey

Sap Green

Gouache

Titanium White

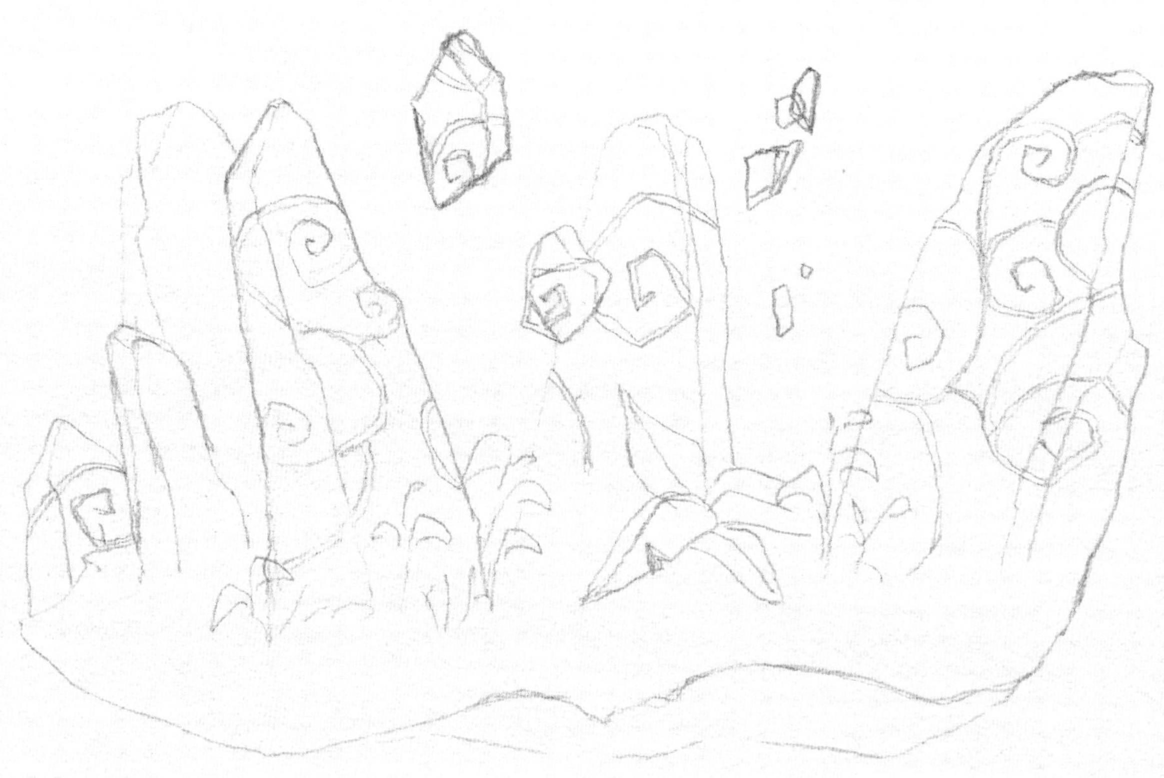

Step 1

Use the illustration to draw or trace the sketch onto your watercolor paper. Rocks are organic shapes; feel free to add more of them floating about the scene. The key shapes to keep are the strong, slanted boulders sticking up from the ground, surrounded by smaller broken pieces of rock.

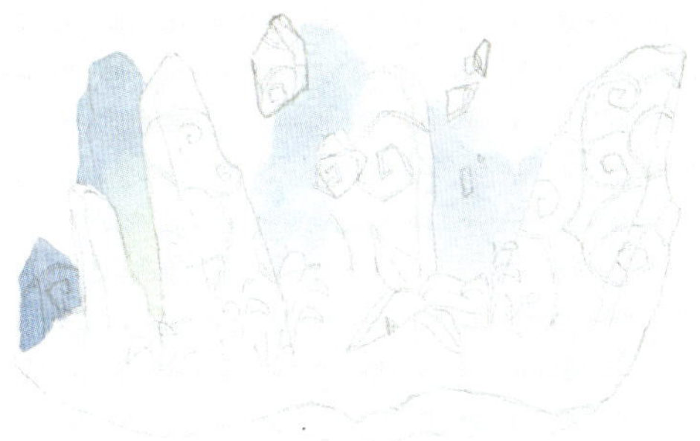 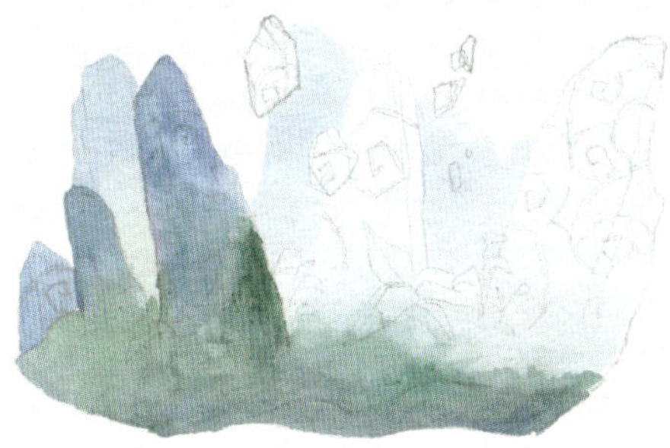

Step 2

Start with your round brush 10, and work quickly on a wet layer. Use Deep Blue mixed with a lot of water, and start painting the silhouette of rocks in the distance, making similar shapes as the ones sketched. While the paint is wet, dab spots of diluted Violet, applying *The Wet-on-Wet Technique* described in Chapter 1 (see page 16). As you paint further down, create a gradient with water, and fade the color into the page.

For rocks that grow closer, create a gradient from Deep Blue and then diluted Gamboge toward the bottom.

Let this layer dry thoroughly.

Step 3

Continue painting with your round brush 10 and a wet layer for this step. Raise your sketchbook or paper at a slight angle as described in *The Bead Method* from Chapter 1 (see page 15), and start by wetting the paper where the rocks on the left side are sketched. Then, while the page is wet, dab wet paint into it: first Deep Blue, then Violet, then Crimson Red Lake. Let the paint create textures and blend naturally.

Then, as you paint toward the bottom of the rock where the ground is, introduce spots of Deep Green + Crimson Lake Red onto the wet page. Working quickly while the page is wet, paint the rest of the ground with Payne's Grey + Deep Blue to give the illusion of more rocks in between the moss.

Use water to fade the colors toward the right, so there's a smooth transition to those rocks when we paint them in the next step.

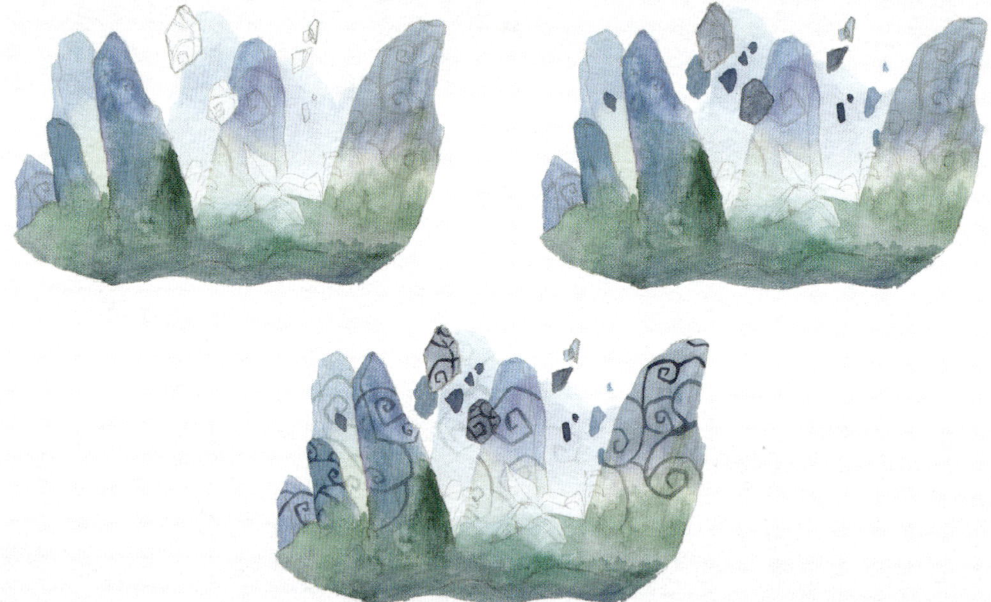

Step 4

Continue working on a wet layer. Dip your round brush 10 in a fair amount of water, and use Payne's Grey to start creating a gradient on the rocks. While the page is still wet, dab spots of Violet and Deep Blue over the Payne's Grey.

As you paint toward the bottom of the rocks, use water to fade the grey, and dab Gamboge. Then, clean your brush, and use more water to lighten and spread the color further downward, creating a smooth fade.

Now, while those colors are still wet, dab spots of Deep Green + Crimson Lake Red, connecting the colors with the fade from the previous step.

Step 5

Switch to your round brush 2 for this step. Use Payne's Grey + Deep Blue diluted with a fair amount of water to cover the small floating rocks. Paint more of these hovering rocks by marking the paper with the paint in abstract shapes.

Step 6

Now that our moody, misty scene is established, we can move on to defining the magic of the runes. Switch to your round brush 0 for this step. Use Payne's Grey + Deep Blue with a little bit of water, and paint over the swirling runes on the rock. Add more water to your mixture to paint the engravings toward the bottom more transparently.

For the rocks in the distance, use a lot of water + a touch of Gamboge with your Payne's Grey + Deep Blue mixture.

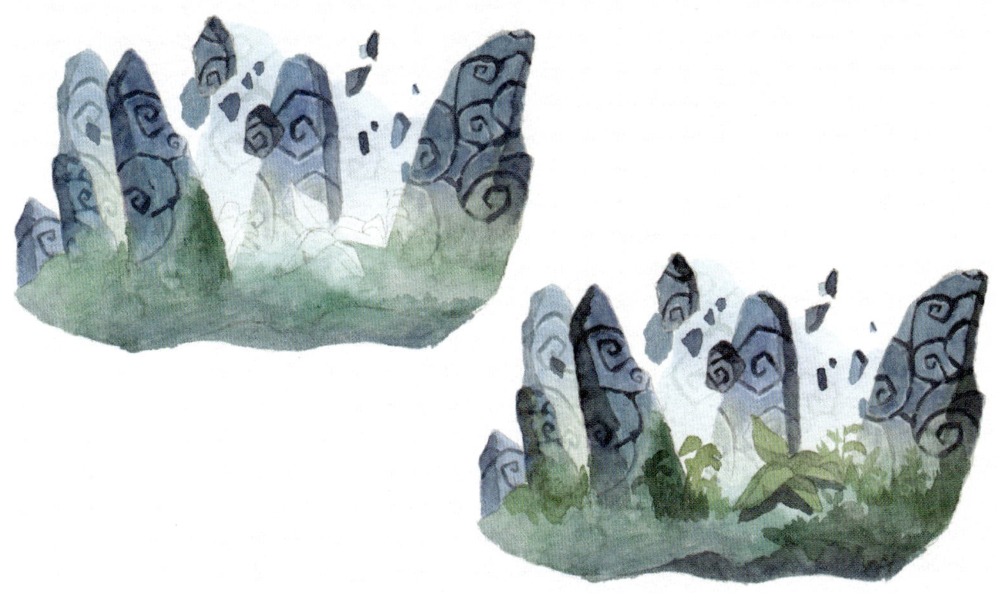

Step 7

Switch to your round brush 2. Mix Payne's Grey + Deep Blue with an equal amount of water, and use *The Glazing Method* (page 16) to paint the shadows on the rocks to give them form. Let your brushstrokes be loose but jagged, stopping in some places to let the paint dry, and then continuing. This creates more variation, texture, and interest in a watercolor painting.

Then use a thick mixture of Payne's Grey to darken the swirling rune lines. Be careful not to fill the entire lines; we don't want the illustration to look too uniform. Paint darker lines on the upper parts of the engravings, giving them a 3D appearance.

Next, wet your round brush 2, and use diluted Deep Blue to paint even more form on the rocks. Keeping in mind the light source striking from above, paint over the light areas of the rock. Leave a thin unpainted line where the engravings create a "lip" on the rock, letting the white of the paper peek through. This enhances the 3D appearance on the rocks even more.

Step 8

Let's bring in the greenery in this step. Use your round brush 2. Mix Sap Green + a touch of Crimson Lake Red to create a low-saturated green. Use an equal part of water, and start painting the grass blades and leaf shapes on the ground. Glaze some spots of this color to the rocks.

While that's drying, mix Deep Green + Payne's Grey, and apply this color to deepen the shadow side of the rocks and beneath the big leaves. Also apply this color to the bottom of the illustration, the rocky ground beneath the moss where some falls over the edge. Mix more water into this color, and apply it to the shadow on the large leaves.

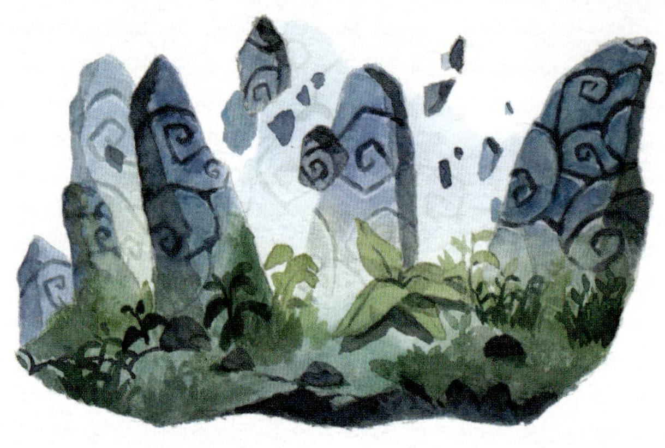

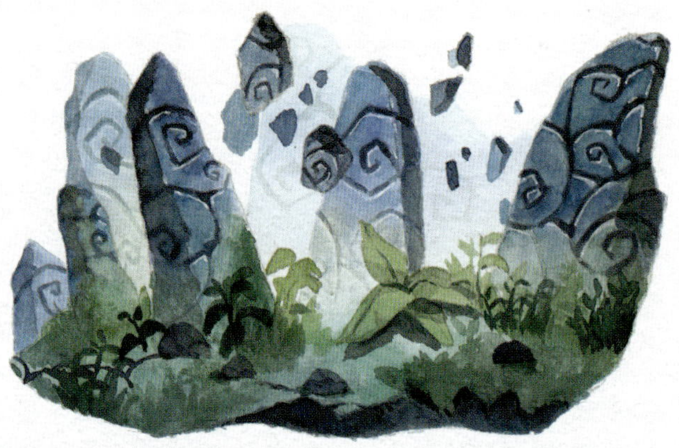

Step 9

We're almost done with this rock ritual. Mix Payne's Grey + Deep Green to make a dark green-blue color, and use your round brush 2 with very little water to paint more silhouettes of leaves and grass blades on the ground, creating variation and interest.

Paint more small pebbles and stones on the ground with a thick mixture of Payne's Grey, and paint a small shadow around each pebble. Also paint little cracks and fissures on the rocky ground.

Step 10

And lastly . . . the most delicious detail. Use Titanium White gouache to exaggerate the highlights on the "lip" of the rocks.

With that finishing touch, we've completed our first rock ritual. Great job, follow wizard! With every tutorial, we are one step closer to completing this dimension, and your watercolor powers grow ever stronger.

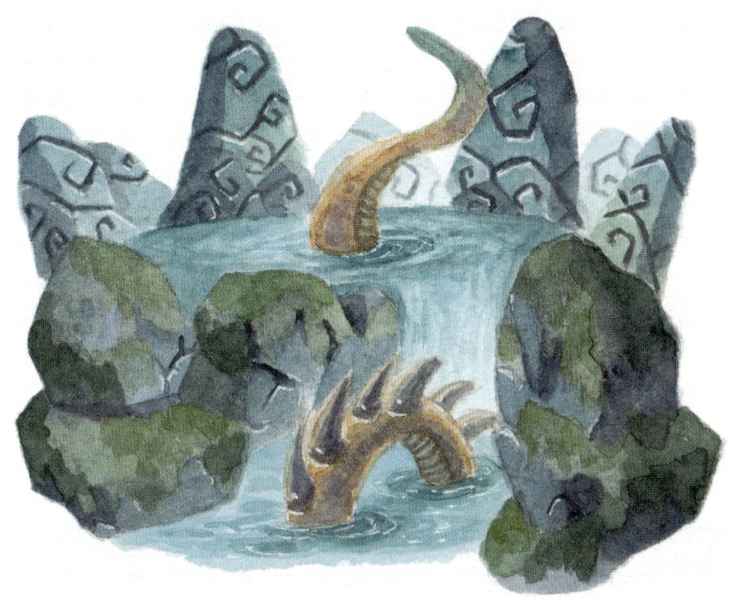

A Simple, Safe, Slithering Stream

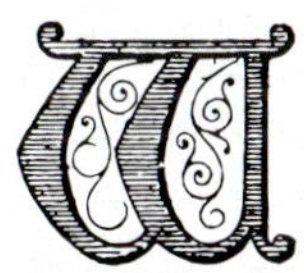

ater is essential to any world. Our forest dimension is no different. especially now that we have human visitors.

In this tutorial. we're going to paint a simple little stream. which our visitors can use to restock their water supplies safely. Well. somewhat. In the stream. there is a primordial serpent. Unfriendly or not—it's up to the adventurers to discover.

Brushes

Round brush 10, 0, 2

Colors

Deep Blue

Gamboge

Payne's Grey

Violet

Cerulean Blue

Deep Green

Crimson Lake Red

Yellow Ochre

Gouache

Titanium White

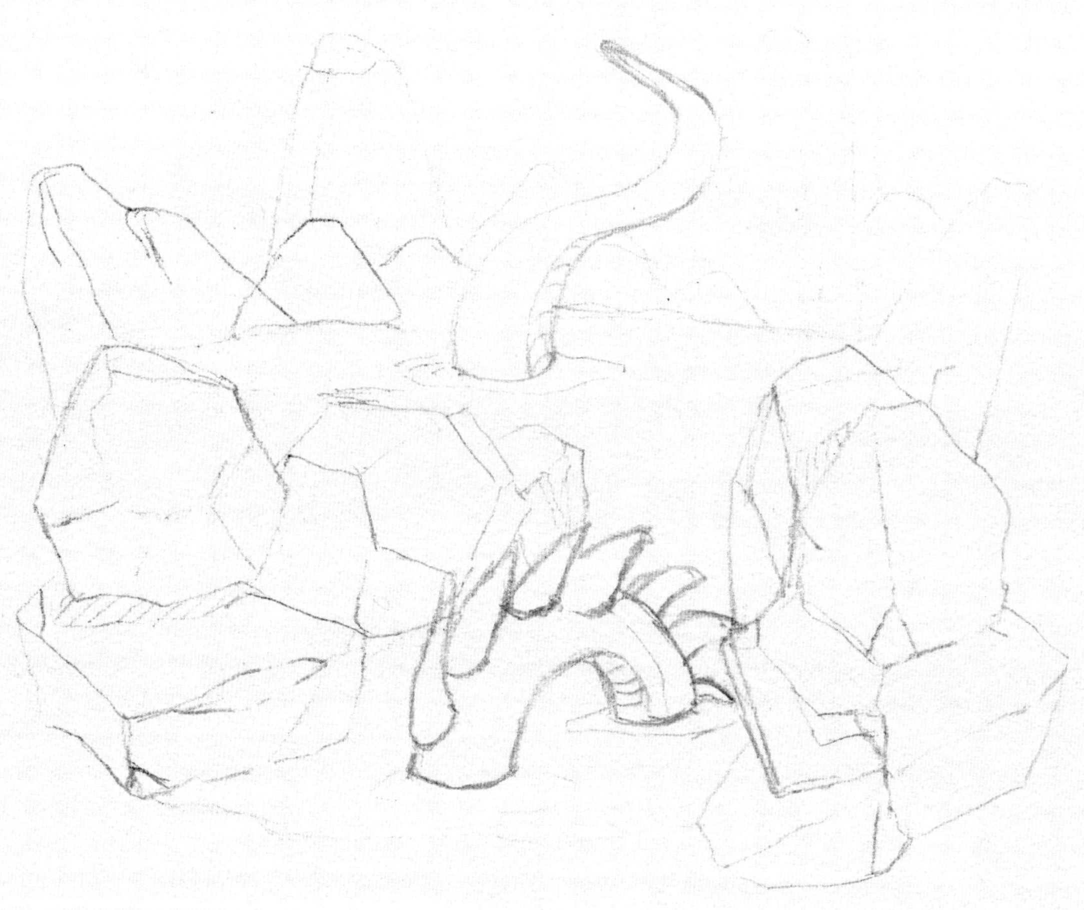

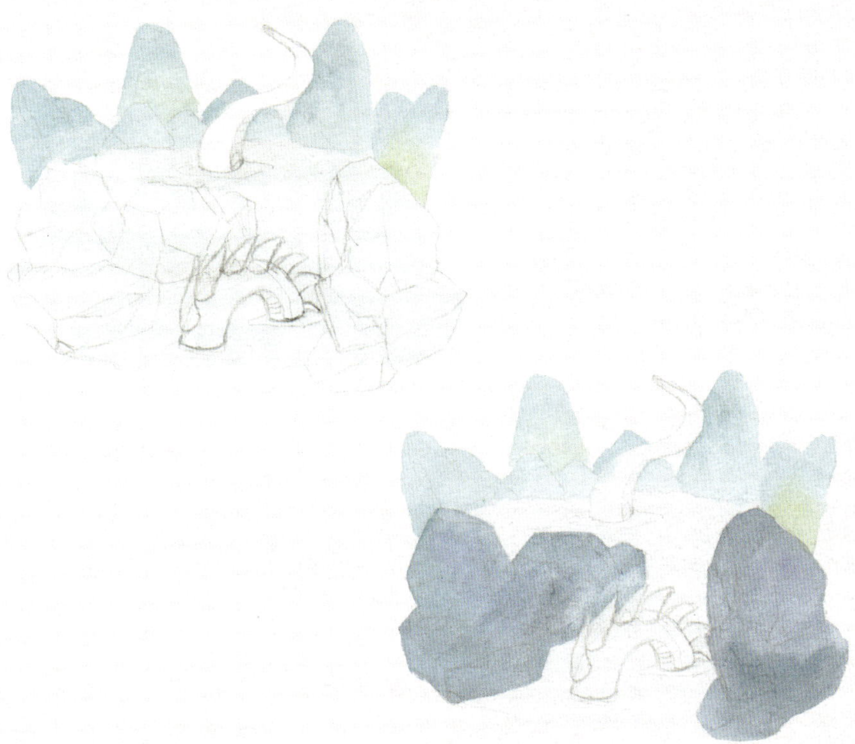

Step 1

Draw the provided design onto your sketch-book or watercolor paper using an HB pencil. Draw the boulders similarly to the previous tutorial, and feel free to add more rocks or floating boulders. The key shape to keep is the body of the serpent emerging from the water. Ensure that you can clearly see a curving tail in the upper pond, and a neat curve in the lower pond.

Step 2

Start with your round brush 10, and work quickly with wet paint. Raise your paper slightly at an angle (as described in *The Bead Method* from Chapter 1, page 15), and use Deep Blue diluted in water to paint the background rocks. Start from the top, and as you

paint toward the bottom, create a fade into Gamboge. Dry your brush, and use *The Lifting Technique* from Chapter 1 (see page 18) to lift the paint from the page on the bottom of the rocks to create a smooth fade into the paper.

Step 3

Continue working with the same technique as the previous step. This time, use Deep Blue + a touch of Payne's Grey with a fair amount of water, and paint the rocks in the foreground. Cover the surface of all the rocks. While the paint is still wet, dab some spots of Violet randomly on the rocks, to allow for some color variation.

Let these layers dry thoroughly.

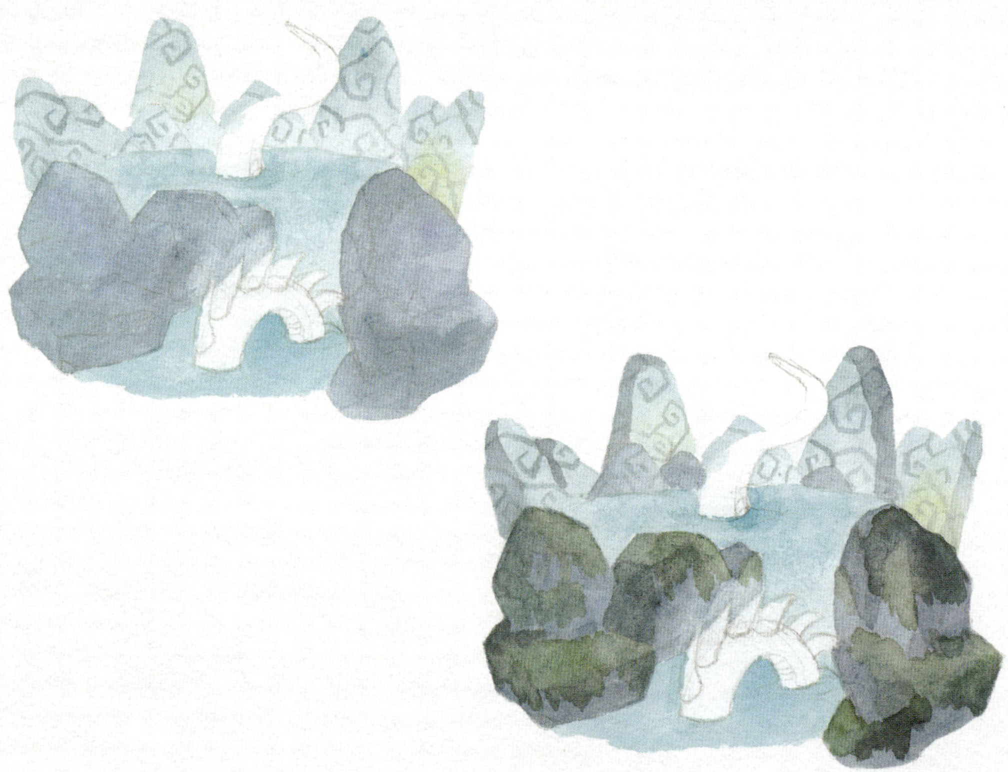

Step 4

Use diluted Cerulean Blue with your round brush 10 to paint over the area of the water.

While that's drying, switch to your round brush 0 to start detailing the runes and engravings on the rocks. Use Deep Blue + Payne's Grey to carefully paint swirling shapes. Add a touch of Gamboge to the mixture to paint the engravings over the yellower areas.

Step 5

Switch to your round brush 2. Paint a layer of shadow on the background rocks using Payne's Grey + Deep Blue with an equal part of water.

For the foreground rocks, paint the surfaces of the rocks that are facing away from the water in Payne's Grey + Deep Blue also. To avoid letting the colors look too uniform, work in loose, quick strokes, letting the paint dry in some areas and overlapping colors in other areas.

Then, while the paint is still semi-wet, start introducing the colors of moss on these rocks. Rocks near water will undoubtedly be overgrown with moss. Use Deep Green + Gamboge for moss in the light areas on the rocks, and Deep Green + Crimson Lake Red for the moss in the shadow areas. Keep the form of the rocks in mind when painting this moss in light and shadow; let some of the moss fall over the edges.

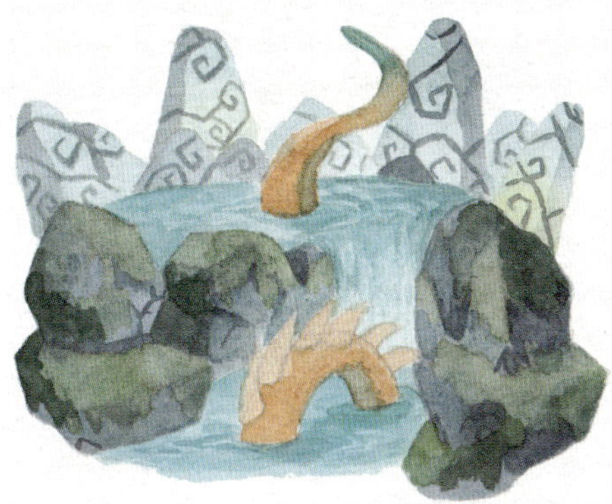

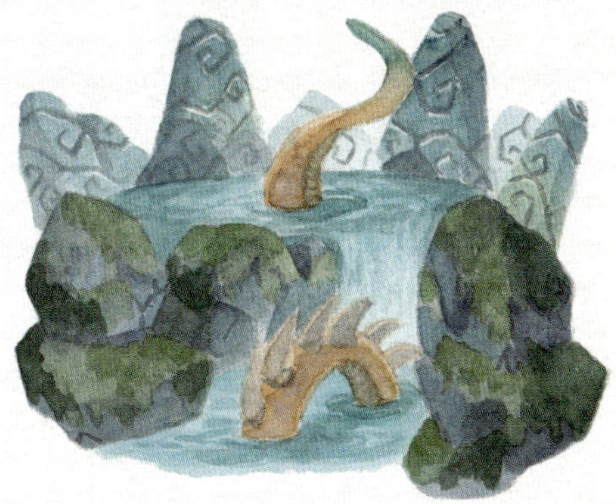

Step 6

Use a round brush 2 for this step. First, let's paint some shadow and definition on the water. Use Cerulean Blue + Deep Blue to paint loose swirls in the water. For the pool above, paint the swirls in a circular shape, to define the current toward the waterfall. For the bottom pool, paint most of these swirls and shadows around the body of the serpent.

Then use Yellow Ochre diluted with water to paint the body of the serpent. While the paint is wet, create a gradient into Cerulean Blue for the tail end of the serpent, and the inside of the curving body.

Next, use Payne's Grey to paint small lines and cracks on the boulders on the bottom, and deepen the engravings on the rocks above.

When the Yellow Ochre on the serpent is dry, paint another layer of Yellow Ochre along the curve of the body, leaving the upper parts of the curve unpainted as a highlight.

Step 7

Continue painting with your round brush 2. Use Deep Blue to paint a layer over the rocks in the upper background. While painting, remember to leave a blank space on the upper "lip" of the engravings, creating a more 3D form on those rocks. Use the same color to paint more ripples on the water.

Next, use Payne's Grey to deepen the shadows on the rocks on the bottom, where the moss falls over the edge.

Then use Violet to glaze shadows on the horns along the serpent's back and body. Also paint another layer of Deep Green + Gamboge over the moss to define it further.

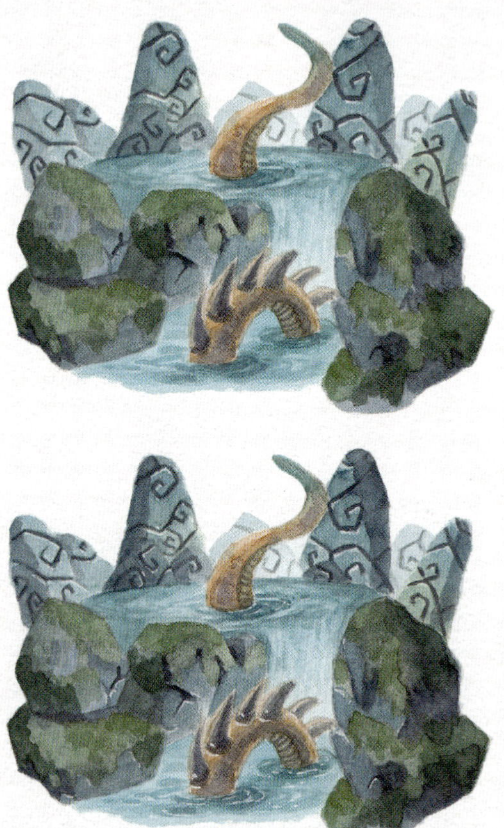

Step 8

Switch to your round brush 0 to make more detailed lines. First, use Payne's Grey to paint over the engraving lines on the rocks above. Do the same with the little lines and cracks on the rocks on the bottom.

Next, use Violet to deepen the shadows on the serpent's body and horns using *The Glazing Method* (page 16). Then use Deep Blue to paint over the shadow on the water, closely around the serpent's body.

Step 9

We're almost done with this serpent's little home. The last few details are going to make the painting pop. First, darken the shadow side of the rocks in the upper pond using Payne's Grey.

Finally, use Titanium White gouache to paint spots of sparkling water at the crest of the ripples.

Once the sparkles are done, our serpent is ready to be unleashed to the world! Those mossy boulders sure do look inviting to relax on and enjoy the sounds of the waterfall, don't they?

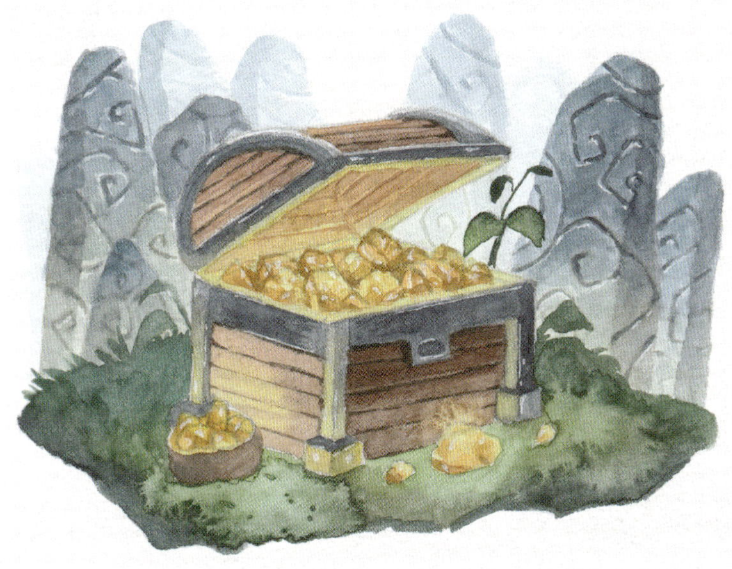

A Goblin's Gemstone Stash

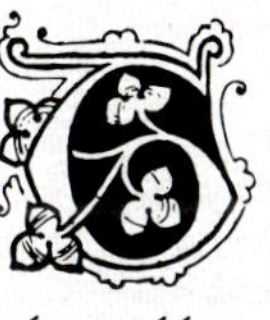reasure. Imagine it. Wealth, fame, glory. These things attract even the noblest of monks and knights from across kingdoms. But who collects such large masses of wealth and stashes them in one place? Can you imagine what a large task it is to gather that amount of gems and gold, and then hide it from the known world? It takes years. We have one beautiful species to thank for that: GOBLINS.

Chances are you have encountered a goblin at least once in your life, whether or not you were aware of it at the time. All those household items that mysteriously go missing? That was a goblin (or its distant relative, a brownie).

In this tutorial, we're going to paint a chest full of treasure, belonging to one hardworking goblin—my good friend in mischief, Wobbly. If an adventurer reaches this far into our dimension, they shall be granted this great wealth . . . and immediately face Wobbly in a duel to the death.

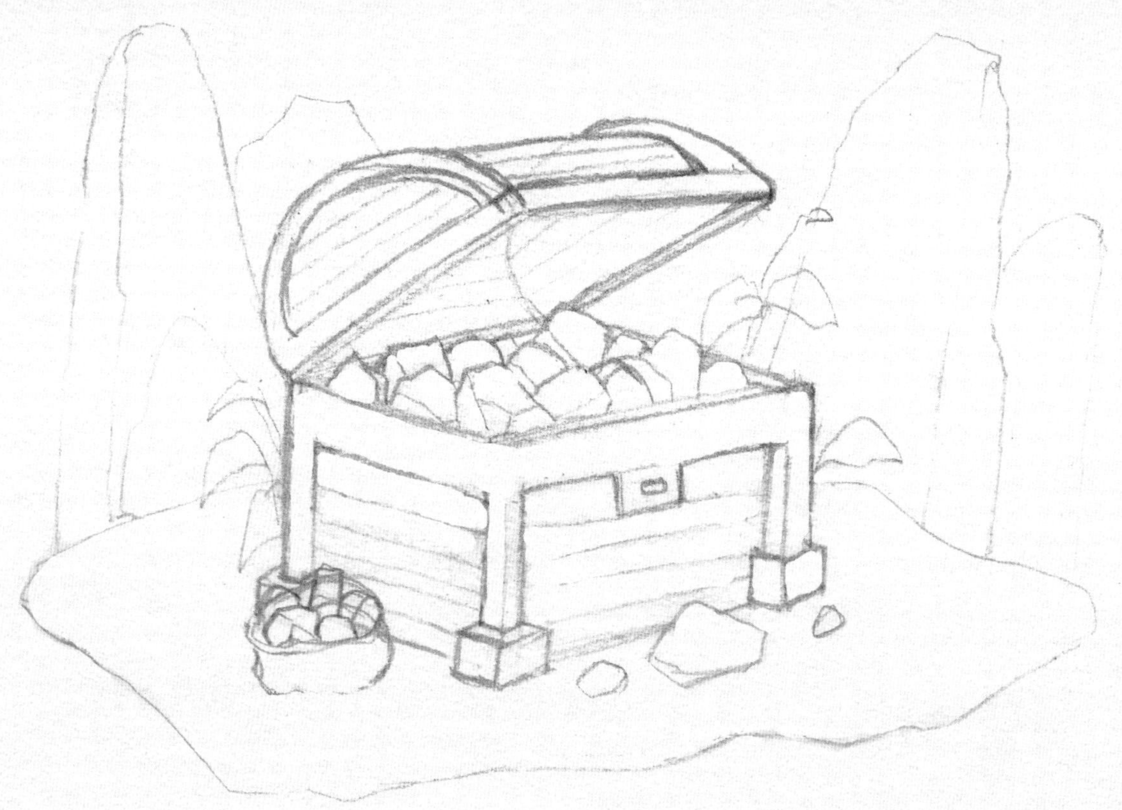

Brushes

Round brush 10, 2, 0

Colors

Deep Blue	Burnt Umber
Gamboge	Deep Green
Payne's Grey	Crimson Lake Red
Violet	Burnt Sienna
Lemon Yellow	Ultramarine Blue
Yellow Ochre	

Gouache

Titanium White

Step 1

Draw or trace the sketch onto your water-color paper using an HB pencil. Draw the boulders in the background similarly to the previous tutorial. Think of the treasure box as a simple 3D cube.

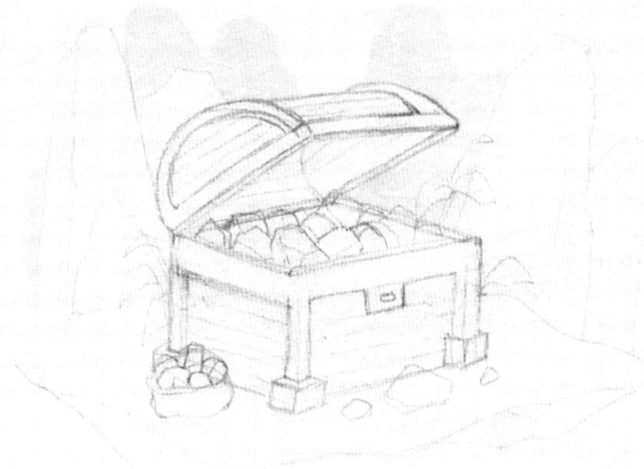

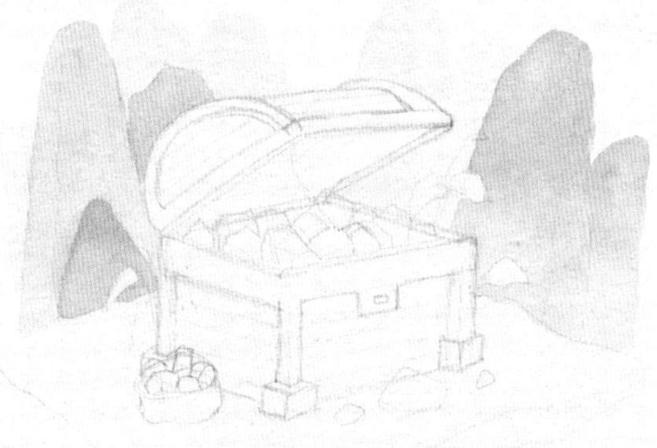

Step 2

We will start by painting the furthermost rocks in the background. For this step, use a round brush 10 dipped in a fair amount of water. Use Deep Blue diluted in a lot of water to paint the silhouette of the distant rocks, using similar shapes as the ones you sketched out. Fade the color into Gamboge toward the bottom of the rock, using *The Wet-on-Wet Technique* from Chapter 1 (see page 16).

Step 3

Use the same process from Step 2 to paint in the rocks closer to the treasure chest. Use Deep Blue + Payne's Grey on a watery layer to fade the color into Gamboge toward the bottom. While the paint is wet, dab some spots of Violet into the water, creating some color variation on the rock. Let this wet layer dry thoroughly before continuing on to the next step.

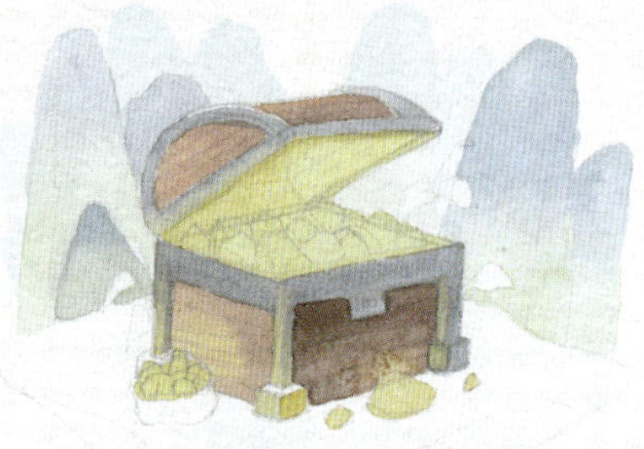

Step 4

In this step we're going to lay out the base colors for the treasure chest. Switch to your round brush 2.

First, use Lemon Yellow with an equal part of water to cover the inside of the chest, as well as the gemstones on the ground and in the small pouch. While the paint is still wet, dab some spots of Gamboge in random areas, allowing for color variation.

Next, use Yellow Ochre to begin painting the wood on the top. While it's still wet, dab Burnt Umber onto the paper, and let the colors granulate together on the page naturally. Use the same process for the hemisphere shape on the side of the chest lid.

Then use Payne's Grey to paint the metal parts of the chest. Dab Lemon Yellow on the planes that directly face a gemstone and receive glowing light from it.

Apprentice Notes:

Don't try to control the paint too much; let the colors flow freely, mix together, granulate, and react with the paper. These textures are unique to watercolor and create more beautiful illustrations.

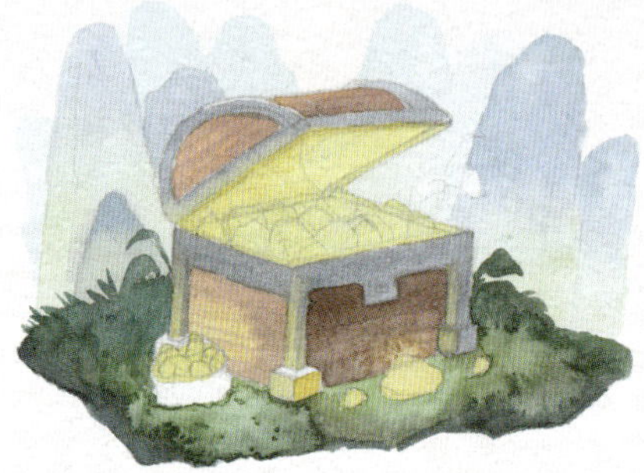

Step 5

Let's paint the ground in this step. For this step, you will need to be loose, free, and a little bit chaotic. We will be working opaquely. Use your round brush 2, and an equal part of water. First, use Lemon Yellow + Deep Green to paint the highlighted grass around the gemstones on the ground. Working quickly while the paint is still wet, use Deep Green + Gamboge + a touch of Crimson Lake Red to paint around the glow. Paint the grass furthest from the glow with Deep Green + Crimson Lake Red. While these colors are still wet, dab a bead of plain water into the paint. Watch how the water spreads the paint across the page like lightning.

Toward the bottom rocky area, below the grass, use Deep Green + Payne's Grey. Let all these colors naturally react together, creating their own details on the ground, such as leaves, pebbles, and foliage that we don't have to paint ourselves.

Let this layer dry thoroughly before continuing.

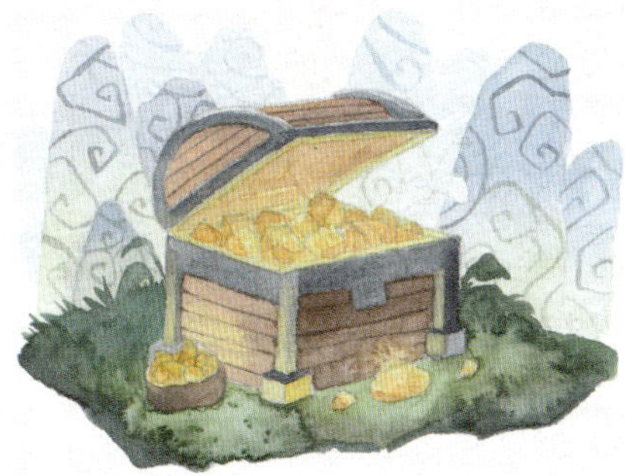 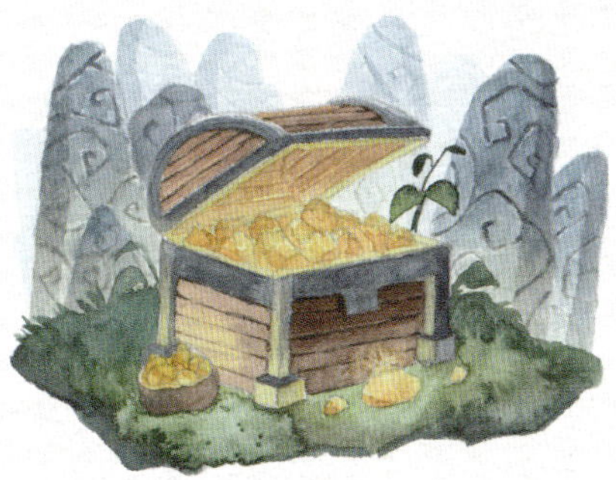

Step 6

Continue using your round brush 2. First, use Burnt Sienna + Ultramarine Blue to paint the small pouch. While the paint is still wet, dab some spots of Ultramarine Blue where the pouch would create a shadow on itself.

Next, mix Gamboge + a touch of Crimson Lake Red to get a light-orange color, and paint the different edges of the gemstones. Paint spots of this orange color randomly, creating *suggestions* of jagged edges and form on the stones. Use this same technique with various shades of this orange; add more Crimson to get a darker orange, and more Gamboge to get a deeper yellow.

Use *The Glazing Method* (page 16) to paint another layer for the inside of the lid using Gamboge + Crimson Lake Red + a touch of Burnt Umber. Leave the edges of the planks unpainted, creating a "lip" on the lid and wood. Then glaze another layer of Payne's Grey over the metal parts of the lid, keeping in mind where the light source is striking from (the gemstones).

Next, switch to your round brush 0, and use Burnt Sienna + Ultramarine Blue to paint over the lines in the wooden planks on the outside of the chest. While that's drying, use Payne's Grey to paint the swirling runes on the rocks in the background.

Step 7

Use your round brush 2 dipped in a fair amount of water to paint over the rocks in the background with Deep Blue + Payne's Grey, once again using *The Glazing Method*. Leave the areas on the "lip" of the engravings unpainted for a 3D effect.

Next, switch to your round brush 0 for all the little details and outlines. Use Payne's Grey and paint in quick strokes in the same direction as the metal, leaving some of the previous layer showing through. This creates a "shine" to appear metallic.

Then mix Burnt Sienna + Ultramarine Blue, and darken the lines on the wooden planks. For the planks inside the lid, use Burnt Sienna + a touch Crimson Lake Red.

When the layer for the rocks in the background is dry, mix Deep Green + Crimson Lake Red, and paint the stem and leaves of a plant just behind the treasure chest. For the leaves facing toward the glowing chest, add Deep Green + Lemon Yellow into the wet paint, and let the colors blend together naturally.

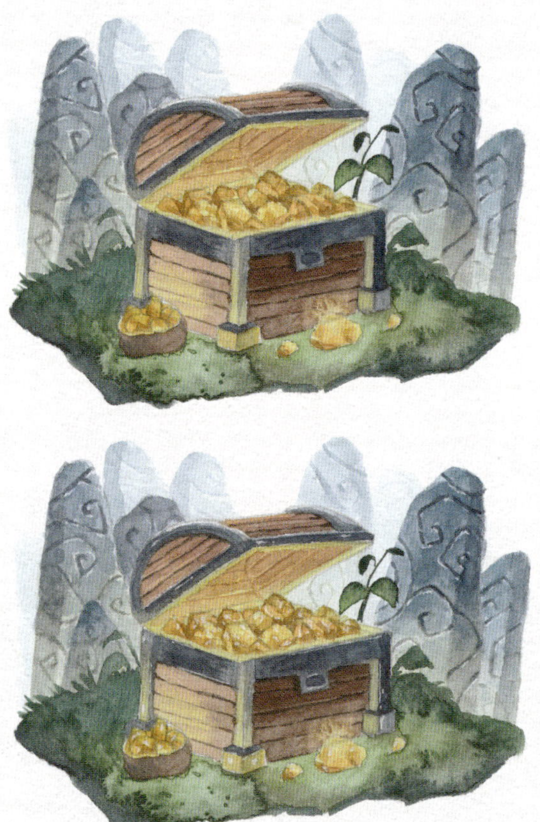

Step 8

Let's paint more definition on the star of the show: the gemstones themselves. Using your round brush 2, mix Gamboge + Crimson Lake Red + a touch of Deep Green to create a reddish-brown color. Apply this color carefully on the edges of the rocks, outlining the shape and the side of the gems that will be inside the box. Use the same technique for the gems on the ground and in the pouch.

While that's drying, glaze another layer of Payne's Grey on the deepest shadows of the metal, and paint an oval shape on the lock of the chest.

Step 9

At long last, we can paint the final delicious detail: the sparkly white highlights.

Use Titanium White gouache to paint spots of white on the metal and the gemstones, bringing out their shape and color and luxuriousness.

With those final marks, we have completed our creation of an invaluable treasure chest! This wealth of gems belonging to Wobbly is worth hundreds of kings. Only the most noble adventurer can ever lay eyes upon it and take it home. Well done, fellow wizard.

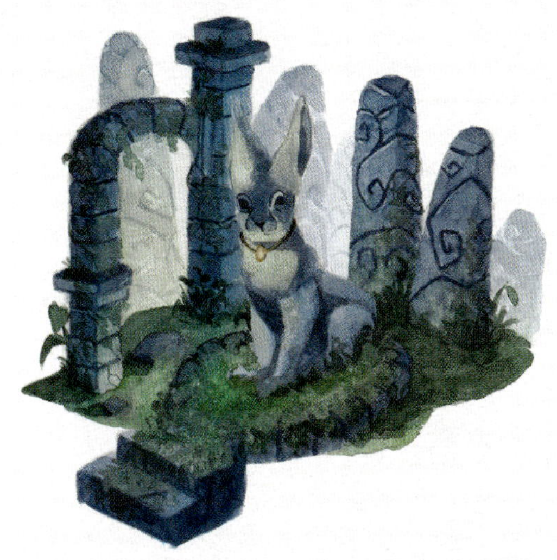

Rocks of Past, Moss of Present

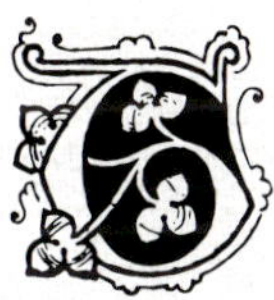

here was once a rabbit wizard named Corvid. Very little is known about her or her research. The only proof we even have of her existence is a stone statue of her likeness–poised in an ever-knowledgeable expression. Her statue sits atop a stone pedestal. surrounded by ruins of a building that was once her abode. Some say the statue is not just a carving: It is Corvid herself cursed to stone.

In this tutorial. we're going to paint Stone Corvid in the ruins of her temple. Every good dimension has ruins for adventurers to stumble upon . . . and a trap that will awaken the wizard.

Brushes

Round brush 10, 2, 0

Colors

Deep Blue

Gamboge

Violet

Payne's Grey

Deep Green

Lemon Yellow

Crimson Lake Red

Gouache

Titanium White

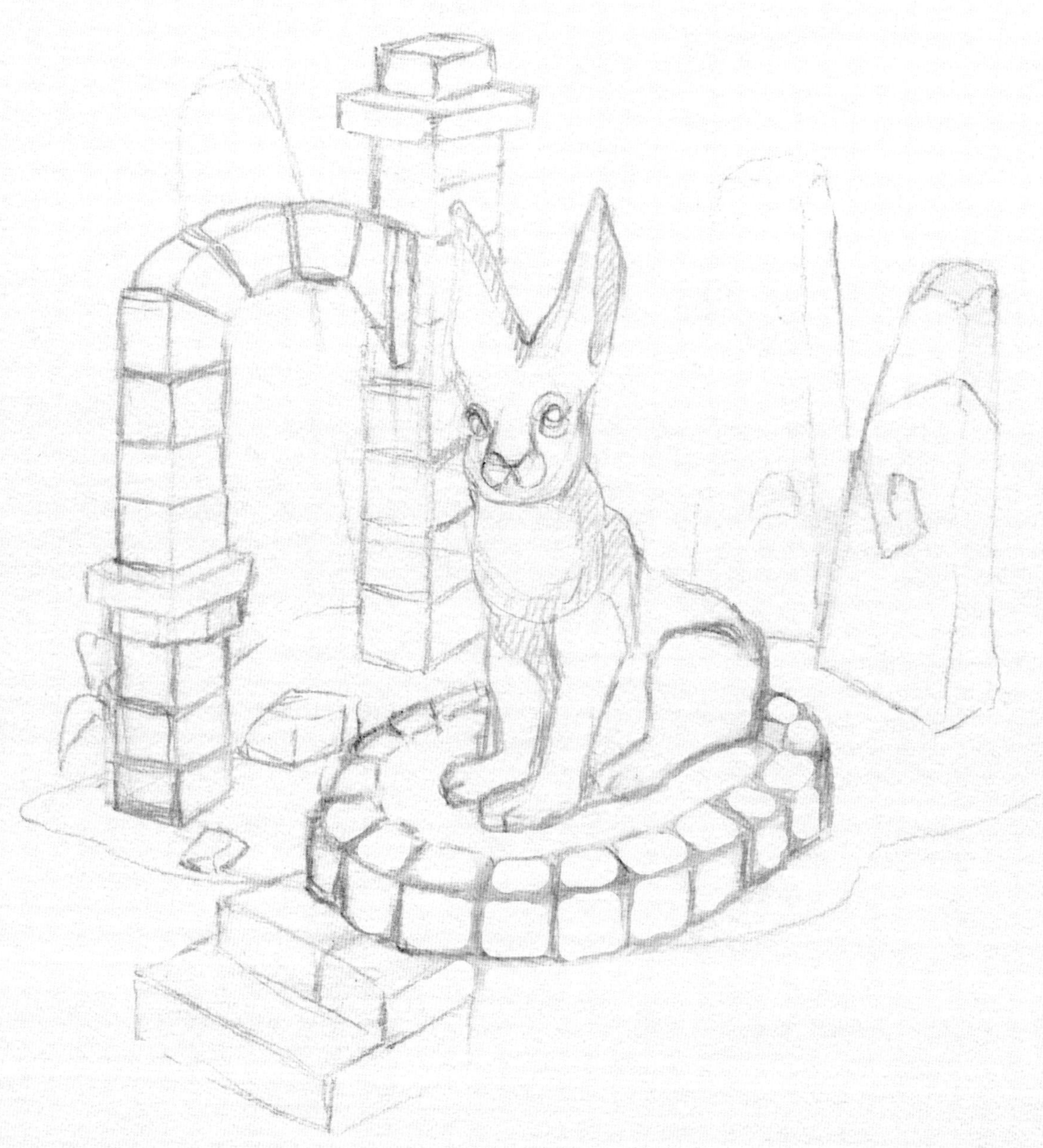

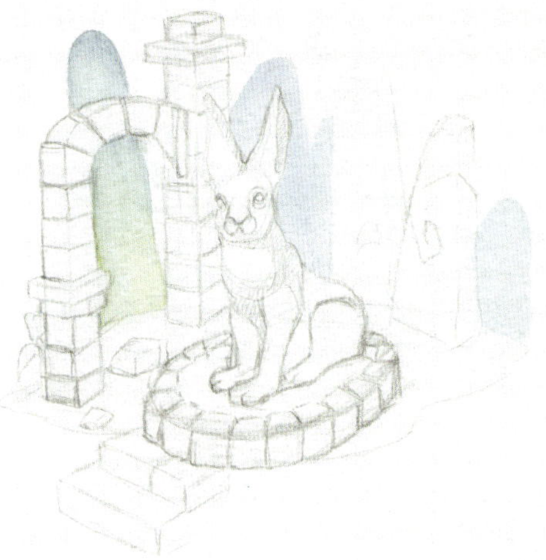

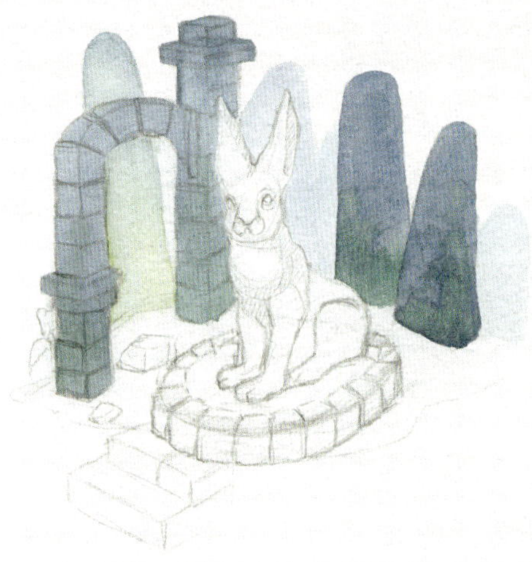

Step 1

Draw or trace the sketch onto your watercolor paper, using my drawing as a reference for the rabbit statue's pose and the surrounding ruins. The rabbit's pose is the key shape to draw, as well as the ring she is seated on. In the background, draw more boulders similar to the previous tutorials.

Step 2

Start painting the background rocks in the distance with a fairly wet round brush 10. Use Deep Blue diluted in water, and raise your sketchbook at a slight angle so the paint flows downward naturally, as described in *The Bead Method* from Chapter 1 (see page 15). While the Deep Blue is still wet, dab spots of Gamboge into the water. Wipe your brush dry, and use *The Lifting Technique* described in Chapter 1 (see page 18) to lift the paint at the bottom of the rock to create a fade into the paper.

Repeat this technique on the other background rocks, using Deep Blue and spots of Violet. Let these wet layers dry thoroughly before continuing.

Step 3

Now we can lay the base colors for the ruins in the middle ground. Mix Deep Blue + a touch of Payne's Grey with a fair amount of water. Apply this color to the brick arch, the pillar, and the two rocks on the right. While the paint is wet, dab spots of Deep Green + Deep Blue + a touch of Payne's Grey on the bottom and corners of these rocks to indicate the beginnings of moss. This is still a fairly wet layer, so the colors will granulate and blend together as they dry, as described in *The Wet-on-Wet* Technique from Chapter 1 (see page 16).

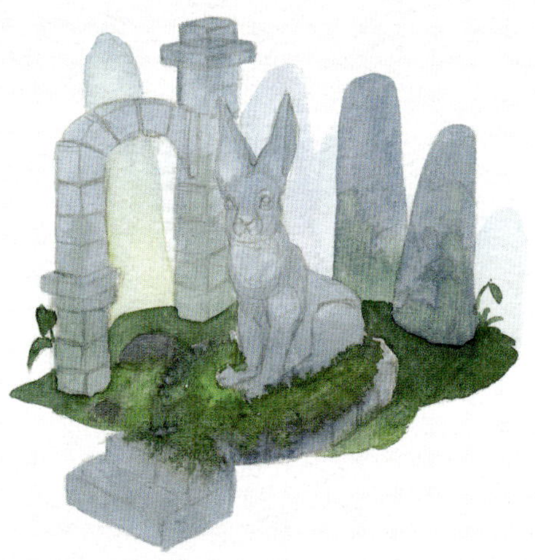 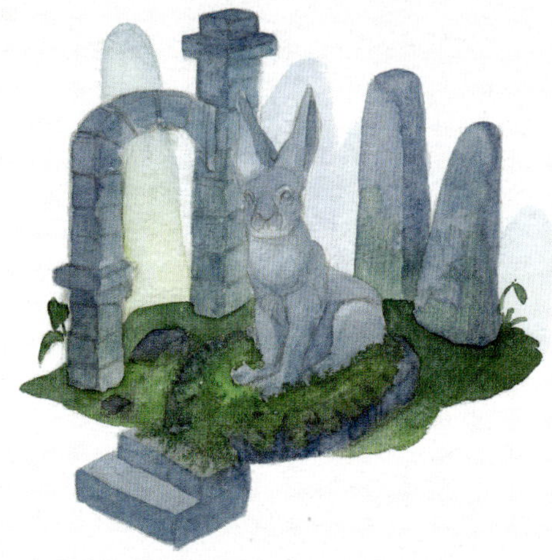

Step 4

Continue using your round brush 10 and a wet layer. Work quickly before the paint dries. First, apply Deep Blue + Payne's Grey on the rabbit statue. Now you will use *The Lifting Technique* (page 18) again. While the paint is still wet, quickly use a dry round brush 2 to lift the paint from the chest, snout, and ears of the rabbit. Later we will paint a glowing necklace on her. Apply this grey-blue color to the bricks on the pedestal, the steps downward, and the lone rocks on the ground.

Then mix Deep Green + Lemon Yellow + a touch of Crimson Lake Red, and paint the pedestal beneath her feet. Let this bright-green color granulate and mix with the Payne's Grey + Deep Blue, which will create the texture of wild moss.

Next, start painting the ground with Deep Green + Gamboge + a touch of Crimson Lake Red. Toward the pedestal where the ground would be highlighted from the glowing gemstone, dab spots of the same color mixture.

Let this layer dry thoroughly.

Step 5

Switch to your round brush 2. To define the shadows and form, mix an equal part of water with Payne's Grey, and paint over the left side of the pillar and the arch. For the tall rocks on the right, glaze the shadow on the right side.

For the rabbit statue, glaze the shadow color on the ears, at the top of the face, and at the back of the body. Keep in mind the glow that we will paint later, coming from a necklace resting on her chest.

Also add this shadow color to the stone steps and pedestal.

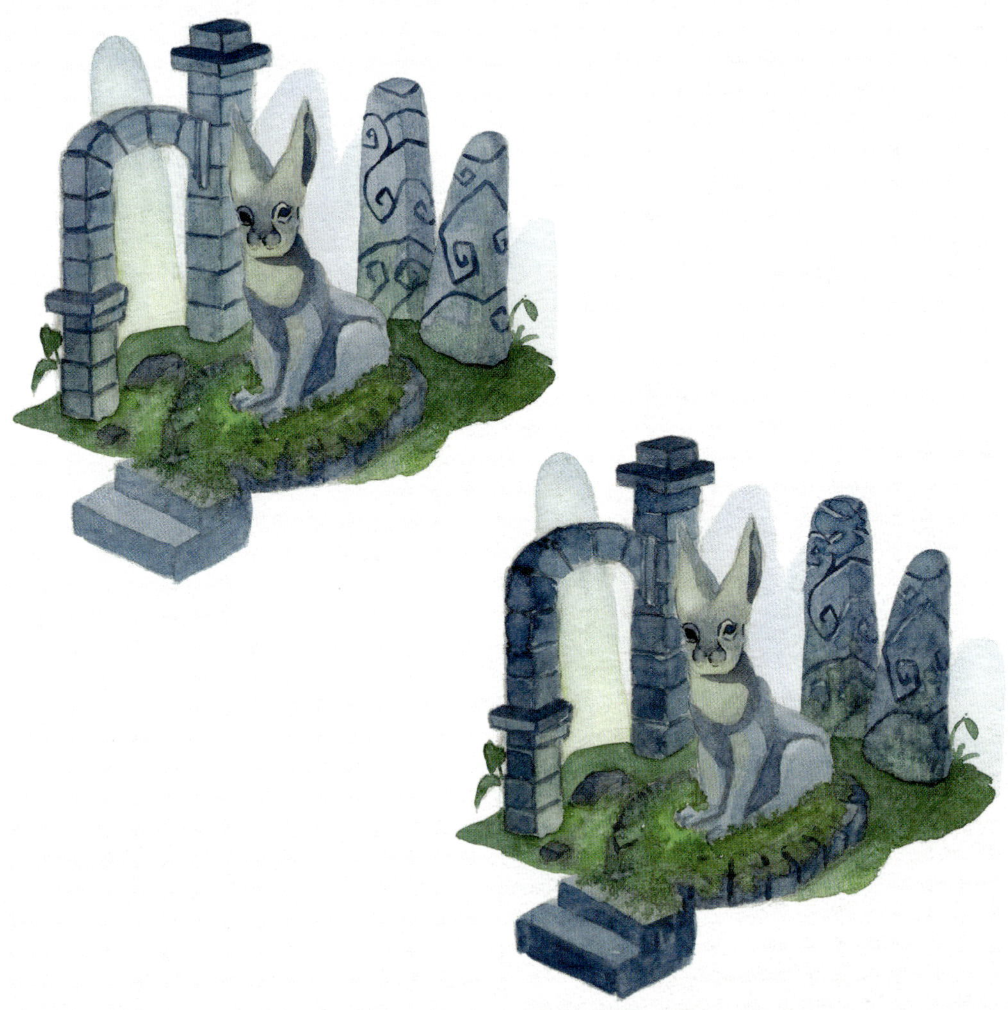

Step 6

Use your round brush 0 and Payne's Grey for this step. With a sturdy touch, paint over the lines on the pillar, arch, runes, and body of the statue. Then use Lemon Yellow with a lot of water, and apply it over the areas on the rabbit statue's chest and ears.

Step 7

Switch back to your round brush 2. Using Deep Blue + Payne's Grey with an equal part of water, paint over the shadow areas of all the rocks and pillars. Let your brush-strokes be loose and sketchy; let the paint dry in some areas and pool in other areas randomly so it creates texture and variation. While the paint is wet, dab Deep Green into the wet paint to indicate moss.

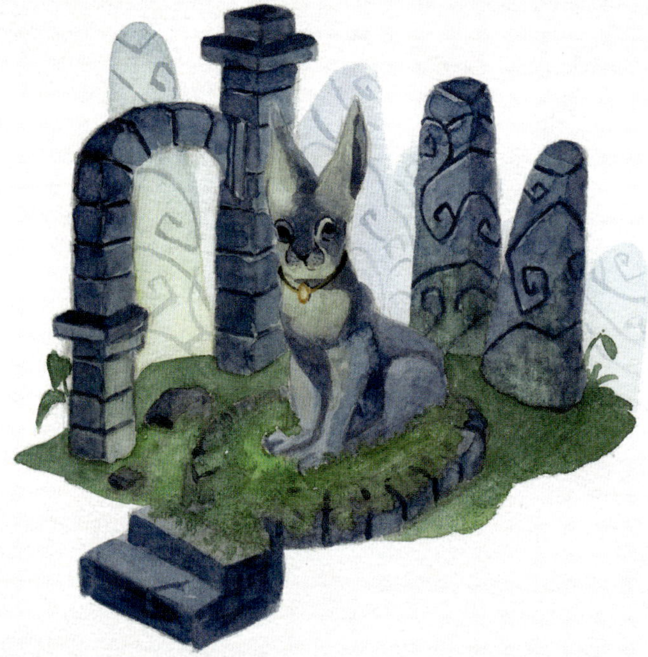

Step 8

Use your round brush 0 to paint the neck-lace. Mix Titanium White gouache to paint an oval shape on the rabbit's chest for the gem of a necklace. Then mix Lemon Yellow + Crimson Lake Red + Titanium White, and paint the string around the neck.

Next, define the shadows on the rabbit to make the light stand out more. Use Payne's Grey for this. Paint over the areas on the head that face upward away from the light, and the lower body toward the back. Use the same color to paint over the rune lines and cracks in the stones.

Then use Deep Blue with a lot of water to paint the engravings in the background rocks.

Finally, use Payne's Grey to paint over the string of the necklace where it is in shadow.

Step 9

We're almost done with this illustration! Let's finish up the background rocks and then neaten up the ground with more detail.

Use your round brush 2. Mix Deep Green + Lemon Yellow + a touch of Crimson Lake Red, and paint chaotic and loose spots on the pillars in rough leaf shapes. Then create a dark-green color by mixing Deep Green + Crimson Lake Red, and paint the vines that connect these leaves and wrap around the stone.

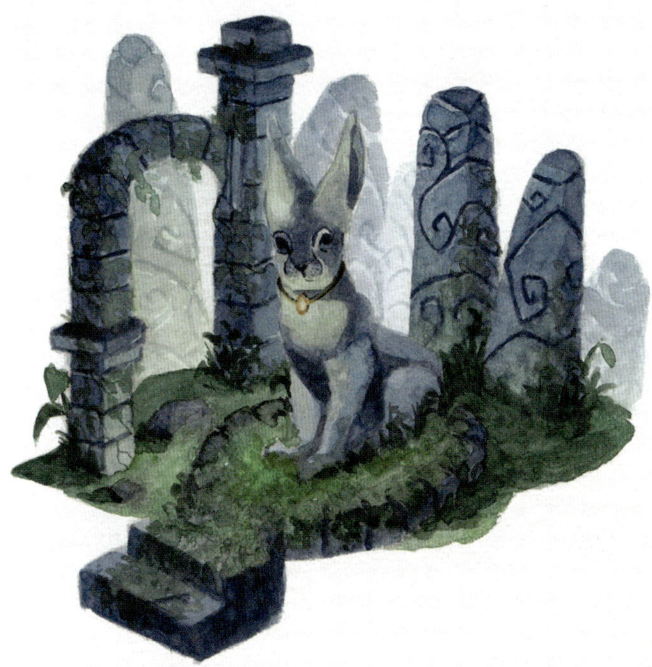

Use the same dark-green color to paint a shadow on the left of the stones on the ground and leaves below the foot of the statue and rocks behind it, as well as the stone steps.

Then use Payne's Grey diluted in a lot of water to glaze another layer on the rocks in the background. Be careful to leave the upper "lip" of the engravings unpainted, creating depth and form on those stones.

Next, use white gouache—or a white pencil—to paint the highlights on the stone, the "lip" on the engravings, and a small dot on each eye of the statue.

As a final step, erase any pencil lines that are still visible once all the paint is thoroughly dry.

With that, the Ruins of Corvid are complete. Any visitor may now stumble upon the overgrown moss to discover the glowing necklace and the story of the rabbit wizard. Well done on unleashing yet another feat of magic upon the world.

Apprentice Notes:

We've mingled with plantae, fungi, and stone. And now, dear wizard, we can transcend your abilities to the final level. Are you ready?

Chapter Five
And a Hint of Salt

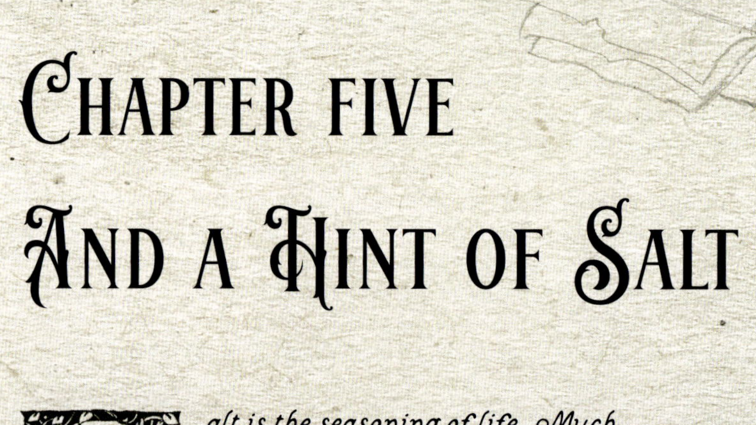

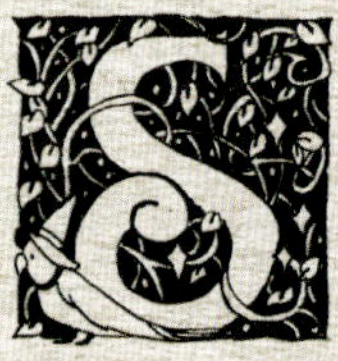

alt is the seasoning of life. Much like how salt enhances food, highlighting its flavor, every wizarding dimension needs this ingredient to give it an extra flair.

In this chapter, we're going to unleash some of the chaotic imagination you've kept tucked away, to paint complete scenes and learn more about the ancient world of wizards and sorcery. From books that were never meant to be written, to dragons and eggs, and a sturdy wizard's tower, this final chapter brings together all we've painted so far to add the finishing touches to our dimension.

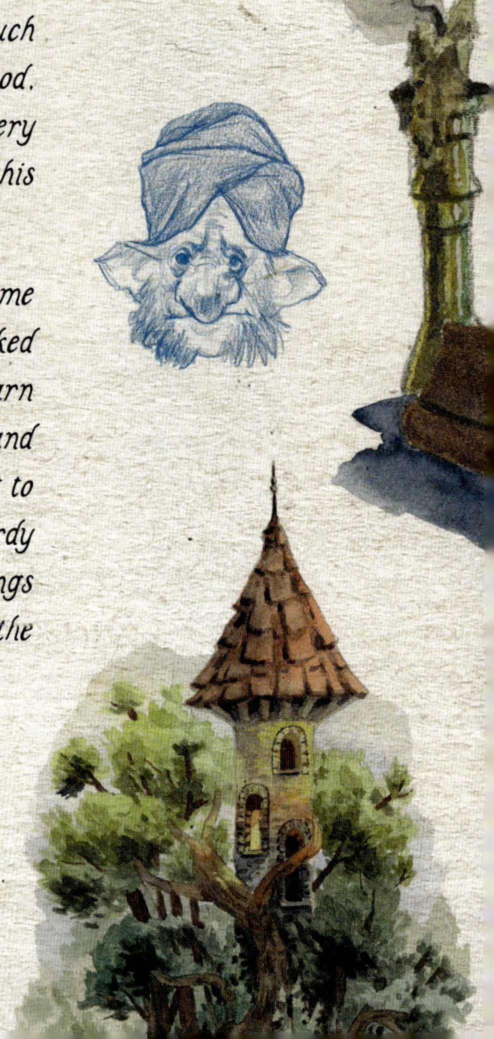

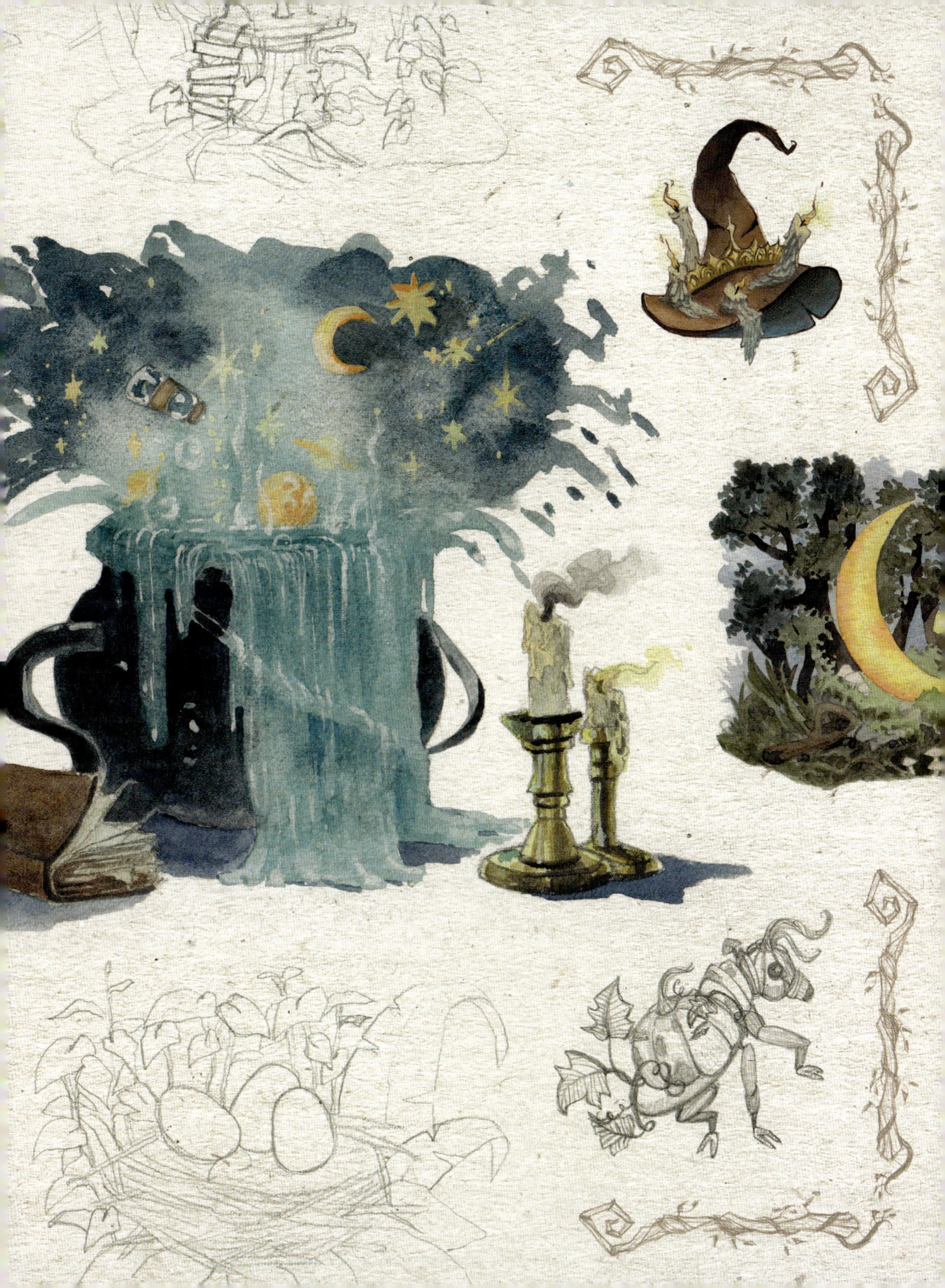

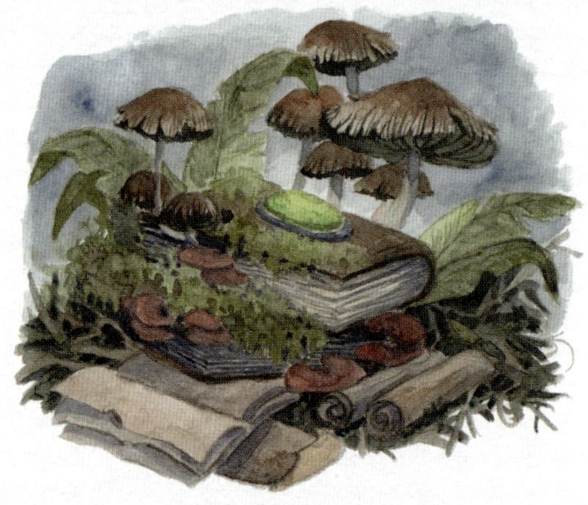

The Book of Mosscraft

izards and powerful books (that they shouldn't have written in the first place) go together like bread and butter. They are a staple among the world of sorcerers, mages, and the like. We are studious and academic, but don't confuse that with orderly. Wizards thirst for knowledge—even the cursed and forbidden knowledge often held in an equally cursed and forbidden book.

In this tutorial, we're going to paint a powerful book called *Mosscraft*. Inside, it holds the secrets of the Earth: the truth behind what forces govern seeds and spores to do what they do. This sacred knowledge involves the very programming of molecules laid out in writing. Our dimension is the safest place to store such a dangerous tome.

Brushes

Round brush 2, 0

Colors

Lemon Yellow

Deep Green

Burnt Sienna

Ultramarine Blue

Sap Green

Crimson Lake Red

Payne's Grey

Yellow Ochre

Deep Blue

Vermillion

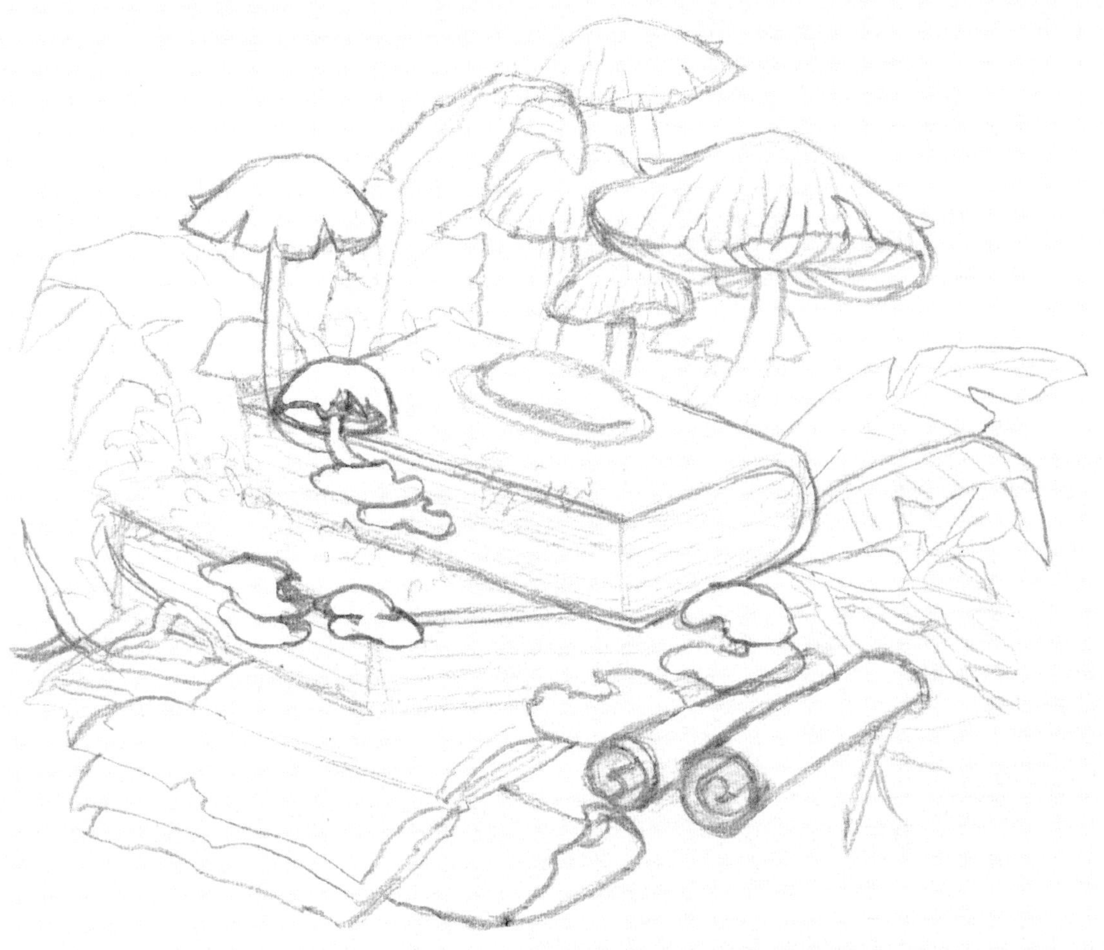

Step 1

Sketch or trace the pencil illustration onto your watercolor paper, using my drawing as a reference. Think of the book as a rectangular prism, and then draw the gemstone and pages on it. Feel free to alter the design around the book as much you like; add more of your favorite mushrooms and leaves.

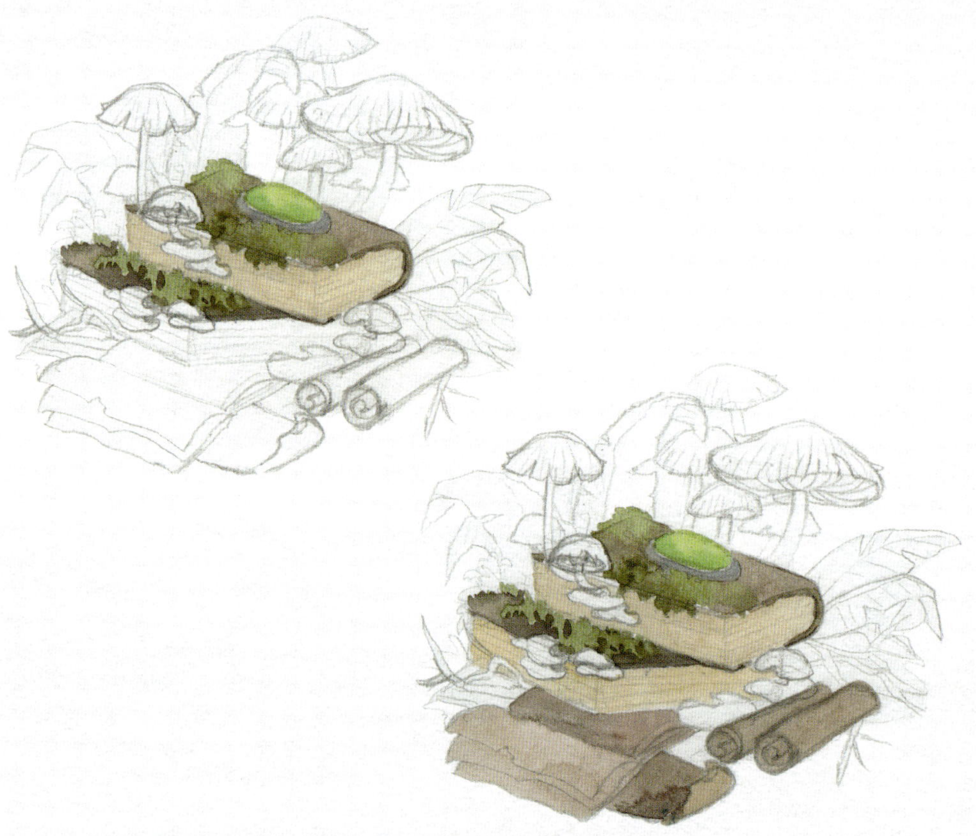

Step 2

Let's begin laying down the base colors for this illustration. Dip your round brush 2 in a fair amount of water. First, mix Lemon Yellow + Deep Green to get a cool, eerie green color, and paint the gemstone on the book's cover. Then mix Burnt Sienna + Ultramarine Blue, and paint the brown cover of the book. While the paint is still wet, start painting suggestions of moss and decay on the cover using Sap Green + Crimson Lake Red + Lemon Yellow.

For the metal ring around the gemstone, use Payne's Grey. Use a light wash of Yellow Ochre for the pages of the book.

Step 3

Paint the second book's pages with a light wash of Yellow Ochre, using a similar process to the previous step. Then mix Burnt Sienna + Ultramarine Blue for the pages below the second book. On the lighter side, mix a touch of Yellow Ochre into the Burnt Sienna + Ultramarine Blue color. Use the same color for the scrolls.

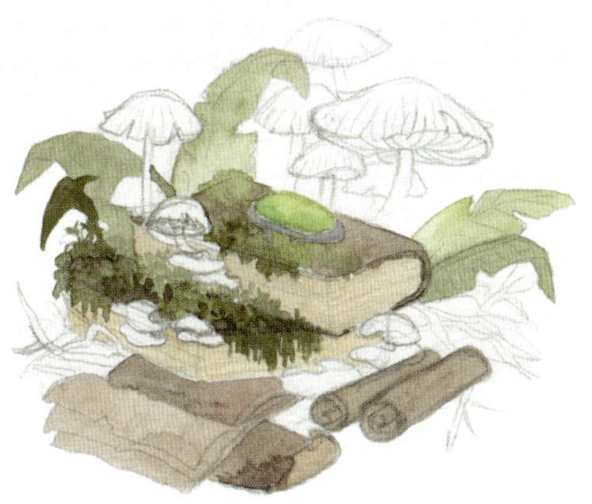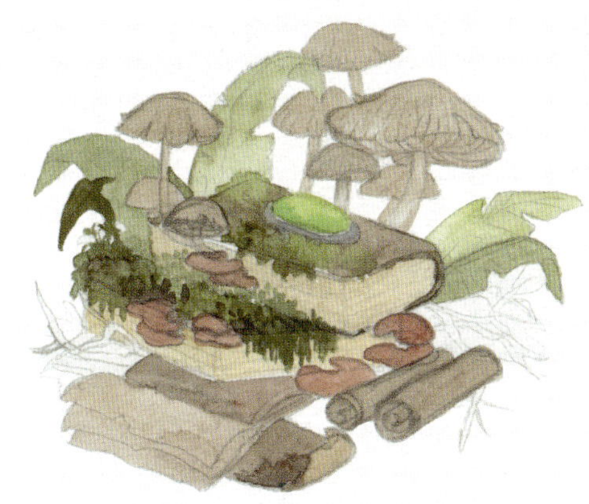

Step 4

Continue painting the greenery. This step is a little tricky because we want the leaves to be visible shapes on their own, but also to reflect a little of the glowing gem on the book. To accomplish this magical feat, we're going to use *The Lifting Technique* described in Chapter 1 (see page 18).

Create a dark, desaturated green by mixing Sap Green + Crimson Lake Red, and paint over the leaf on the left.

Move from left to right. For the next leaf, add more water to your mixture + a touch of Lemon Yellow. Apply this color to the entire leaf. While the paint is still wet, use a dry brush to lift the paint at the bottom of the leaf where it intersects with the book.

Move to the right-most leaf, and use the same technique: Paint the surface, then wipe your brush dry and lift the paint on the part facing the gem.

While the leaves are drying, use the same dark-green color to paint more moss on the second book; this moss grows on the cover and also falls off the edge overlapping the pages.

Step 5

Mix Burnt Sienna + Deep Blue with a lot of water. Paint this color across the mushrooms. Then create a dull red by mixing Vermillion + Burnt Sienna, and paint the curving lichen on the pages.

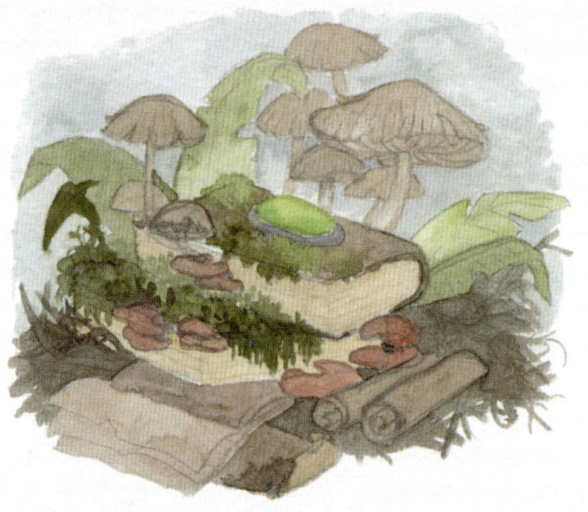 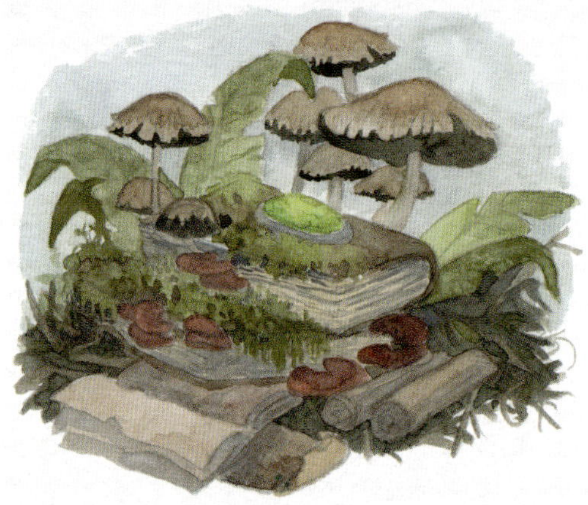

Step 6

Now let's lay the base color for the grassy ground. Mix Burnt Sienna + Deep Blue with an equal part of water. Cover the entire area of the ground. For the edges, use short and quick brushstrokes to create the shapes of sticks and branches jutting out beneath a pile of more sticks.

Next, clean your brush and mix Ultramarine Blue + Payne's Grey, diluted with a lot of water. Use this color to paint the background of the illustration. Be careful to avoid the shapes of the mushrooms and leaves.

Step 7

Mix Deep Blue + Burnt Sienna with an equal part of water. Use this color to paint the underside of the mushrooms.

Then use Payne's Grey to paint angular shadows on the stems of the mushrooms. Continue using the same color to create shadows for the pages on the books and scrolls, using *The Glazing Technique* described in Chapter 1 (see page 16).

Now use Payne's Grey + Sap Green to paint the shadows on the sticks on the ground, using *The Inverse Painting Technique* described in Chapter 1 (see page 17). Use the same color to paint the shadows on the giant leaves, defining their form more. Also use the same color to paint spots of green on the ground, suggesting leaves.

Next, use Payne's Grey to outline the lines of the pages of the first book. Finally, use Payne's Grey + Crimson Lake Red to paint the red mushrooms' shadows.

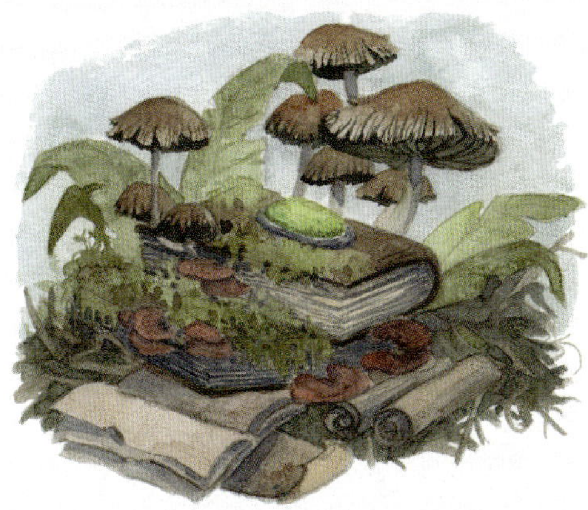

Step 8

Switch to your round brush 0 for this step. We're going to outline the shapes and strengthen the shadows to make the gem illuminate. Use a thick mixture of Payne's Grey, and start painting the mushrooms. Paint the lines beneath their gills and angular shadows on their stems. Then, paint the lines of the pages on the books, keeping in mind that the bottom book is farther away from the light, so it will have darker shadows.

Use the same color (Payne's Grey) to paint the shadow on the open pages and the rolled scrolls. Also paint the lines of the metal ring around the gem on the book.

Then apply another wet layer of Burnt Sienna across the mushroom caps, on their top. Finally, mix Sap Green + Crimson Lake Red to paint an outline on the bottom of the gemstone, where it sits on the metal ring.

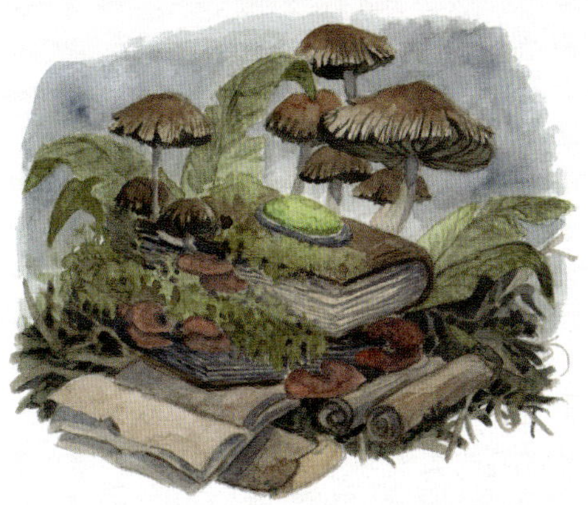

Step 9

For this final step, switch back to your round brush 2. Mix Payne's Grey + Ultramarine Blue with a lot of water, and paint the outer edges of the sky background, enhancing the light on the stone.

Then add another layer of Burnt Sienna + Deep Blue on the mushroom caps.

Next, use a thick mixture of Payne's Grey + Sap Green, and deepen the shadows of the sticks on the ground using *The Inverse Painting Technique* (page 17). Use the same color to draw the lines on the giant leaves.

Finally, this illustration is done! Our adventurers shall find these books, and tether themselves to cursed knowledge . . .

The Wizard's Tower of Chambers

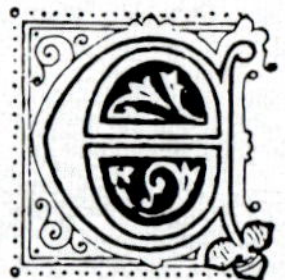

very wizard needs a tower. And every tower needs to fit certain criteria: It needs to be dramatic, extravagant, mysterious.

In this tutorial, we're going to paint our personal tower, a place to relax and wind down after the day's scheming. Our visitors might even stumble upon this tower and finally get the chance to meet the creator of this lovely dimension.

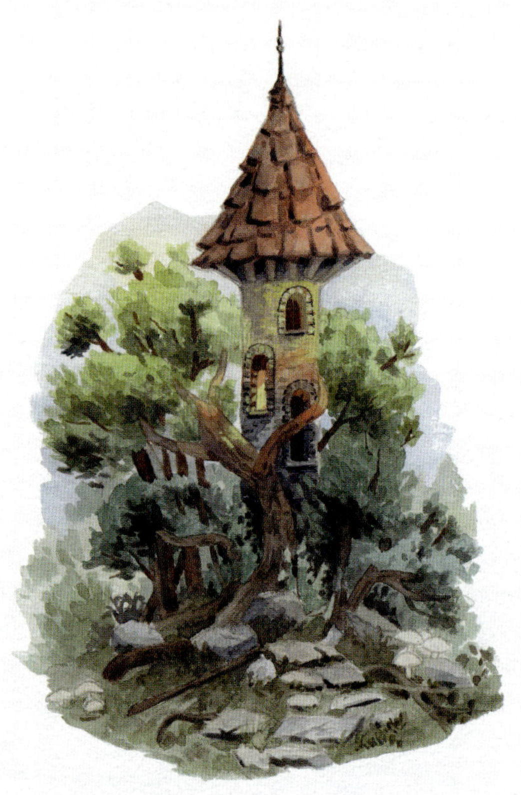

Brushes

Round brush 10, 2, 0

Colors

Vermillion

Gamboge

Burnt Sienna

Yellow Ochre

Payne's Grey

Sap Green

Ultramarine Blue

Crimson Lake Red

Deep Blue

Gouache

Titanium White

Hansa Yellow Medium

Burnt Sienna

Ultramarine Blue

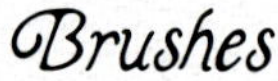

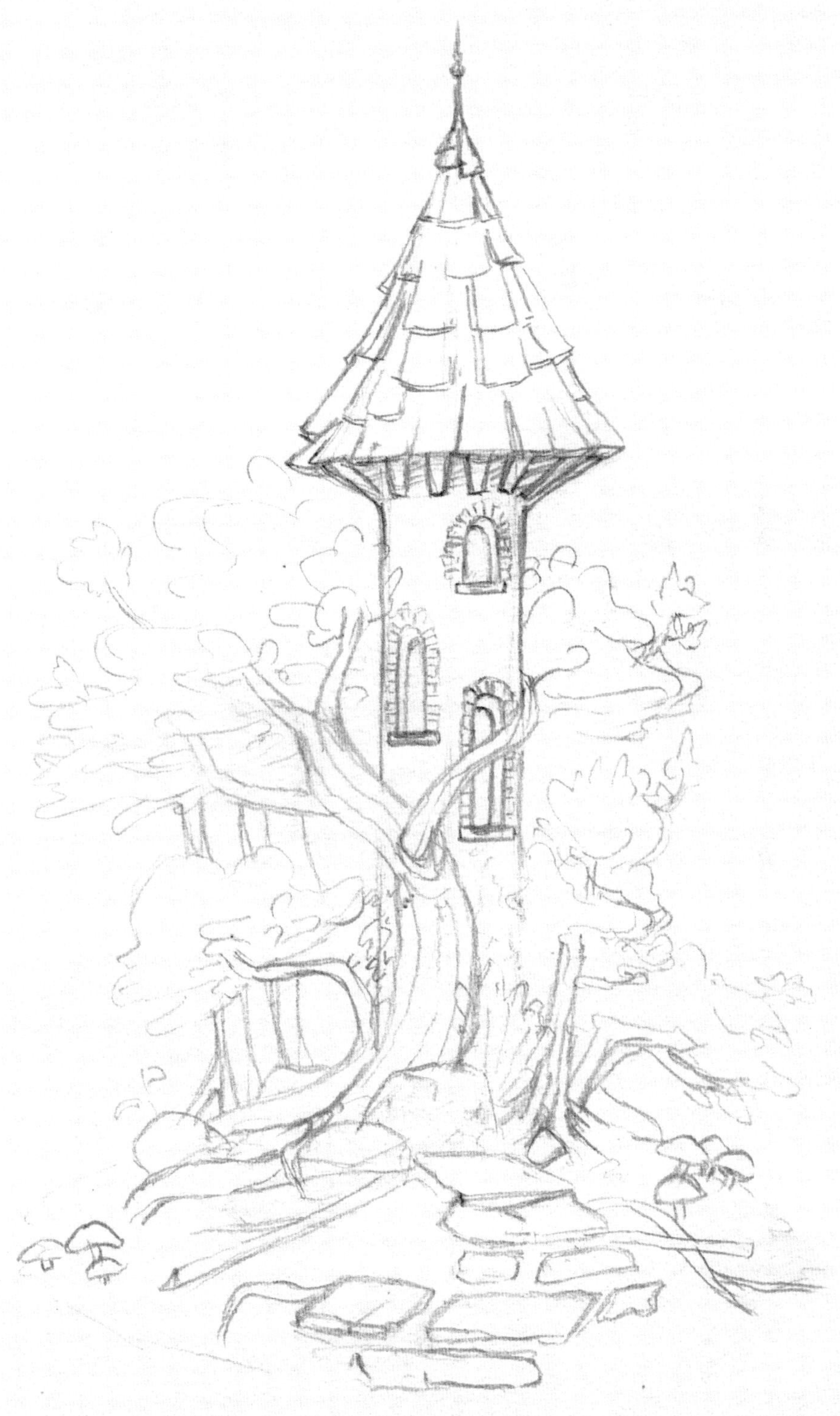

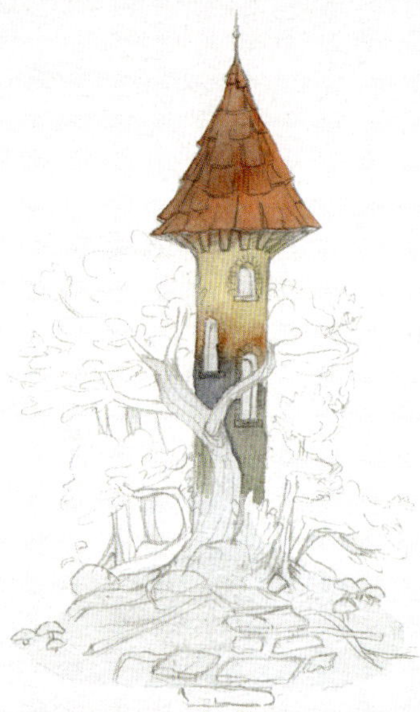 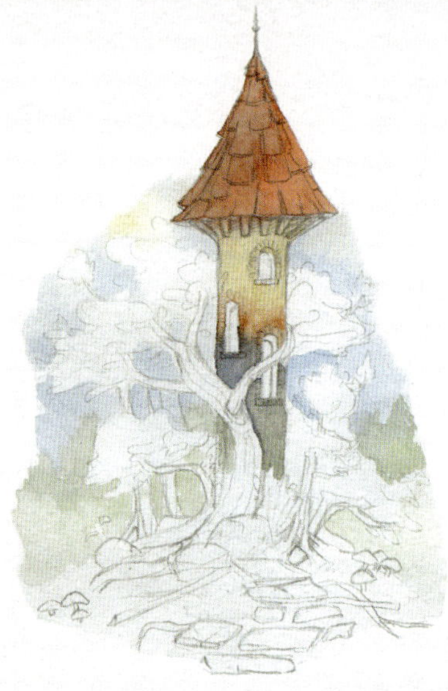

Step 1

Draw the base sketch, using my drawing as a reference. Feel free to alter the composition according to your imagination—noting that the key piece to keep in the illustration is the looming wizard tower with the pointed ceiling and its curving windows.

Step 2

Work quickly on a wet layer using your round brush 10 and *The Bead Method* described in Chapter 1 (see page 15). First, mix the color of the roof using Vermillion + Gamboge + a touch of Burnt Sienna. Apply this color to the entire surface of the roof.

Next use a light wash of Yellow Ochre for the top portion of the tower, until the top of the second window. While the color is still wet, dab Burnt Sienna across the tower in an angle. And finally, at the bottom of the second window, use Payne's Grey for the shadow part of the tower. To suggest that

the tower is reflecting all the green trees around it, dab Payne's Grey + Sap Green at the furthest bottom of the tower.

Let the water blend the colors together naturally. Continue to the next step after a few minutes of waiting to let the colors dry completely.

Step 3

In this step, we're going to lay out the base for the background. Continue using your round brush 10 dipped in a fair amount of water. Start with a light wash of Yellow Ochre to paint the upper areas, imagining where glowing sunset clouds would be. Then use Ultramarine Blue + Payne's Grey diluted with a lot of water to paint the rest of the sky.

Further down, use Sap Green + Yellow Ochre + a touch of Payne's Grey to suggest foliage in the background.

Let this layer dry thoroughly.

Step 4

Time for the greenery and surrounding forest. For this step, keep the lighting of the scene in mind: Imagine a glowing orange-yellow sunset. The light will strike the upper parts of this scene, affecting the colors of the tower, the trees, and the sky.

First, mix Sap Green + Gamboge, and paint the upper bunches of the trees' leaves. Imagine some trees are behind others. Paint these with Sap Green + Crimson Lake Red.

Moving lower into the shadow, mix Sap Green + Deep Blue + a touch of Payne's Grey. The color of the shadows will be cooler, using more blue and Payne's Grey the lower we paint.

Keep your brushstrokes loose but intentional: Imagine the shadows cast on a shrub that is *behind* another shrub, as described in *The Inverse Painting Technique* in Chapter 1 (see page 17). Imagine the little bunches of leaves that sprout from a larger tree, and paint a suggestion of them.

Also remember to leave some space between tree canopies for the branches and tree trunks.

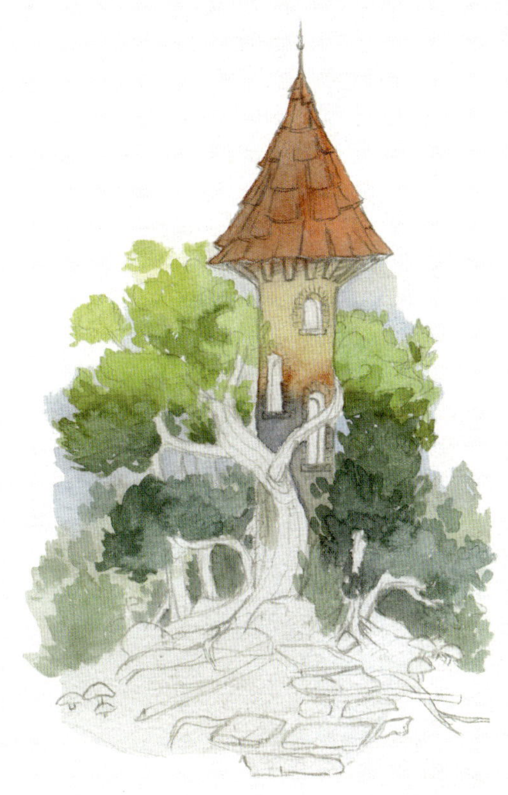

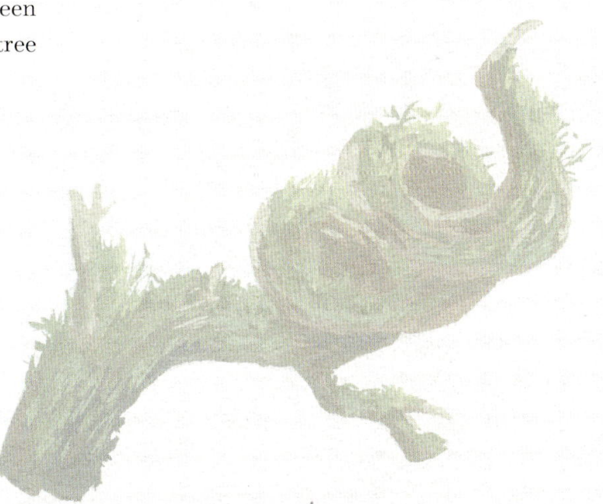

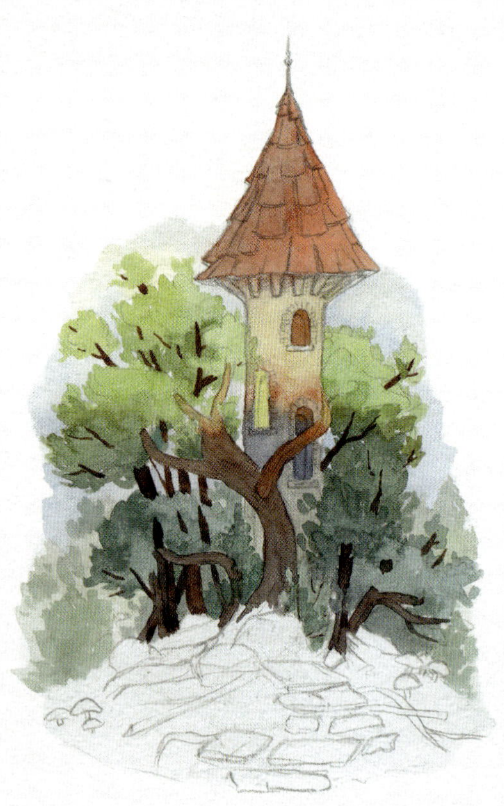

Step 5

Switch to your round brush 2. Let's begin painting the sticks and branches on this scene. Some parts of the large trunk curving around the tower will be lit with the sunset glow. Use a gradient of Yellow Ochre, then Burnt Sienna, then Burnt Sienna + Ultramarine Blue.

For the rest of the branches, use Ultramarine Blue + Burnt Sienna. Paint trunks and narrow branches. Leave gaps in between, giving the effect of the branch going through the foliage.

Next, use Burnt Sienna to paint over the first window. Then use the same color to paint only the top of the third window, before creating a gradient into Payne's Grey.

Finally, use Gamboge to paint the second window (the one facing away from the sunset glow). This window will have the light of someone working inside.

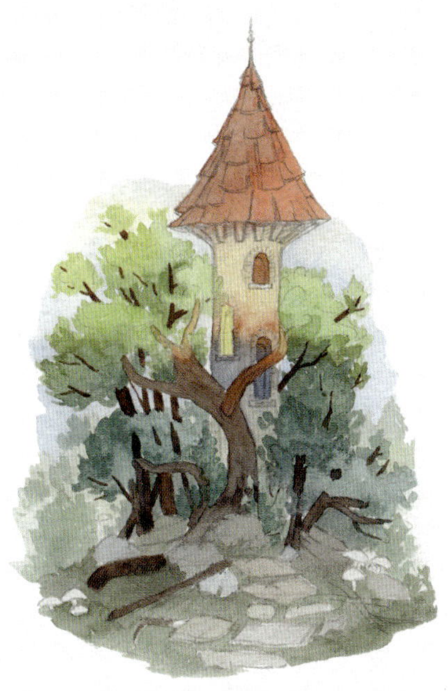

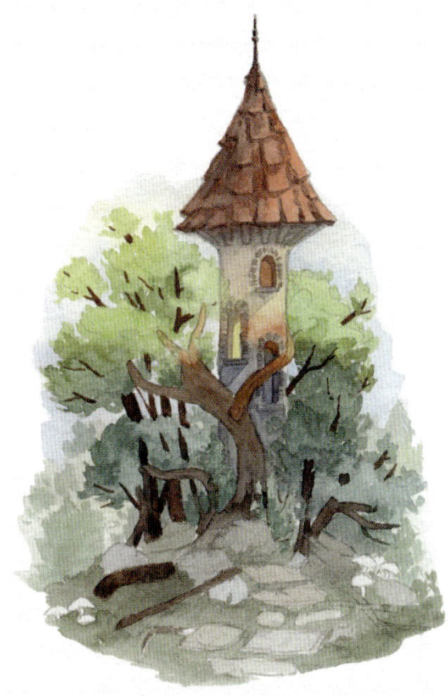

Step 6

Let's fill up the remaining unpainted areas. First, paint all the stepping stones and rocks around them using Payne's Grey + Yellow Ochre, diluted with a fair amount of water. Paint them in different shades of the two colors randomly: some stones with more Yellow Ochre in the mixture, others with more Payne's Grey in the mixture.

Use the same brown color from Step 5 (Burnt Sienna + Ultramarine Blue) for the tree roots.

Then for the grass, mix Sap Green + Payne's Grey + Burnt Sienna. While painting the ground, be careful to avoid the tiny mushrooms.

Step 7

Now we can begin the fun parts: pushing the contrast in the light and shadow.

Begin painting the roof tiles on the tower. Use Crimson Lake Red + Payne's Grey to paint a thin wash over the left side of the tower, enhancing its circular shape. Then, while the paint is still wet, use the same color to outline the shadows on the roof tiles, and paint the pointed spire at the top.

Now use Payne's Grey to paint the shadow on the left side of the tower and directly below the roof. Use the same color to paint the tiny spots of the stones around the windows, as well as angular shadows beneath the windows and window sills. Paint the rest of the bottom of the tower Payne's Grey, darkening the forest floor and enhancing the light even more.

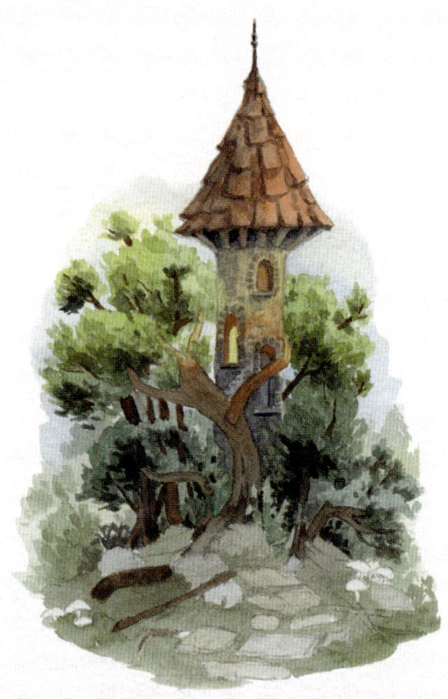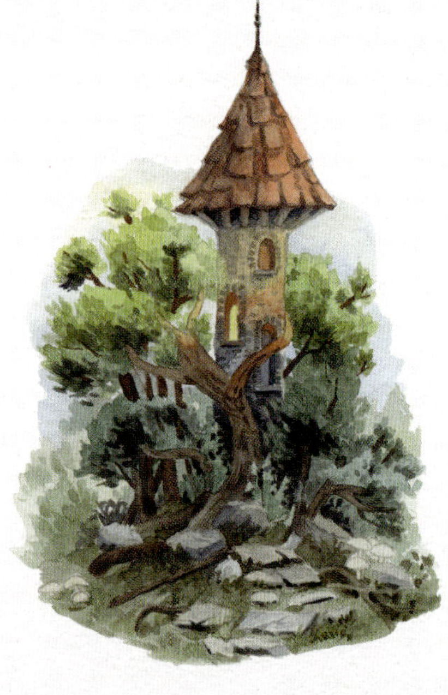

Step 8

Switch to your round brush 0 for painting these detailed shadows. Use a thick mixture of Payne's Grey to paint the shadows inside the tower's rafters beneath the roof. Dilute the grey with a bit of water, and paint little spots to suggest stone bricks across the tower and to deepen the lines on the windowsills.

Next, use Payne's Grey + Sap Green + a touch of Crimson Lake Red to begin painting the dark shadows on the leaf canopies on the bottom trees. For the tree shadows on the top, use Sap Green + Crimson Lake Red. Slowly layer these shades over each other, creating little spots of interest and shape.

Step 9

Use your round brush 2 for this step. Mix Sap Green + Payne's Grey, and begin painting the spots on the grass where sticks intersect, and boulders and mushrooms cast shadows, applying *The Inverse Painting Technique* from Chapter 1 (see page 17). Then mix Sap Green + Yellow Ochre, and paint in quick brushstrokes to create spots that suggest different varieties of grass growing on the forest floor. Use pure Payne's Grey to paint the shadows on the boulders, painting sharp lines to indicate cracks.

Then mix Burnt Sienna + Payne's Grey, and paint some of the lines of the tree bark.

Finally, use a thin wash of Yellow Ochre + Crimson Lake Red to paint the small mushrooms.

Step 10

For this final step, we're going to bring out some gouache paint to fix some of the lighting. First, using your round brush 0, use Payne's Grey to paint angular shadows across the curving tree branches.

Now bring out your gouache. Use Titanium White gouache + Hansa Yellow Medium, and paint the upper part of the tower, bringing back the glow on the building. Use the same color to paint spots of light on the tree bark that's outside the glowing window.

Then use Burnt Sienna gouache to paint the inside of the window, and Burnt Sienna + Yellow Ochre watercolor for the inner rim. Do the same thing for the third window (on the bottom), and blend the color into Ultramarine Blue + Burnt Sienna. Use the same color (Ultramarine Blue + Burnt Sienna) to paint the outer brick linings of the windows, emphasizing their shape, as well as the line of the brick that turns inside the window.

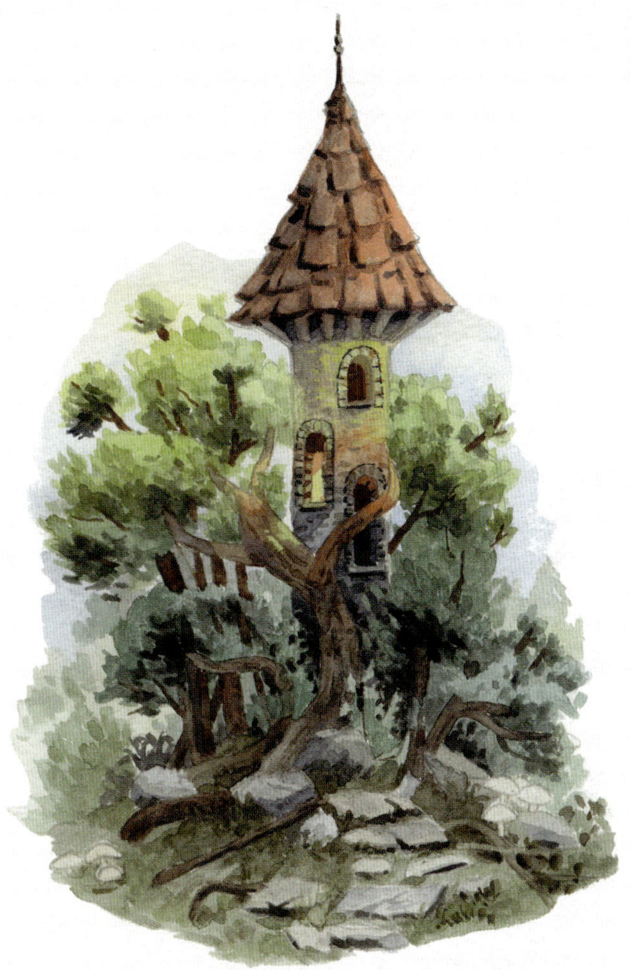

Finally, like a flick of your staff, use Vermillion watercolor, and paint an angular shadow on the window with the yellow internal light.

And with that, we've successfully constructed our own wizard's tower, where we can make a cup of tea—and plan our next scheme.

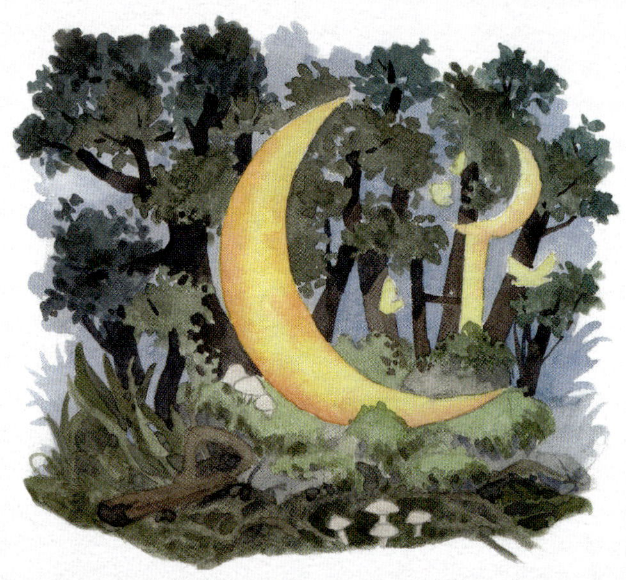

The Waning Moonflies

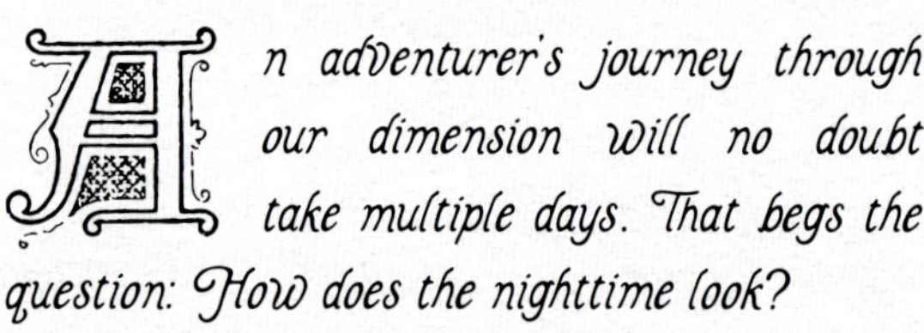
An adventurer's journey through our dimension will no doubt take multiple days. That begs the question: How does the nighttime look?

Our dimension will have not one, but two moons, with a whimsical glowing waterfall. And these moons shall forever stay in the same phase. And to make it extra whimsical, these moons will not be in the sky: They will be among the trees and rocks on the ground. As such, a magical species of moonflies will sprout from the light of these moons, creating an awe-inspiring scene for visitors to gaze upon.

Brushes

Round brush 10, 2

Colors

Gamboge

Vermillion

Ultramarine Blue

Payne's Grey

Deep Green

Crimson Lake Red

Sap Green

Burnt Sienna

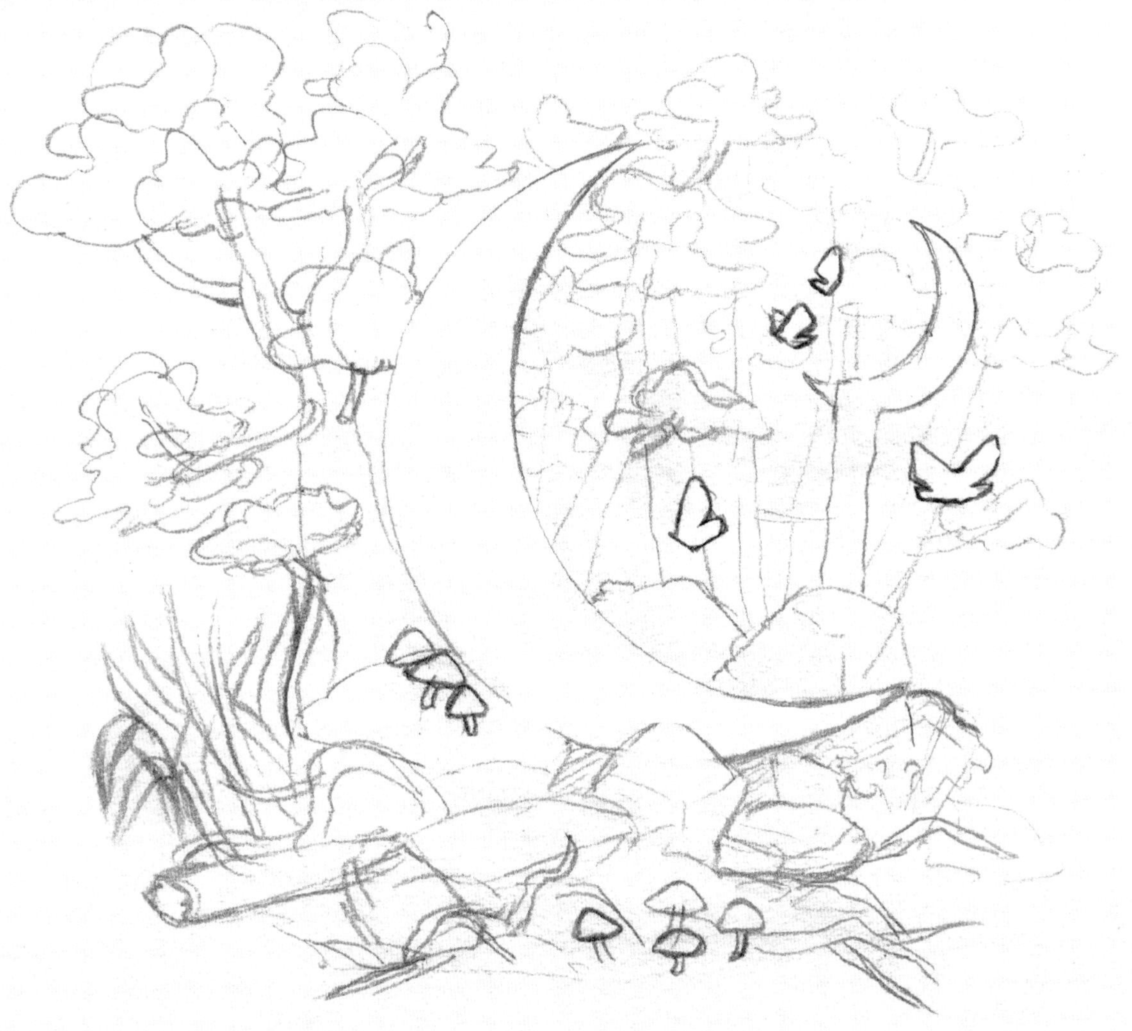

Step 1

Draw the pencil sketch onto your water-color paper, using my drawing as a reference. Here the key shapes are the moons—use a compass or circular object to draw a perfect crescent. The rest of the scene can be altered according to your imagination.

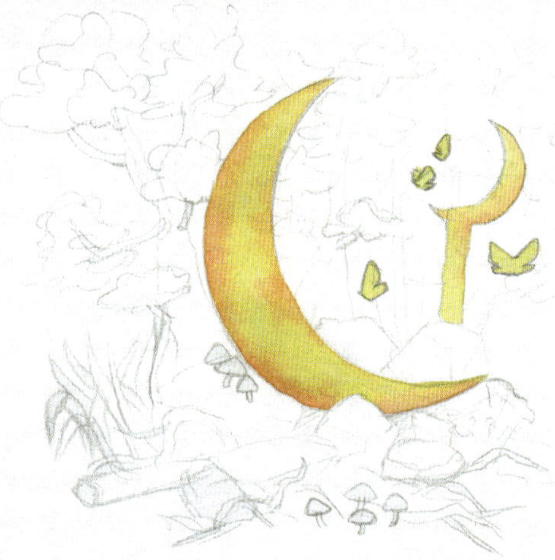

Step 2

Begin with your round brush 10, dipped in a fair amount of water. Use pure Gamboge with an equal part of water to paint the moons and all the moonflies. Then, working quickly while the paint is still wet to apply *The Wet-on-Wet Technique* described in Chapter 1 (see page 15), mix a touch of Vermillion into the Gamboge, making a bright-orange color. Quickly dab spots of this color on the outer edges of the moons, and watch how the pigments mix into each other naturally.

While the paint is still wet, dab more Vermillion into the outer edges.

Let this layer dry thoroughly

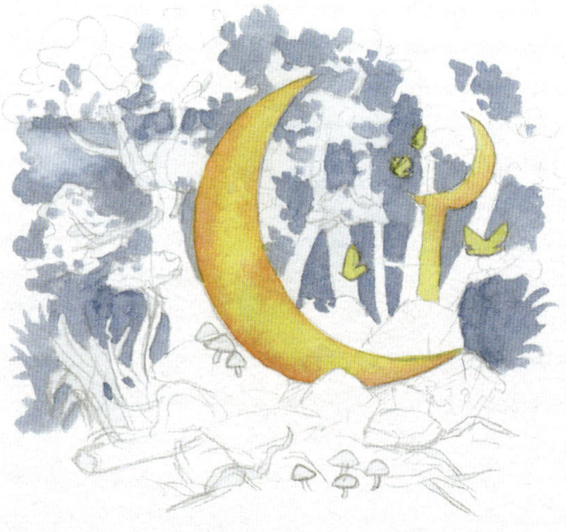

Step 3

Since we're painting a nighttime scene, mix Ultramarine Blue + Payne's Grey, and begin painting the dark sky using your round brush 2. On the outer edges, mimic the shape of the leaf canopies and grass blades to create a cohesive piece. Be careful to avoid the trees and branches—but paint spots in between the tree canopies to show some of the sky color peeking through the leaves (which we will paint later.)

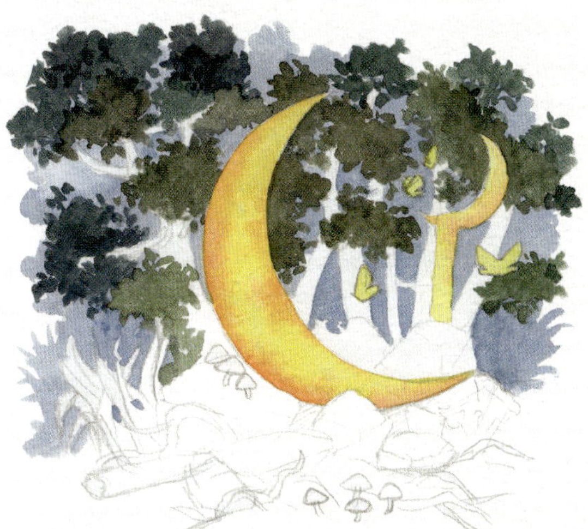

Step 4

For this step, you will be mixing two shades of green. The first green is Deep Green + Payne's Grey + a touch of Crimson Lake Red. Apply this color to the tree canopies that are farthest away from any of the moons and moonflies.

To create the second green, which is warmer, mix Sap Green + a touch of Crimson Lake Red. Apply this color to all the leaf canopies that are close to the moons or facing the moons.

Use short but careful brushstrokes to create circular leaves on the canopies, overlaying the different shades.

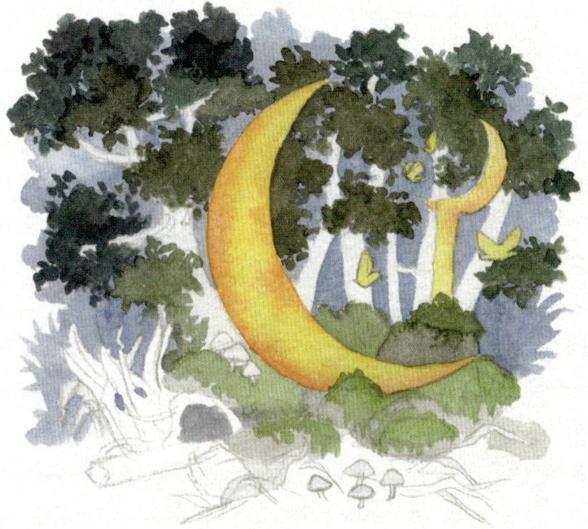

Step 5

Now let's begin painting the moss-covered rocks. Use Payne's Grey + a touch of Gamboge diluted with a lot of water. Paint all the rocks surrounding the large moon. Then mix Sap Green + Gamboge + a touch of Crimson Lake Red to desaturate the green a little, and paint the moss on top of the rocks. Be careful to avoid the moon itself.

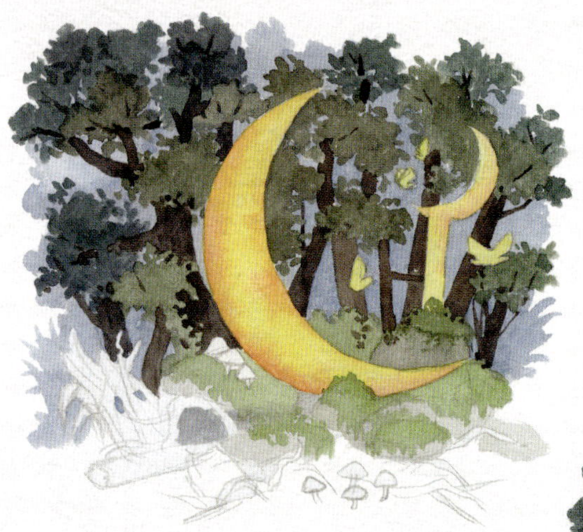

Step 6

Mix Burnt Sienna + Ultramarine Blue + Payne's Grey to get a dark grey-brown color. Using your round brush 2, paint all the tree trunks and little branches sprouting between the leaf canopies.

Add more Burnt Sienna in the mixture to paint the tree branches that are closest to the moons.

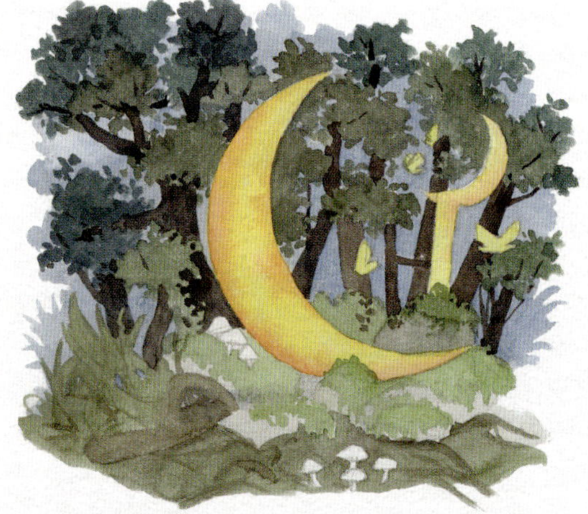

Step 7

Now paint the grass using Sap Green + a touch of Burnt Sienna to get an olive-green color. Apply this color to the entire surface of the ground, carefully painting those strands of grass on the left, and avoiding the tiny mushrooms.

Wait for that layer to dry for a few minutes. Then apply another layer of Burnt Sienna over the larger sticks and fallen logs on the ground, using *The Glazing Method* (page 16) to deepen their form.

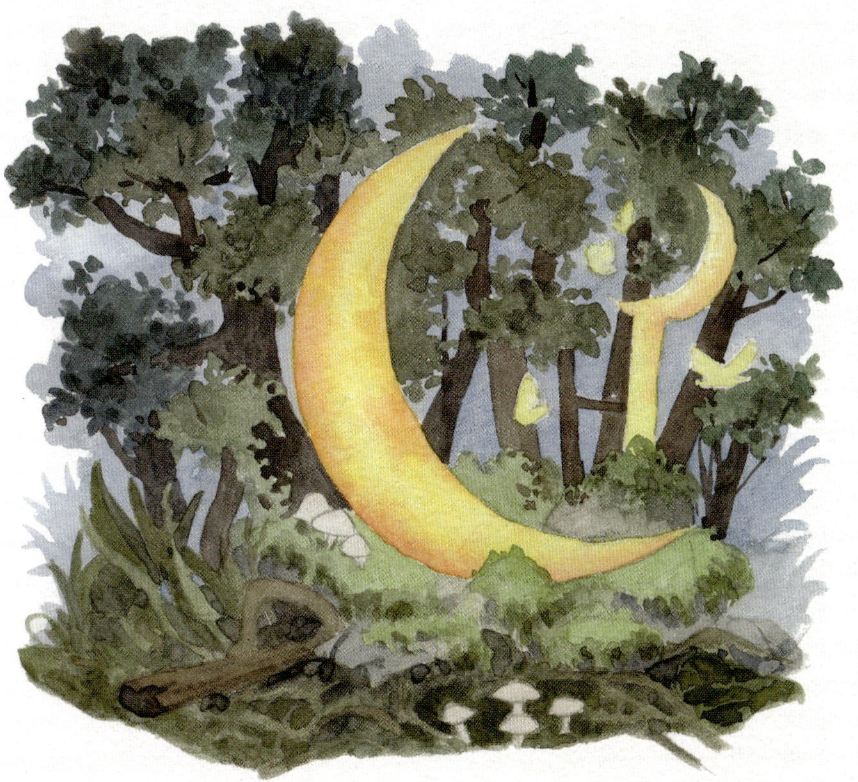

Step 8

With your round brush 2, begin defining the shadows on the grassy ground. Use Payne's Grey + Sap Green, and apply spots of this color beneath the rocks, strands of grass, sticks, and tiny mushrooms, bringing out their shape with *The Inverse Painting Technique* (page 17).

Then use pure Payne's Grey to paint the shadows on the rocks, where the moss hangs over the edge.

Use Sap Green + a touch of Crimson Lake Red to paint shadows on the moss itself, where the moss faces away from the glowing moon.

Wait a few minutes for that to dry. Then, erase any pencil lines that are still visible, especially around the moonflies.

The next thing that needs our attention in this painting are the trees in the background. To define them with shadows, mix Sap Green + Crimson Lake Red + Payne's Grey. Apply this color to the bunches of leaves that face away from the glowing moons and moonflies.

While that's drying, glaze another layer of Burnt Sienna over the large log on the left and the stick curving above it, bringing them forward with the glow.

Finally, use pure Payne's Grey to deepen the circular end of the fallen log on the left, using *The Glazing Method* (page 16).

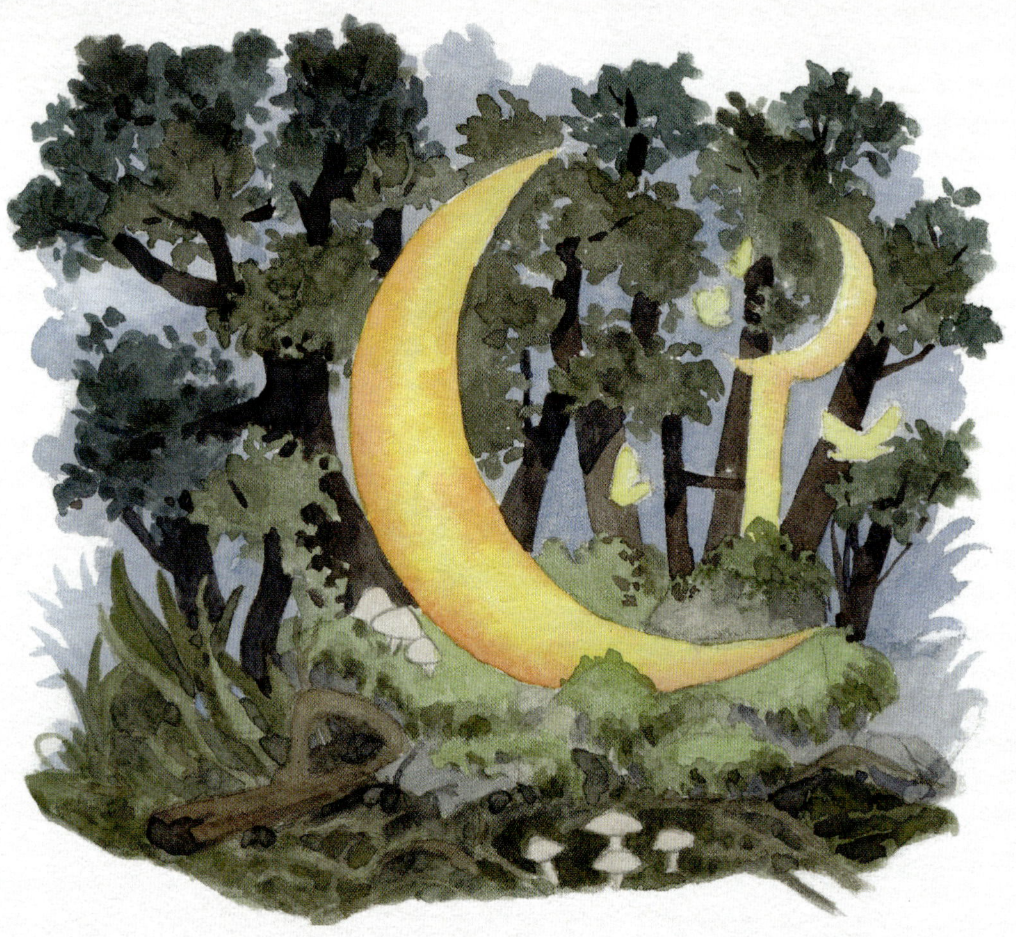

Step 9

The only magical elements left to paint now are the angular shadows across the tree branches. Use pure Payne's Grey, and apply these shadows on the upper branches that reach into a tree canopy. This final touch brings out the glow of the moons better, creating a finished scene.

With that, dear wizard, you've successfully used your arcane abilities to install a wondrous scene for our adventurers to bask in. Well done!

The Lantern Teahouse

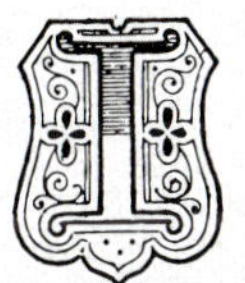 don't know about you, dear wizard, but I love a good storm. Thunder and rain present the perfect opportunity to boil a large kettle of tea, sit inside with warm candlelight, and watch the dark sky.

In this tutorial, we're going to paint a giant lantern that fell from its post long ago and has now been renovated into a little teahouse. I'm sure our adventurers, after battling dragons and poisonous mushrooms, will savor a good, cozy shelter. They will certainly need it, because the storms in our dimension can get pretty intense.

Brushes

Round brush 2, 0

Rigger brush 0 (optional)

Colors

Yellow Ochre

Lunar Blue

Sap Green

Payne's Grey

Crimson Lake Red

Lemon Yellow

Burnt Sienna

Phthalo Blue

Burnt Umber

Titanium White

Step 1

Draw the sketch onto your watercolor paper, using my drawing as a reference. Think of the lantern as a cube, and then draw the vines and hook on it. Inside, draw some furniture and an oval shape for the light bulb. The rest of the scene can be altered to your imagination; add more trees and vines as you see fit.

Step 2

Using your round brush 2, begin painting the light inside the lantern with a light wash of Yellow Ochre. While the paint is still wet, use *The Wet-on-Wet Technique* described in Chapter 1 (see page 15) to dab more Yellow Ochre on the right side of the lantern, indicating the shape more.

Paint a small oval shape of the same color on the top of the light, indicating the flame.

Step 3

Continue painting with your round brush 2. Use Lunar Blue with an equal part of water, and paint the dark, stormy background. Be careful to avoid the tree branches and trunks.

Then mix Sap Green + Payne's Grey, and paint the ground. Because this will be a wet and rainy scene, leave areas of white paper showing through to indicate puddles.

Let this layer dry completely before moving on to the next step.

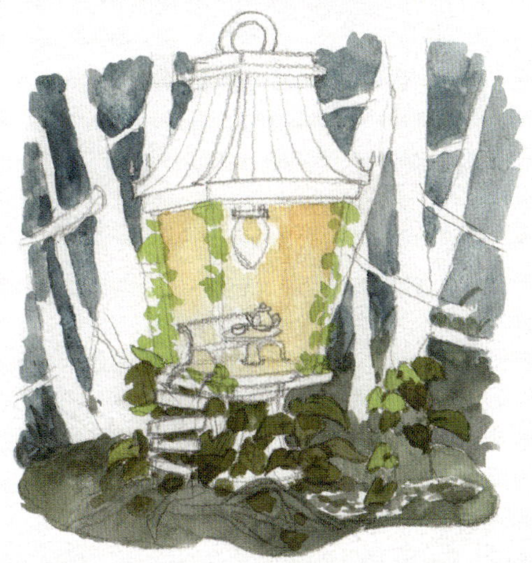

Step 4

Let's begin painting the leaves surrounding the lantern. Mix Sap Green + Payne's Grey + Crimson Lake Red, and paint the leaves that are beneath the lantern, disappearing into shadow.

For the light leaves, use Sap Green + Lemon Yellow. To indicate creeping vines along the sides of the lantern, dab spots of this color in leaf shapes.

Step 5

Use Burnt Sienna + Yellow Ochre to paint the top step of the ladder. Then mix Burnt Sienna + Payne's Grey to paint the rest of the steps descending into the shadow.

Next, use Payne's Grey + Yellow Ochre to paint the left side of the top metal part of the lantern. Then use pure Payne's Grey for the right side and the ring on the top. Use the same color for the base of the lantern—the part that touches the ground surrounded by the leaves.

For the metal below the roof of the lantern, use Payne's Grey + Phthalo Blue.

Step 6

Mix Burnt Umber + Payne's Grey + a touch of Phthalo Blue with an equal part of water. Paint the tree branches in the background, using more Phthalo Blue in the mixture to paint the trees closer to the foreground.

Step 7

Now let's paint the furniture inside the lantern. First, use Yellow Ochre + a touch of Payne's Grey to create a dull mustard color. Apply this color to all the surfaces that face *away* from the direct light striking from above: the backrest of the bench, the leg of the table, the curve of the kettle, and the cup. Also apply this color carefully to the right side of the lantern, creating shadows on the wall and texture.

While that's drying, mix Burnt Sienna + Payne's Grey, and paint the outline of the steps on the ladder, as well as the rope and two dots on either side of each plank.

Then go back to the bench. Using Payne's Grey diluted with water, deepen the shadow parts: the side of the bench and the shadow the kettle and cup cast on the table.

Use Yellow Ochre + Payne's Grey for the light fixture above the lantern. Then use Payne's Grey for the topmost rectangle.

When that's dry, erase the pencil lines.

Step 8

Begin refining the details on the leaf-littered floor. Use Sap Green + Payne's Grey to paint more shapes of leaves scattered across the ground. Then use Sap Green + Burnt Sienna, and paint the rest of the ground in quick spots, creating texture and color variation. Use this same color to paint the shadows around the leaves you established.

Then use Sap Green + Payne's Grey to paint more leaves wrapping around the tree branches.

Next, use the Burnt Umber + Payne's Grey mixture from Step 6, and paint numerous smaller sticks sprouting among the chaos of leaves and trees in the background. Paint more leaves on those background sticks, using Sap Green + Payne's Grey.

Now use pure Payne's Grey to darken the bottom of the sky.

Switch to your round brush 0. Use Burnt Umber + Payne's Grey, and deepen the shadows on the lamp's stand, in between all the leaves. Also use this color to paint the shadow parts of the roof of the lantern, and the curves.

Finally, use some of the sky color (Lunar Blue) to paint over the white of the puddles, where the water will reflect the sky.

Step 9

This scene is almost done. The last step is to paint the rain! For this step, use Titanium White watercolor, and a long rigger brush 0. The rigger brush is optional; if you don't have a rigger, you can alternatively use your round brush 0. Dip your brush into the watery paint. Then, with a super-delicate stroke, paint drops of rain falling vertically.

Paint droplets falling on a leaf, and then pooling on the leaf below, and then dropping off that leaf, cascading like a waterfall.

Also apply spots of white highlights on the top plank of the ladder and the puddles.

With those final white spots of light, this scene is complete. Our visitors can reward themselves after a long and perilous journey with freshly brewed lantern tea.

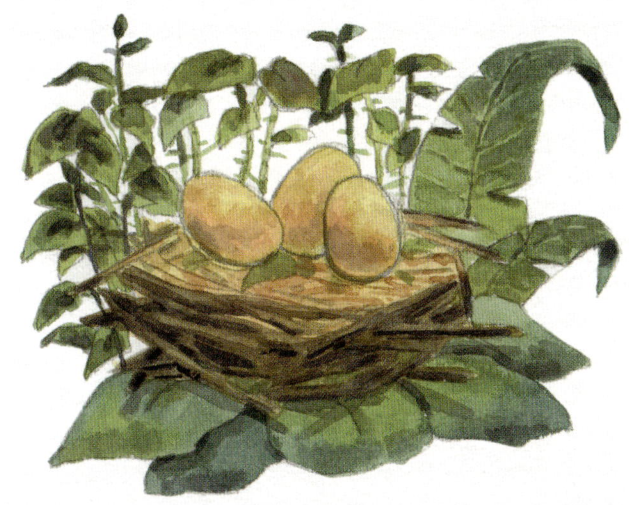

The Moss Dragon's Nest

very wizard's dimension has a dragon. It's tradition. It wouldn't be a complete adventure without our heroes feeling the anticipation of something gargantuan breathing in the dark or hearing the terrifying roar of these creatures in the distance.

The Moss Dragon is a unique species that camouflages itself onto a rock, appearing as moss. Nature's first green is gold, so this dragon's eggs glow brightly in their nest, emitting great power that causes the flora around it to erupt in growth. In this tutorial, we're going to paint this dragon (or three) and invite them into our watercolor dimension.

Brushes

Round brush 10, 2, 0

Colors

Gamboge

Yellow Ochre

Vermillion

Sap Green

Crimson Lake Red

Deep Blue

Burnt Sienna

Payne's Grey

Gouache (optional)

Titanium White

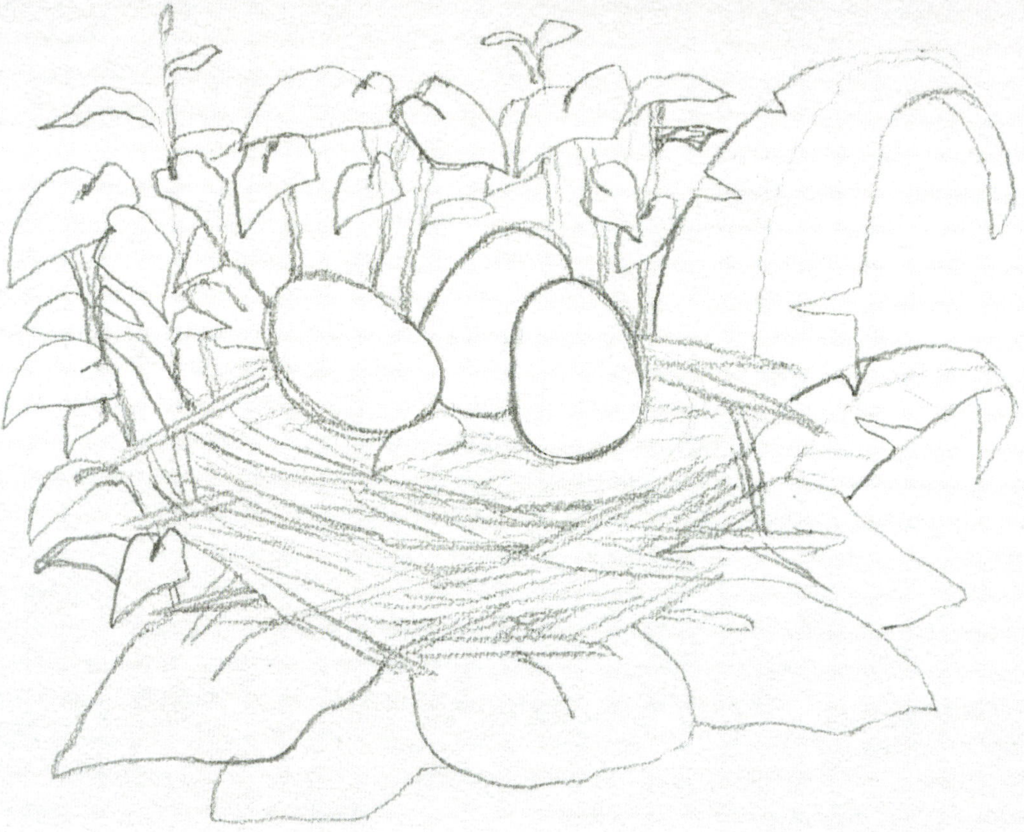

Step 1

Draw or trace the base sketch onto your watercolor paper, using my drawing as a reference. Think of the nest as a bowl shape, and then draw short, straight lines to indicate twigs. Besides the nest itself, the key shapes to draw are the oval eggs nestled inside.

Step 2

Use your round brush 10 for this step. Mix Gamboge + Yellow Ochre with an equal part of water, and paint the three eggs inside the nest. While the paint is still wet, use *The Wet-on-Wet Technique* described in Chapter 1 (see page 16) to dab spots of Yellow Ochre + Vermillion into the paint, on the curve of the oval eggs.

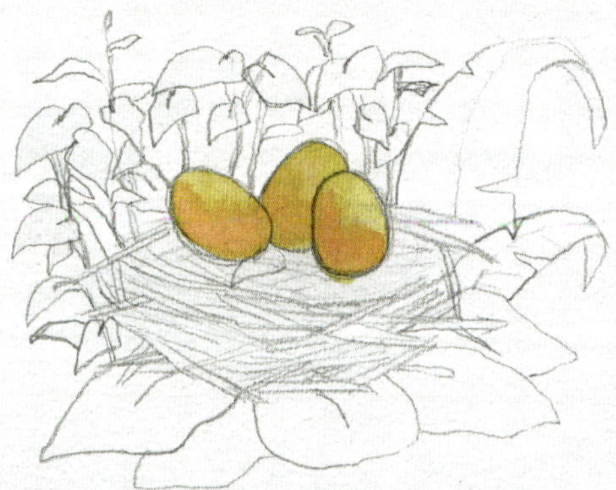

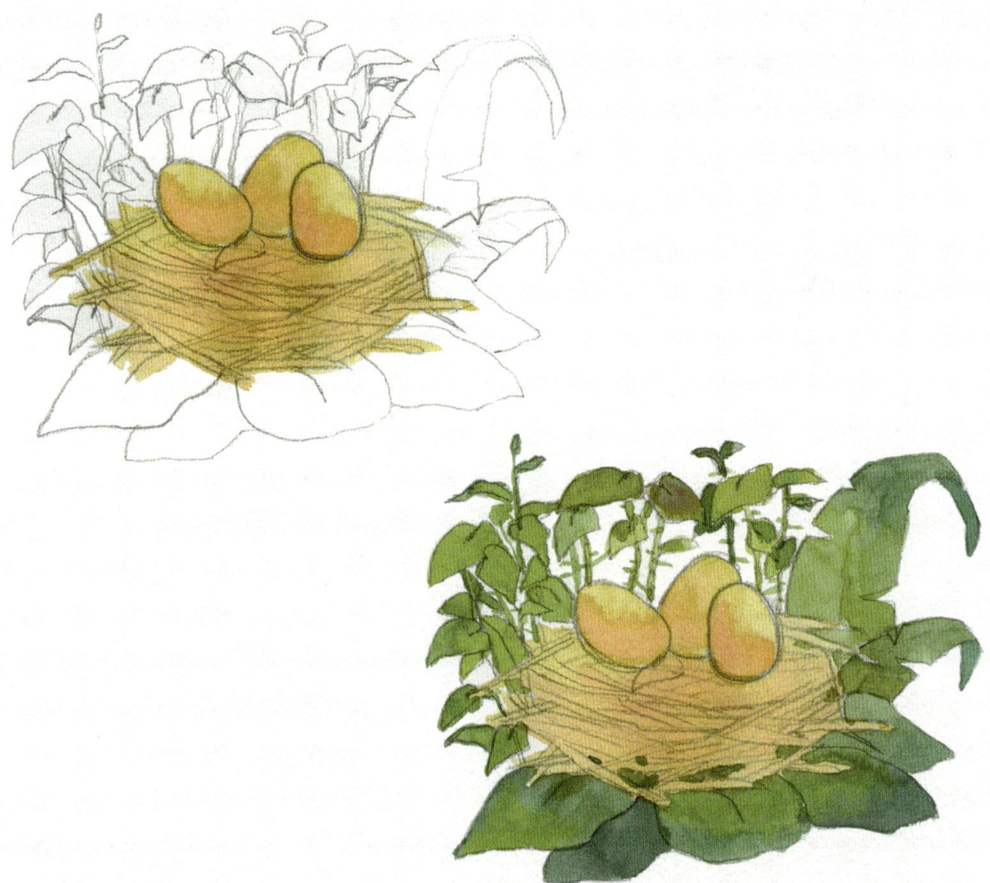

Step 3

Continue with your round brush 10. You will be using the process you painted the eggs with to paint the base color for the sticks in the nest. First, use a light wash of Yellow Ochre + Gamboge, and cover all the sticks. Then, with *The Wet-on-Wet Technique* (page 16), dab spots of wet Vermillion + Yellow Ochre into the paint.

Let the paint dry completely before moving on to the next step.

Step 4

Switch to your round brush 2. Start painting the leaves around the nest using Sap Green + Gamboge + a touch of Crimson Lake Red. Use this color for the parts of the leaves that face toward the nest.

Transition that color into dark blue-green by mixing Sap Green + Deep Blue + Crimson Lake Red. Work while the paint is wet, and allow the two colors to granulate together, creating texture and interest.

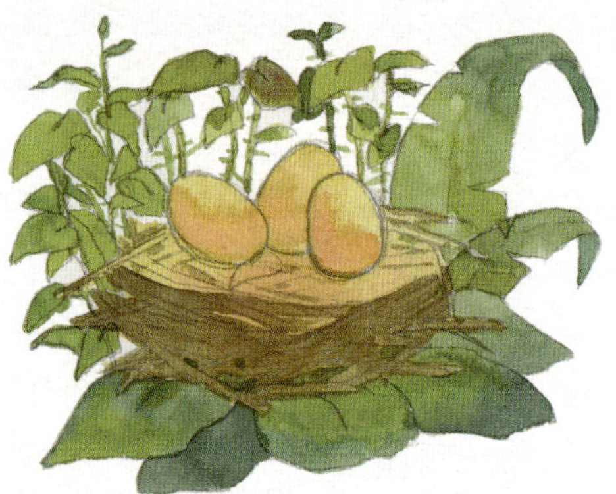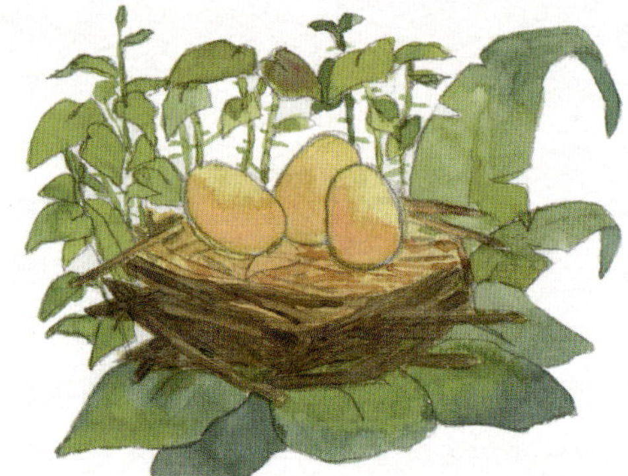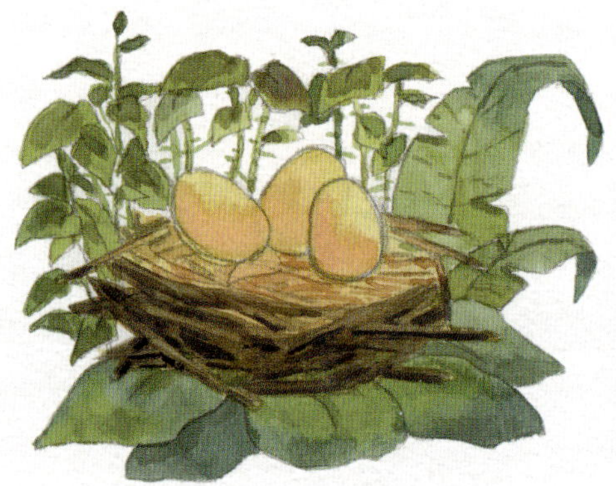

Step 5

We can now begin creating a glow coming from within the nest. Use a thin wash of Burnt Sienna + Deep Blue, and paint the front of the nest. Keep in mind the "bowl" shape of the nest, and let some darks overlap the light to create depth.

Step 6

Next, paint another layer of Burnt Sienna + Deep Blue on the shadow side of the sticks, paying more attention to each shape and the shadow it will cast.

For shadow on the inside of the nest, use Burnt Sienna + Yellow Ochre.

Step 7

Switch to your round brush 0. Use Payne's Grey to darken the lines and shadows of the sticks in the dark.

Then mix Sap Green + a touch of Payne's Grey to paint little shadows on the leaves and stems behind the nest, defining their shape and form a bit more. Repeat the same technique on the leaves on the bottom of the nest.

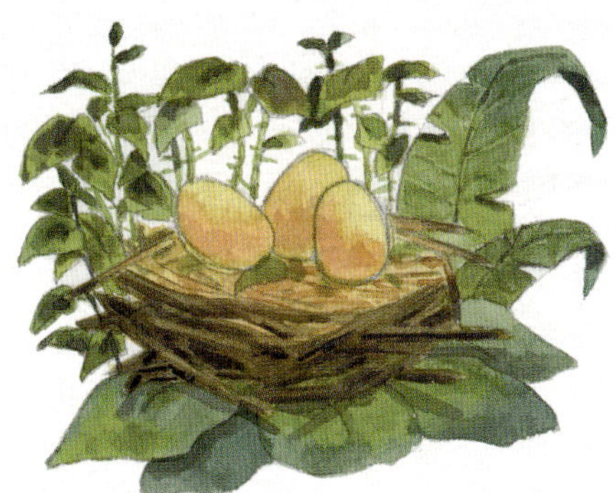

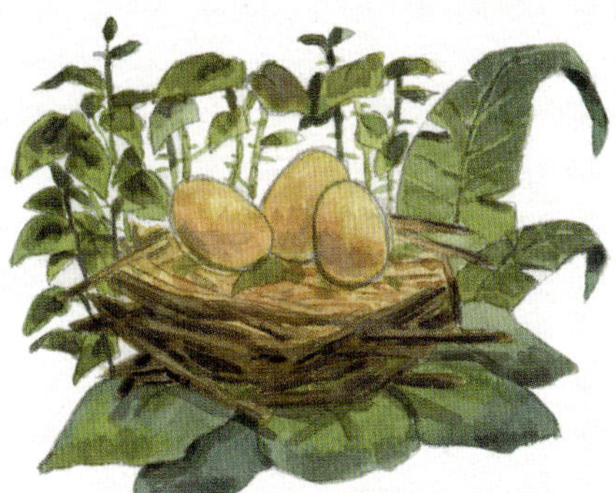

Step 8

Continue using your round brush 0 and Payne's Grey. Dilute the color with an equal part of water, and paint the shadows of the sticks cast across the ground leaves. Apply the same color on the curve of the two triangular leaves on the right-hand side, as well as the shadows on the little leaves and stems above the nest.

Then mix Sap Green + Yellow Ochre, and paint the front of those triangular leaves, creating detail by avoiding a thin line for the color beneath to peek through, suggesting the veins on the leaf. Apply this same color for suggestions of leaves inside the nest itself.

Finally, use a thin, watery mixture of Yellow Ochre + Vermillion to paint the curve on the oval eggs, creating hints of texture and variation.

Step 9

We're almost done with this nest! We just need a few final touches in the shadow areas to define the forms of the different objects in our scene. First, use a very watery mixture of Payne's Grey, and dab it across the curve of the eggs, indicating their round form.

Then use Payne's Grey + Sap Green to deepen the shadow spots on the bottom leaves and the veins on the triangular leaves on the right. As you paint farther upward on those leaves, darken the shadows using more Payne's Grey. This creates more form, and it enhances the glow effect.

And that marks the completion of this dragon nest! Somewhere within this dimension, the dragon who laid these eggs stealthily hunts our adventurers. That's a job well done for us wizards.

Apprentice Notes:

To create yet more interest on the dragon's eggs, use Titanium White gouache to paint shiny spots.

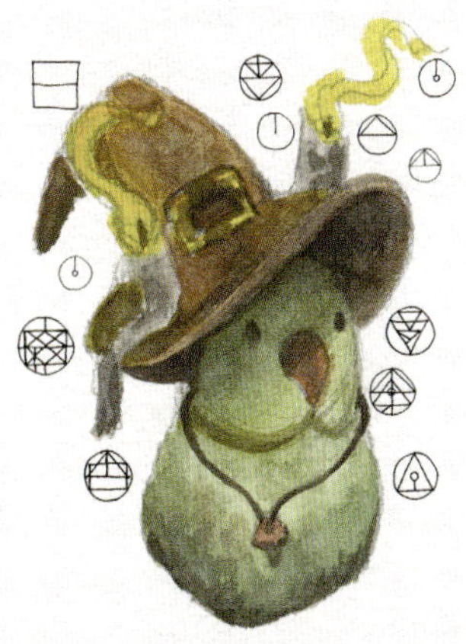

AFTERWORD

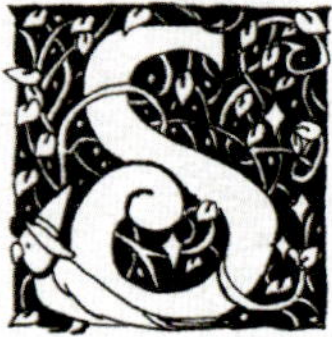

o, you've created your very own watercolor dimension. That means we've reached the end of the line, and our journey together ends here. I am honored to have been part of your initiation into all things sorcery and wizardry. I hope that this book not only inspired you and tingled your inner child-like mischievousness but also sparked a bonfire of curiosity. What you have achieved is no small feat. A wizard and their dimension are like . . . well, two very important things that go great together.

Though our collaboration ends here, your personal wizard journey has only begun. You have yet to climb the corporate ladder—and by that I mean you have yet to use your powers to taunt as many unsuspecting heroes and heroines as you can. Direct your ever-green imagination to the magic of the world, and paint it with your magic staff. I have no doubt you will use the knowledge from this book to create wonders and impact the wizarding community with ground-breaking discoveries.

What branch of sorcery will you further study and specialize in? Perhaps your interest lingered in Chapter 2, and you wish to heal the world with medicinal plants and tree components. Perhaps your natural desires will lead you to delve further into darker studies and be on the necromantic frontier, growing mushrooms in your wake. Or, perhaps, you simply love a good rock.

Perhaps there are more subjects we haven't even touched in this book, and they are out there for you to envelop: the elements, the stars, dust, galaxies, and beyond.

Go on. Be a wizard.

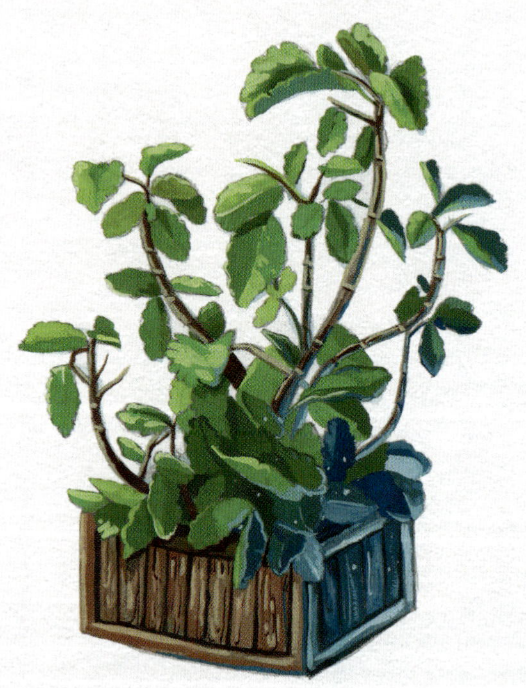

Acknowledgments

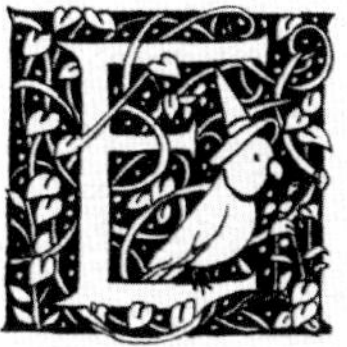 very witch or wizard has their coven, a tribe of people they can depend on for anything the world throws at them. This book would not have been possible without the incredible support of my coven.

My parents are the best parents anybody could ask for; their unconditional love and support have allowed me to pursue art as a career, an unconventional occupation that is not often encouraged in our community. Thank you to Mom for endless tingling conversations about adventures in India, history, magic, science, astrology—all over morning chai. Thank you to Pops for being the sturdy ground I need whenever work feels overwhelming. Being an artist naturally keeps me in my own mind a lot, painting and thinking of new ideas for stories, with my nose in my sketchbook, especially when I'm working on a big project like this book—and I can't thank my parents enough for looking after our home when that happens.

Thank you to my little sister, who was the first to read all my stories during bedtime, for all your imaginative ideas and plot twists, and for constantly tolerating my weirdness wherever we go. I am forever grateful I have you to create the craziest songs with during load shedding.

Next, thank you to Jude, my incredibly patient partner and adventure buddy, whose encouragement and love have been invaluable.

My art tribe friends—namely Chyavan, Virush, Trisha, and Sunny—are a constant source of inspiration and adventure. I can't forget my online art tribe: all the kind people who love my work enough to follow me, become a patron, purchase a print or artwork, send me a wonderful DM or email, meet me at artist alleys, or even just enjoy my artworks behind the scenes in silent wonder. Your encouragement keeps me going, quite literally.

I also want to thank team Prime Art, especially Kelly, Sue, and John, for their unshaking belief in my work, and for investing in my art. Having access to high-quality art supplies is an insane privilege and honor for any artist, and I never take our relationship for granted.

A big thank you to all the people who made this book a dream come true. Thank you to my editor, Sarah, for her understanding, encouragement, and patience while I learned so many new things during this process. Thanks also go to the entire publishing team at Page Street for printing my imagination on paper and giving me this amazing opportunity to share my stories with so many people. From the editing to the design to the marketing, Team Page Street were the real wizards-behind-the-scenes.

Last, but not least, thank you, dear reader, for picking up this book. I believe a story is only alive when a reader ignites the words, so thank you for lending me your imagination.

About The Author

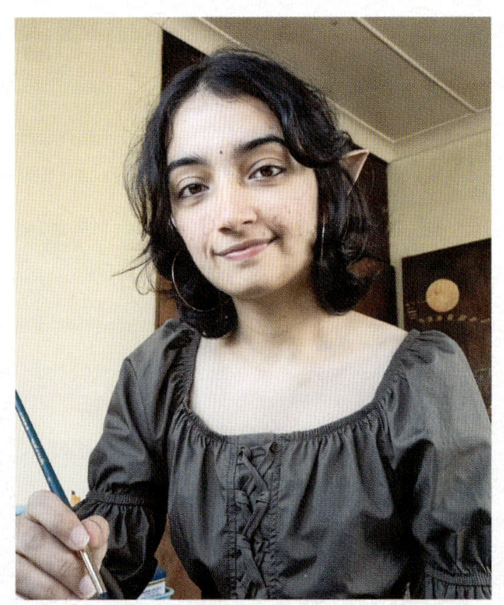

Kiara Maharaj (Kiara in the Forest) is an illustrator, writer, and wizard from the bottom-most tip of Africa. She often feels less like a human and more like a species of fungi you'd find feeding off the nutrients on dead wood. She spends most of her time in her sketchbooks, creating new worlds and adventurous characters, and writing mis-adventures for her fantasy short story series The Polkadot Files. When she's not writing or painting, she and her ringneck parrot play ball together and cook up new ideas for spells.

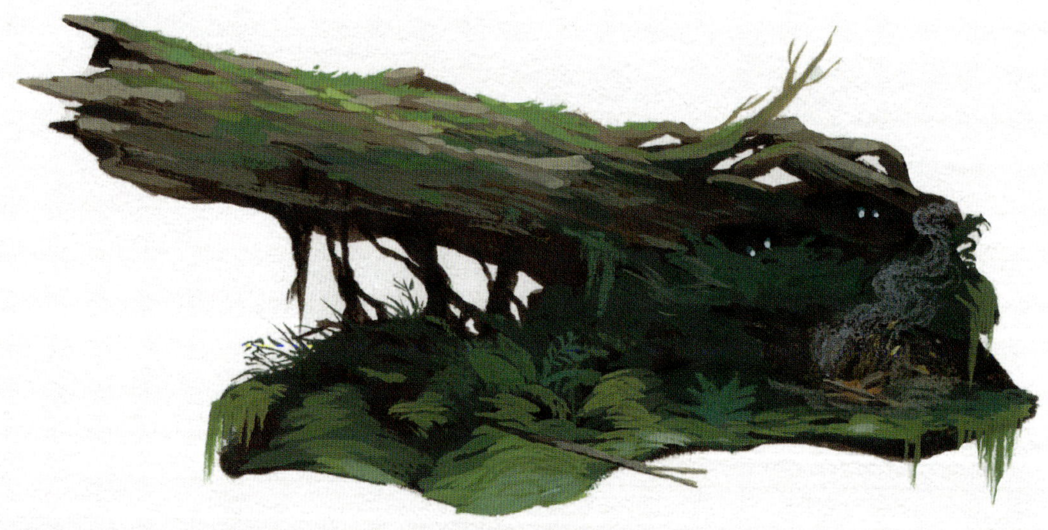

Index

B

bead method
    Dimension Never Reveals its Directions, A, 29
    Eyes from the Shadows, 49, 51
    Fresh Flowers for the Homesick, 75
    Grove of Wonders, The, 87
    Place for Adventurers to Rest, A, 54, 55
    Portal to the Unknown, 81
    Rocks of Past, Moss of Present, 157
    Rune Magic and Rock Rituals, 139
    Secrets of the Spores, 124
    Shadow Creatures of the Shade Tree, 62
    Simple, Safe, Slithering Stream, A, 145
    Tale of the Skeleton Tree, The, 34
    Talking Leafhead Tree, The, 69
    Techniques Used in this Book, 15
    Tentacles in the Tree Stump, 41
    Wizard's Tower of Chambers, The, 172
Book of Mosscraft, The, 164–169
brushes, in Supplies List, 11

C

cat, in Fungivore in the Underbrush, A, 114–120
Caves of Cadmus the Uncanny, The, 130–136
Characteristics of Watercolor versus Gouache, 13–14
Common Shapes and Color Combos, 20–21, 47, 62, 66

D

Dash of Mushrooms, A, 92–127
Dimension Never Reveals its Directions, A, 26–31
dry brush technique
    Fresh Flowers for the Homesick, 78
    Grove of Wonders, The, 91
    Techniques Used in this Book, 19
drying effect, in Characteristics of Watercolor versus Gouache, 14

E

Eyes from the Shadows, 45–51

F

Fresh Flowers for the Homesick, 73–78
frog, in Dimension Never Reveals its Directions, A, 26–31
Fungivore in the Underbrush, A, 114–120

G

glazing method
    Book of Mosscraft, The, 168
    Caves of Cadmus the Uncanny, The, 133, 134, 136
    Dimension Never Reveals its Directions, A, 30
    Fresh Flowers for the Homesick, 76, 77
    Goblin's Gemstone Stash, A, 153
    Path of the Toadstool, The, 112
    Pixie Party House, The, 98
    Rune Magic and Rock Rituals, 141
    Simple, Safe, Slithering Stream, A, 148
    Tale of the Skeleton Tree, The, 35, 36
    Techniques Used in this Book, 16–17
    Tentacles in the Tree Stump, 43, 44
    Waning Moonflies, The, 182, 183
Goblin's Gemstone Stash, A, 149–154
Grove of Wonders, The, 85–91

H

Handful of Rocks, A, 128–161
hat, wizard's
    Fungivore in the Underbrush, A, 114–120
    Mushroom Wizard, The, 100–106
    Tale of the Skeleton Tree, The, 32–38
Hint of Salt, And A, 162–195

I

inverse painting technique
    Book of Mosscraft, The, 168, 169
    Fungivore in the Underbrush, A, 118, 120
    Mushroom Wizard, The, 104
    Path of the Toadstool, The, 111
    Pixie Party House, The, 99
    Secrets of the Spores, 125
    Techniques Used in this Book, 17
    Waning Moonflies, The, 183
    Wizard's Tower of Chambers, The, 173, 176

L

Language of Shapes, The, 20
Lantern Teahouse, The, 11, 185–190
layering, in Characteristics of Watercolor versus Gouache, 14
lifting technique
    Book of Mosscraft, The, 167
    Fresh Flowers for the Homesick, 76
    Place for Adventurers to Rest, A, 59

Rocks of Past, Moss of Present, 157, 158
Simple, Safe, Slithering Stream, A, 145
Techniques Used in this Book, 18
light box, in Trace the Sketch, How to, 22

M

moon, in Waning Moonflies, The, 178–184
Moss Dragon's Nest, The, 191–195
mushrooms
Book of Mosscraft, The, 164–169
Dash of Mushrooms, A, 92–127
Fungivore in the Underbrush, A, 114–120
Mushroom Wizard, The, 100–106
Path of the Toadstool, The, 107–113
Pixie Party House, The, 94–99
Secrets of the Spores, 121–127
Waning Moonflies, The, 178–184
Mushroom Wizard, The, 100–106

O

opacity, in Characteristics of Watercolor versus Gouache, 13–14
owl, in Tale of the Skeleton Tree, The, 32–38

P

paint
Characteristics of Watercolor versus Gouache, 13–14
Supplies List, 10
palettes, in Supplies List, 11
paper, in Supplies List, 11
Path of the Toadstool, The, 107–113
pencils, in Supplies List, 12
pens, in Supplies List, 12
Pixie Party House, The, 94–99
Place for Adventurers to Rest, A, 52–59
Portal to the Unknown, 79–84

R

rabbit, in Rocks of Past, Moss of Present, 155–161
rocks
Caves of Cadmus the Uncanny, The, 130–136
Goblin's Gemstone Stash, A, 149–154
Handful of Rocks, A, 128–161
Rocks of Past, Moss of Present, 155–161
Rune Magic and Rock Rituals, 137–142
Simple, Safe, Slithering Stream, A, 143–148
Rocks of Past, Moss of Present, 155–161
Rune Magic and Rock Rituals, 137–142

S

Secrets of the Spores, 121–127
serpent, in Simple, Safe, Slithering Stream, A, 143–148
Shadow Creatures of the Shade Tree, 60–66

Simple, Safe, Slithering Stream, A, 143–148
snail, in Mushroom Wizard, The, 100–106
staff, wizard's, in Caves of Cadmus the Uncanny, The, 130–136
Supplies List, 10–12

T

Tale of the Skeleton Tree, The, 32–38
Talking Leafhead Tree, The, 67–72
teacup, in Fresh Flowers for the Homesick, 73–78
Techniques Used in this Book, 15–19
Tentacles in the Tree Stump, 39–44
Tools and Tricks of the Trade, 8–23
Trace the Sketch, How to, 22–23
treasure chest, in Goblin's Gemstone Stash, A, 149–154
trees
Eyes from the Shadows, 45–51
Fresh Flowers for the Homesick, 73–78
Grove of Wonders, The, 85–91
Lantern Teahouse, The, 11, 185–190
Place for Adventurers to Rest, A, 52–59
Portal to the Unknown, 79–84
Shadow Creatures of the Shade Tree, 60–66
Tale of the Skeleton Tree, The, 32–38
Talking Leafhead Tree, The, 67–72
Tentacles in the Tree Stump, 39–44
Two Tablespoons of Trees, 24–91
Wizard's Tower of Chambers, The, 170–177
Two Tablespoons of Trees, 24–91

W

Waning Moonflies, The, 178–184
wet-on-wet technique
Caves of Cadmus the Uncanny, The, 132
Eyes from the Shadows, 47, 48
Fungivore in the Underbrush, A, 117
Goblin's Gemstone Stash, A, 151
Grove of Wonders, The, 89
Lantern Teahouse, The, 187
Moss Dragon's Nest, The, 192, 193
Mushroom Wizard, The, 102, 103
Path of the Toadstool, The, 110
Pixie Party House, The, 97
Rocks of Past, Moss of Present, 157
Rune Magic and Rock Rituals, 139
Secrets of the Spores, 123
Shadow Creatures of the Shade Tree, 62
Talking Leafhead Tree, The, 69
Techniques Used in this Book, 16
Waning Moonflies, The, 180
Wizard's Tower of Chambers, The, 170–177